First among Friends

First among Friends

Interest Groups, the U.S. Supreme
Court, and the Right to Privacy

Suzanne U. Samuels

Foreword by Nadine Strossen

Westport, Connecticut
London

Libary of Congress Cataloging-in-Publication Data

Samuels, Suzanne U.

First among friends : interest groups, the U.S. Supreme Court, and the right to privacy / Suzanne U. Samuels ; foreword by Nadine Strossen.

p. cm.

Includes bibliographical references and index.

ISBN 0-275-97824-9 (alk. paper)

1. United States. Supreme Court. 2. Judicial process—United States. 3. Briefs—United States. 4. Pressure groups—United States. 5. Government litigation—United States. 6. Privacy, Right of—United States. I. Title

KF8742.S26 2004

347.73'26—dc22   2004044228

British Library Cataloguing in Publication Data is available.

Library of Congress Catalog Card Number: 2004044228

ISBN: 0-275-97824-9

First published in 2004

Praeger Publishers, 88 Post Road West, Westport, CT 06881

An imprint of Greenwood Publishing Group, Inc.

www.praeger.com

Printed in the United States of America

The paper used in this book complies with the Permanent Paper Standard issued by the National Information Standards Organization (Z39.48-1984).

10 9 8 7 6 5 4 3 2

To my partner and best friend, Steven

Contents

Foreword

First among Friends is a groundbreaking study that examines the role of amici curiae, or "friends of the Court," briefs on the Supreme Court's handling of cases involving the right to privacy. By relying on the personal papers of the Justices, as well as the briefs of the parties and thei amici, Samuels is able to track the influence of interest groups on the Court's decision-making process. She looks at cases involving abortion, aid in dying, family relationships, and antisodomy statutes and concludes that interest groups have played a central role in presenting the Justices with information and helping them to craft legal arguments in these cases. *First among Friends* highlights the importance of certain amici, especially government agencies, well-established civil rights and civil liberties organizations, and groups with extensive scientific or medical expertise.

Often, the Justices are compelled to choose between dueling experts, each presenting either different information or a different analysis of the same information. *First among Friends* shows that the Justices not only are adept at choosing between friends, but are increasingly reliant upon their briefs. These trends were clear in the 2002–2003 term, when the Justices decided *Lawrence v. Texas*. In this landmark case, the majority embraced an analysis of the historical basis for antisodomy laws that had been offered by many amici, but rejected by the Court's majority, in the 1986 *Bowers* ruling.

The role of amici will likely become even more prominent in the future, as the Justices are called upon to evaluate laws that involve increasingly complex scientific and technological issues. *First among Friends* makes a significant contribution to our understanding of how the Justices reach decisions, especially in the controversial and important area of constitutional privacy.

Nadine Strossen
President, ACLU

Preface

"Choose a research project that interests you," I counsel my undergraduates, "something that makes you angry, intrigues you, or simply makes you want to know more." My interest in law and fascination with how judges decide cases began when I was an undergraduate myself, and was piqued by my graduate and law study at the University at Buffalo. While in the J.D./Ph.D. program at Buffalo, I was very interested in understanding how social movements and pressure politics affected judicial lawmaking. Many of our law professors urged us to reject the conception of law as insulated from the larger society and to think instead about law as part of the social and political landscape.

The seeds of *First Among Friends* were planted when I began to think seriously about what role groups had in the decision-making process. I must admit that I was at first thrilled by the possibility that groups, particularly those seeking to protect individual rights and liberties, might be able to influence this process. I was fairly idealistic, and hoped that well-informed and well-meaning judges might be able to craft policy that took into account the needs of those individuals and groups that were poorly represented in the more "democratic" legislative and executive branches. Over time, I became skeptical about interest group lobbying, particularly in the courts, and began to worry that some groups might be able to "capture" the courts as they had many agencies and legislative bodies.

First Among Friends is the culmination of nearly a decade of my work on interest group lobbying and the U.S. Supreme Court. It proceeds from the assumption that groups try to influence policy by employing all available avenues and that they lobby courts as they do the other branches of government. I have always been interested in the right to privacy, and as this project began to take shape, I knew that I wanted to focus on this right, because it is almost entirely a creation of the U.S. Supreme Court. I also knew that I wanted to do a qualitative study. Precisely because I was interested in the development of law over time, I decided that my study would be one that focused on how interest groups influenced the opinions written by the Justices, and not just their votes. *First Among Friends* is an examination of how amici curiae briefs are incorporated into all the Justices' opinions—majority, concurring and dissenting. There are some instances in which the Justices rely very heavily upon these briefs, even using whole portions of the briefs without attribution. Focusing on the arguments and data provided me with a rich opportunity not only to learn a lot about some of the most controversial issues facing our society, but to discern how the amici briefs were employed by the Justices.

I have thoroughly enjoyed working on this project, and much of this enjoyment has come from the encouragement and support of my colleagues. I presented parts of this book at the annual meetings of the American Political Science Association, Midwest Political Science Association, Northeast Political Science Association, and Law and Society Association. I am thankful to my colleagues at these organizations for their enthusiasm about this project, and especially to Sue Behuniak, Lee Epstein, and Nadine Strossen for their strong support and wonderful collegiality. Thanks also to Steve Halpern for first encouraging me to work on this project. I am indebted to the estates of Justices Hugo Black and Thurgood Marshall for granting me access to their personal papers. I am also grateful to the librarians at the Manuscript Division of the Library of Congress for helping me to access the personal papers of Justices Hugo Black, William Brennan, John Harlan and Thurgood Marshall, and to the Woodrow Wilson School at Princeton University for offering access to the papers of Justice William O. Douglas.

I am also very thankful to my colleagues and friends at Seton Hall University, especially Mary Boutilier, Jo Renee Formicola, Joe Marbach, and Jeff Togman. They provided not only strong encouragement for me to move forward, but a very supportive environment in which to do so. I will always be in debt to my students at Seton Hall, especially my seminar students, who saw this project at different stages and were always eager to learn more about it. Thanks to the Seton Hall University Research Council for providing travel funds to support my research at the Library of Congress and Princeton University. I am grateful to Stacey Lee Donohue, who was always there to lend a listening ear (and a reading eye!) and for whose friendship I am so very thankful. Thanks also to my mother, Camille Uttaro Stern, and to my brothers, sisters-in-law, nieces and nephews, who asked about "that book" and then listened, and listened, and listened.

This book spanned two lifetimes—one before children, the other after, and as many of us know, these two lifetimes bear little resemblance to each other. My children, Charlotte Rose and Sebastian Raphael, are the brightest stars in my sky, and as perhaps only small children can, they helped me to keep it all in perspective. Just when I could have been swallowed up by this project, they were there asking me to tell them "just one more story," or to play chase, or to help them create a dinosaur cave in our living room. Finally, as always, I am grateful for the companionship and loving support of my husband and partner, Steven, who helped me to stay focused on this project through all of its iterations. He knows more about amicus curiae participation than perhaps any other physician, and he is also very good at doing laundry, cleaning the bathroom and doing the food shopping! I dedicate *First among Friends* to him with my warmest love and deepest gratitude.

Introduction: Decision-Making in the U.S. Supreme Court

Throughout our nation's history, we have pondered the role of the U.S. Supreme Court in the larger polity. In Federalist Paper No. 78, Alexander Hamilton attempted to allay the fears of those who argued that the Court would undermine the fledgling democracy and threaten the rights of both individuals and states by contending that the judiciary was the least dangerous branch of government, because it lacked the powers of sword and shield.[1] Hamilton contended that an independent judiciary was necessary to guard against what he called "the occasional ill-humors in the society."[2] Others, perhaps most notably Thomas Jefferson, argued that the Court was in essence antidemocratic, since the Justices were not elected by the people and might have the power to strike down laws passed by the democratically chosen branches. This debate about whether courts are or should be independent of the either of the other branches of government or the people continues to rage. Furthermore, the debate has intensified in the second half of the twentieth century, as the Supreme Court increasingly has been called upon to adjudicate cases involving highly controversial issues that implicate federal, state, and local laws.

At the heart of much of this debate are discussions about how Supreme Court Justices arrive at decisions in hotly contested cases. While Hamilton and others claimed that the Justices would rely only on strict rules and precedents in reaching decisions, most scholars now understand that these rules or laws are often not strict and that this precedent is malleable. Ambiguities in the law and conflicting legal precedents enable Justices to exercise significant discretion in reaching decisions, especially where an issue is novel or highly controversial. Moreover, instead of being insulated from political pressures, scholars have discovered that the Justices are influenced, both directly and indirectly, by a number of outside actors, among them interest groups, the media, public opinion, Congress, and the executive branch.[3]

This book focuses on one group of actors, the community of private and public interest groups that participate in Supreme Court cases, and explores how these groups have influenced the Court's decision-making process. Specifically, this book examines the role of individuals and groups filing amicus curiae briefs in cases involving the right to privacy and aims at assessing whether interest-group participation has made the Court more or less democratic. The right to privacy was first recognized by the Court in the 1965 case *Griswold v. Connecticut*, a case that examined a state contraceptive ban. Over the last thirty-five years, the Court has considered whether to extend the right to privacy to protect an individual's right to choose abortion, to hasten his or her own death, to engage in consensual sexual relations with a same-sex partner, and to be recognized as part of a nontraditional family. In some instances, the Court has extended this right; in others, it has not.

In the years since the *Griswold* decision, a variety of groups have lobbied the Court in an attempt to influence the Court's interpretation of privacy doctrine. While some have attempted to file as formal parties and others have sponsored litigation, the vast majority have employed amici curiae briefs, and there has been an explosion of amici briefs in abortion, aid in dying, family associational, and gay and lesbian rights cases. This book aims at assessing the impact that amici have had on judicial decision-making and uses these cases as a prism through which to evaluate this influence.

THE COURT AND
CONSTITUTIONAL DEMOCRACY

Alex deTocqueville's well-known observation that hardly any issue arises in the United States that is not resolved sooner or later into a judicial question has never been truer than it is today. Our federal courts, especially the Supreme Court, occupy a unique but in many ways difficult position in our polity. Federal judges and justices are appointed and have life tenure, and the electoral checks placed upon the other two branches are not directly applied to these courts. Not only are Supreme Court Justices unelected, but under the fiat of judicial review, they are called upon to consider the constitutionality of laws promulgated by the elected branches. Alexander Bickel and others have counseled the Justices to adopt the passive virtues and, perhaps most important, an attitude of disinterestedness.[4] However, the Justices have chosen to hear cases that turn on interpretations of these laws, and while the Court only infrequently overturns these laws, the countermajoritarian dilemma of judicial review remains.

Analysts disagree about whether the Court's decisions run counter to the law-making majority; some argue that the Justices only rarely oppose such majorities, even where they threaten to curtail the rights of the numeric minority.[5] Others have contended that the Court is not separate from the other branches, but is a part of the whole, constrained by both external and internal influences including Congress, the president, public opinion, the appointment process, and the Justices' own values and behavior.[6] While some see the Court as primarily a majoritarian institution, others claim that the Court does, and should, protect the rights of the individual, even where these rights do not have the support of the majority.[7]

The large-scale entry of interest groups into the judicial arena has blurred the lines between the branches and has affected the way our democracy functions. Interest-group lobbying of the Court has altered the decision-making process and, it could be argued, has made the Court a more majoritarian, or perhaps pluralist, institution. Just as David Truman and others looked at interest-group lobbying in Congress and the agencies as promoting a more responsive, more democratic government, some have argued that a heightened interest-group presence in litigation before the Court has the potential to make the Court a more democratic institution.[8] Amici briefs were initially intended to circumvent one of the most difficult issues in the adversary system, that is, the lack of representation for parties affected by a dispute but outside the formal boundaries of the litigation. Viewed in this light, the amicus brief permits the Justices to consider many viewpoints and to adopt a decision that takes into account information from a variety of sources. Consistent with the pluralist model of democracy, these briefs compete with each other. The Justices integrate more information and formulate better decisions than they would without interest-group participation. This model of pluralism assumes that the Justices consider all briefs and that amici participation is open to any party that wishes to provide additional information. The Justices are not, however, equally receptive to all amici.

Many scholars assume that interest-group lobbying of the courts is much like lobbying the two elected branches. In fact, much of the literature about group participation seeks to analogize adjudication to other forms of policy-making. The courts are seen as simply another forum for governmental decision-making, and Justices and their decisions are scrutinized by scholars seeking to establish that they have acted out of political or strategic motivations. The literature on interest-group participation in the courts in many ways builds upon this assumption. While groups may not lobby the Court with financial contributions or the promise of votes, they do provide the one resource that the Justices increasingly need, that is, information. In the latter part of the twentieth century, the Court has been called upon to resolve issues that require an arsenal of data that Justices, judges, and lawyers do not necessarily have at their disposal. Interest groups may provide this information; in some instances, Justices and judges have relied upon this information to resolve highly complex and technical issues. As Caldeira and Wright have noted, the Court has become increasingly receptive to these briefs, even as the sheer number of briefs has climbed, largely because the Justices recognize that "most matters before [them] have vast social, political and economic ramifications, far beyond the interest of the immediate parties."[9] More recently, Epstein and Knight have argued that some interest groups, particularly governmental entities, provide the Justices with indispensable information about the policy preferences of other governmental actors. They contend that this information allows the Justices to "generate efficacious policy that is as close as policy to their ideal points."[10] Several analysts have discussed this information function and have hinted that amici aid courts by providing them with information about relevant precedents or policy ramifications for cases.[11]

Viewed in this light, amici briefs provide the Justices with a more comprehensive understanding of the issues at play in a case and help them to overcome one of the most serious shortcomings of the adversary system, that is, that only a limited number of options are presented to courts by litigants. Moreover, it could be argued that by enabling interest groups to enter the decision-making process, pluralism has flourished in this ostensibly least-democratic of the three branches. In 1963, before the boom in amici filings, Samuel Krislov claimed that the use of the amicus brief might be viewed as "mirror[ing] the controversy over the Court's law-making function."[12] Krislov contended that Justices Hugo Black and Felix Frankfurter, often at odds about the Court's role in the polity, sparred about the place of the amicus brief in Supreme Court litigation. According to Krislov, Justice Frankfurter wanted to place the amici firmly within the control of the litigating party, as a way of fitting amici within the adversary framework, while Justice Black strongly supported the expansion of the amici role in order to provide more neutral information to the Justices in their decision-making.[13] This book argues that both Justices "won" this debate: amici increasingly cooperate with the formal parties, but their primary function is to provide medical, scientific, historical, and sociological information to the courts.

By allowing amici entry into Supreme Court debates, the Court's functioning may appear to be consistent with the pluralist model of democracy, but the pluralism that has flourished on the Court has many of the elitist tendencies apparent when one looks at Congress and the agencies. Amici briefs do not ensure that all groups are provided access to the Court; in fact, a number of interests go unrepresented. In 1963, Krislov noted that more sophisticated and better-funded groups had clear advantages in filing amici briefs.[14] Similarly, in 1984, Steven Shapiro concluded that even though many people are affected by Supreme Court litigation, relatively few groups actually file briefs.[15] This book underscores the conclusions of both Krislov and Shapiro and argues that the amici in privacy cases have become even more elite over time. Relatively few individuals file amici briefs, and the briefs that seem to provide the Court with information increasingly are filed by mainstream organizations. These amici are well represented in the administrative and legislative realms and vigorously lobby these other branches. This examination reveals that interest-group influence is far more subtle in the courts than in the other branches and is often apparent only from careful examination of the Justices' decisions and personal papers. Over the last thirty-five years, the Justices have become adroit at integrating amici arguments and data into their decision-making process; as a result, their opinions bear the clearly recognizable imprint of the amici briefs.

The Court is not a legislature: its output is clearly different, and the Court is constrained by distinct and different pressures. Perhaps most significant, the Court must make its decisions by weighing the inputs, that is, by considering the briefs presented by the formal parties and perhaps by the amici curiae. The Court's options are probably significantly more limited than are those of Congress or the agencies. Unlike these other branches, the Court is not free to choose among all alternatives. There is an institutional imperative that the Justices consider only those issues raised in the litigation and that they choose only from the options presented by the litigants. This bounded policy space creates both limitations and opportunities for interest groups participating in litigation. Amici curiae are increasingly important in expanding this policy space by providing information about the policy ramifications of various options considered by the Justices. This is especially true in the realms of abortion, aid in dying, and family and associational relations.

In these cases, the Justices have faced novel issues that require either the creation of new legal theories or the processing of somewhat sophisticated medical and scientific data for their resolution. It may be true that the potential for amici influence is significant in other areas, for example, in statutory or regulatory interpretation. In the constitutional realm, however, amici participation is profound, and many groups file briefs in an attempt to influence the Court's interpretation of constitu-tional provisions. Constitutional adjudication in many ways raises the stakes in terms of potential impact, and I assume that interest-group participation in privacy cases sparks widespread participation by di-verse interest groups. This diversity and the sheer presence of many amici provide an excellent opportunity to examine the role of interest-group participation and to compare the relative successes of the "friends."

Lobbying the Court

As interest-group litigation has become commonplace in cases before the Supreme Court, some scholars and lawyers have treated interest-group litigation as simply another tool in the lobbyist's bag of tricks. Writing in 1976, Jonathan Casper noted that the Court had an important role to play in the American democracy, because it could help "provide effective access [by] placing issues on [its] agenda [and] providing the imprimatur of legitimacy that may affect the ability [of groups] to attract adherents, mobilize resources and build institutions."[16] Others have noted that interest groups make excellent use of the Supreme Court to accomplish their policy goals. Among these scholars are Susan Behuniak, who concluded that the 1989 abortion case *Webster v. Repro-ductive Health Services* demonstrated the burgeoning of interest-group politics before the Court,[17] and Christopher Zorn and others, who have sought to establish that groups serve as intermediaries between the Court and Congress and have developed an "interest-group model" of the legislative-judicial relationship.[18] In discussing the evolution of judicial policy, Richard Pacelle has employed much of the literature used to describe policy-making in the legislative and administrative realms.[19]

Interest groups seeking to affect the adjudication of cases in the Supreme Court may use a number of routes. First, the interest group can attempt to influence the nomination process for the Justices, usually by providing information about the nominee to the Senate Judiciary Committee. Throughout the 1980s and early 1990s, this information role became increasingly common. Groups can also seek to affect the Court's handling of particular issues at either the plenary or the merit stage. At the plenary stage, it appears that the content of briefs is relatively unimportant, as the Justices simply seem to be taking account of the *number* of briefs filed in support or in opposition to a writ of certiorari.[20] Some scholars have concluded that the Supreme Court is a representa-tive body because it allows groups to help set the agenda by choosing which cases to hear by looking at how interested groups are in each case.[21]

Groups may also seek to influence the Court's handling of cases at the merit stage by using one of two alternatives. The group either may sponsor a case, by directly engaging in litigation and providing most or all litigation support, or may file an amicus curiae brief, which supplements the efforts of the formal parties to provide information or make alternative legal arguments. Very few groups perform the sponsorship role because of the costs and procedural obstacles inherent in this course of action. In contrast, there are far fewer procedural limitations to filing an amicus brief, and while the cost of filing an amicus brief may amount to tens of thousands of dollars, many well-established groups do not find this cost to be insurmountable. In fact, the use of amici curiae briefs, once a relative anomaly in litigation, has become commonplace and, some would argue, ubiquitous.[22]

Historical Foundations of Amici Curiae Participation

Our historical record of amici participation reaches back to ancient Rome, where the briefs were utilized as purely informational devices.[23] In the fourteenth century, judges began to employ amici briefs as a mechanism to give voice to those interests that were left unrepresented in the adversary system. Amici were expected to provide impartial information to the judge; they often served the function of "oral shepardizing," that is, informing the judges of case law that the parties ignored or overlooked.[24] This neutrality was central to the amici role. In the medieval period, a revival of the amicus role coincided with the expanded use of group litigation. During this era, such litigation was frequent and appears to have reflected the communal nature of social life,[25] and such lobbying of the courts was commonplace in sixteenth-century England. A shift toward individual, rather than communal, rights and responsibilities, which was at the heart of the Renaissance and carried over to the revolutions of the seventeenth and eighteenth centuries, slowly eroded group litigation. When lawyers and judges rediscovered group litigation in the nineteenth and twentieth centuries, they needed what Stephen Yeazell has termed "elaborate justifications" for allowing such litigation.[26] The most widely accepted form of group litigation in the United States during the 1800s and well into the 1900s was the class action suit.

The first amicus curiae to participate in a case before the U.S. Supreme Court was Henry Clay, who represented the State of Kentucky in an 1819 case involving Kentucky land titles. This case, *Green v. Biddle*, threatened to raise federalism issues, and for this reason, Kentucky sought representation.[27] Throughout the 1800s, amici curiae were almost always lawyers representing governmental entities, and not until the early 1900s did the Court allow private litigants to participate as amici. The seeds for a greater amicus role were planted in the early 1900s by the legal realist movement, which called for judges to incorporate social science data into their decisions.[28] Samuel Krislov contends that governments participating as amici assumed the traditional role of neutral observer; however, this changed when private litigants began to file briefs. According to Krislov, the amicus brief has been transformed throughout the last century, from an instrument of "neutrality to partisanship, from friendship to advocacy" and has increasingly been used as a tactical device.[29]

In the late 1940s, several groups, most notably the National Association for the Advancement of Colored People, the American Civil Liberties Union (ACLU), and the American Jewish Congress, employed litigation as a key lobbying tactic.[30] In the landmark *Brown v. Board of Education* cases of 1954 and 1955, a brief by noted social scientists about the effects of segregation on American society provided much of the empirical evidence used by the Justices to strike down school desegregation.[31] Amici were very active in church-state litigation; as Leo Pfeffer has noted, the ACLU, the American Jewish Congress, and Americans United for the Separation of Church and State led the way in filing briefs in cases involving free exercise and the establishment clause.[32] In most areas of the law, however, amicus participation had been negligible up until the mid-1960s. In the period between 1928 and 1966, groups filed amici briefs in 20 percent of cases heard on the merits.[33] By the 1980s, however, interest-group litigation in the Supreme Court had become much more democratic; many more groups and much more diverse groups sought to participate in cases before the Supreme Court.

Amicus Curiae Participation during the Modern Era

There can be no doubt that interest groups have increasingly sought an audience before the Supreme Court. Books and articles in journals and law reviews underscore the great extent to which groups use the Court to press their grievances and advance their interests. Beginning in the early 1960s, scholars have attempted to determine which groups would use the courts. Samuel Krislov argued that groups that were weak in lobbying the other branches had been the leaders in using amici briefs in the 1930s, 1940s, and 1950s.[34] Similarly, examining the strategy employed by the National Association for the Advancement of Colored People, Richard Cortner concluded that groups that could not garner sufficient support for their policy goals in the elected branches could nevertheless succeed in the courts.[35] In 1985, Bradley and Gardner contended that these disadvantaged groups, whom they termed "underdogs," had greatly increased their filing of amici briefs from 1954 to 1980.[36]

Who files and why?

Writing in 1990, Caldeira and Wright concluded that amicus participation was "organizational by nature" and that states made up the largest number of amici at the certiorari stage.[37] State attorneys general have wide discretion in deciding whether to file an amicus brief,[38] and the quality of the states' briefs is perceived by the Justices to be variable, with California and New York filing briefs that appear to be well-regarded by the Court.[39] Over the last twenty-five years, states not only have sought to improve their win rates, especially against the private bar, but often have cooperated with each other in the preparation and filing of briefs, frequently signing on to each other's briefs.[40] Among public and private interest groups, both conservative and liberal groups use the courts, but they differ in their tactics.[41] While liberal groups have tended to assume both a direct sponsorship and amicus role, conservative groups have relied almost exclusively on the amicus brief. At the plenary level, however, the states are clearly outnumbered and outmatched by the Solicitor General's office, which participates often and has a very high success rate.[42] Public interest law firms and citizen groups have become much more visible at this stage; however, business, trade, and professional associations seem to be the most active groups and file the largest number of briefs at both the plenary and cert stages.[43]

There tends to be a significant degree of cooperation among amici and between amici and the formal parties. They share information, create strategies, and divide up arguments.[44] It bears noting, however, that groups tend to file independently, despite the costs attendant to an individual brief.[45] This decision to file a separate amicus brief rather than joining with other like-minded friends is probably motivated by their belief that the sheer number of briefs filed in support of a particular litigant could have an impact on the Court's adjudication.[46]

Attorneys for amici are often drawn from the elite legal circle of Washington lawyers, and these lawyers are often very closely involved in coordinating party and amici activity.[47] Many of these lawyers specialize in appellate advocacy and are repeat players before the Supreme Court.[48] Widespread amicus participation is a characteristic of the U.S. Supreme Court; there is significantly less amicus participation at the lower levels.[49] Despite the small number of amici in the lower courts, these briefs are cited with relative frequency by the federal intermediate courts and state courts.[50] Amici may be either single-issue or multiple-issue groups. In some issue areas, like abortion, single-issue groups tend to predominate,[51] while in other areas, multiple-issue groups are more common. Many groups that file amici briefs can, and do, participate in other activities aimed at influencing governmental policy. Groups have a multitude of reasons for employing judicial tactics: some of these derive from internal stresses; others are the result of external pressures.[52] Clearly, the ability of a group to pursue a litigation strategy is dependent upon there being sufficient organizational, monetary, and political resources.[53] The amicus role is central for some groups, and amicus committees within these groups regularly review court dockets and select cases in which to participate. For some groups, amicus participation is a key element of public or constituent relations and allows for heightened visibility.[54]

In addition to the internal constraints that drive or permit interest-group participation in the courts, significant external pressures encourage participation. Interest groups enter the courts because they seek to influence policy-making. For these groups, litigation is, first and foremost, a form of political action, and amici file briefs because they think that they can influence the disposition of a case before the Court.[55] For prospective amici, these briefs fulfill a variety of functions. Perhaps most obvious, groups filing these briefs seek to provide the Court with information about the issue under consideration. In some cases, these groups add to the data presented by the formal parties, by offering the Court new sources and information or by helping to flesh out arguments made by the parties in abbreviated form.

Amici may also offer new arguments that the formal parties are unable or unwilling to effectively make. For example, Joseph Kobylka argues that amici served to ensure "argumentational pluralism" in establishment-clause cases, providing the Court with a multitude of approaches to these cases.[56] In some instances, an argument is better made by an amicus, because the formal party lacks credibility to raise a particular issue or makes the decision that it is unable to raise an issue for tactical or political reasons. Where a group has recognized expertise or technical skills, they may file a brief to perform an informational function. Moreover, these briefs may bring a new perspective to the Court and may help the Justices to gain greater insight into the ramifications of the case before it. They may serve as "interest articulators" for the Justices.[57] These briefs may perform this function well in some cases, in others, poorly.[58]

The decision to file a brief also appears to be motivated by a desire to respond either to nemesis groups or to Justices or judges. The altered context created by other groups entering the legal arena or by prior decisions can often propel groups to file amici briefs. Shifting legal norms, texts, institutions, and tactics may shape interactions among conflicting groups over time,[59] and litigation may be employed to either maintain[60] or stunt social movements.[61] For example, Woliver concluded that the rhetoric and symbols used by prolife and prochoice groups in *Webster* shaped the wider abortion debate and influenced each side's approach.[62] Other commentators have noted that in some instances, amici have attracted widespread media attention and have driven issues onto the public agenda.[63] Furthermore, the increase in amici filings is likely also the result of actions taken by the three branches. Koshner contends that the Supreme Court, Congress, and the executive branch facilitated interest-group participation by taking certain affirmative steps. For example, Koshner contends that docket changes and a period of judicial activism encouraged amici filings, as did an increase in legislative activity and an expanded role for the Solicitor General in Supreme Court litigation.[64]

How have changes in the Supreme Court rules altered amicus participation?
The enormous influx of amici briefs into Supreme Court litigation in the last three decades has paralleled changes in the Court's rules governing amicus curiae filing. If the Justices chose to do so, they could use these rules to significantly limit the scope of amicus participation. Most of the rules for amicus participation are encompassed in Rule 37. For example, the Court requires that all amici acquire the written consent of each of the two parties and requires, if such consent is denied, that amici apply to the Court directly for leave to file. According to Rules 37 (2) and (3), such a motion will not be favored. This rule does not apply to amici briefs filed by the Solicitor General, the representative of the federal government in litigation before the Court, nor does it apply to representatives of any federal agency, or to the attorney general of any state, commonwealth, territory, or possession, or to law officers representing any city, county, or town.[65] Despite the existence of these rules, the Justices rarely deny a motion for leave to file submitted by an amicus whose brief has been objected to by one of the parties.[66] Moreover, Justices rarely avail themselves of Rule 37(1), which requires that amici briefs provide only information that is not encompassed in the party briefs and warns against repetitive amici briefs. The Justices may allow an amicus to file, even over the objections of the parties and in spite of the fact that the brief is redundant, because they value these devices for their broad informational function.

While the Court does not usually employ its rules to bar amicus curiae participation, the rules do require that amici reveal important information about who they are and where their interests lie. For example, Rules 37(2)(a) and (b) and 3(a) and (b) require that the amicus specify whether consent was granted by the parties and that it identify which party it supports on the cover of its brief. By complying with these rules, amici provide information to the Justices that assists in sorting out the briefs.[67] Similarly, a highly controversial rule adopted by the Court in 1997 serves another important informational function. Rule 37(6), adopted after substantial notice and comment by interested parties, has two requirements. First, the rule mandates that nongovern-

mental amici disclose whether counsel for a formal party actually
authored either the whole amicus brief or a part of it; second, the rule
requires that amici reveal whether an outside party made a monetary
contribution to the preparation or filing of the brief.[68] Some analysts
have contended that the Court adopted this new rule in response to the
attempt by some formal parties to use the amici briefs to expand on
arguments not presented in party briefs. Since 1984, the Court has
imposed a fifty-page limitation on party briefs, and some parties may
be using the amicus brief, with its thirty-page limit, to provide additional "space."[69]

The second aspect of Rule 37(1), which requires disclosure of third-
party contributions to the preparation or filing of an amicus brief, may
be an attempt by the Justices to sort out the briefs. This disclosure may
alert the Justices that there has been extensive coordination between
individuals and groups in the creation and filing of briefs and may
allow the Justices to readily discern which briefs are merely "seconding" or "thirding" an argument made by someone else. This sorting
device could be very useful, especially in cases where the Justices are
faced with the daunting task of sorting through twenty or more amici
briefs. Taken together, the two aspects of the rule reveal that the Justices
have long since ceased regarding amicus briefs as impartial devices.
The Court now recognizes that these "friends of the Court" are better
described as friends of the parties. The new rules could help the Justices
to more clearly delineate the roles of parties and amici, a distinction that
has become even more clouded as more amici have filed briefs.[70]

What impact do amici briefs have on the Court?

The impact of amici on the adjudication of Supreme Court cases
may be assessed in a number of ways. For example, we may conclude
that an interest group has influenced the Court whenever it brings
issues to the Court that would otherwise not have been considered
or influences the views of the Justices about some wider issue. Casper
called for an expanded definition of litigant success, contending that
such success could be measured by the degree to which the Court
provided "effective access" to those seeking to participate.[71] Most
commentators, however, use a narrower definition of impact and aim
at assessing whether amici have had an influence on how the Justices
have decided a case. Nearly all studies have used direct citations as
the principal indicator of impact.[72] There are significant limitations
to this approach; perhaps the most important is that Justices have
become less willing to directly cite to amici briefs, especially in highly
controversial cases. Despite this limitation, many studies have employed this approach, and nearly all have concluded that amici have
influenced the Court.

Some studies have argued for a study of indirect reliance, contending that amici influence can be discerned even in the absence of direct cites to these briefs. In fact, the first account of amicus influence was given by Alexander Bickel, who employed this broader approach, noting that in *Brown v. Board of Education*, amicus Solicitor General was successful in convincing the Court that local school boards should be responsible for formulating desegregation plans.[73] In the last several decades, amici influence has been discerned in a wide variety of contexts, including abortion, capital punishment, criminal due process, employment discrimination, antitrust, and copyright.[74] In most of these cases, the Justices employed the arguments and data of amici, often without direct attribution.

Among those amici with the greatest influence appear to be the quintessential repeat players, who are usually well known in litigation and are probably recognized as experts by the Justices. The Solicitor General has a unique role in Supreme Court litigation: he or she does not have to receive the permission of the parties to file an amicus brief and is, for all practical purposes, the only amicus that the Court invites to file briefs. The inclusion of a brief from that office greatly increases the chances that the Court will hear the case in question, and the Solicitor General also appears to have an impact on the adjudication of the case at the merit stage.[75] It may be that the filing of an amicus brief by the Solicitor General is used as a cue as to both cert-worthiness and merit-worthiness since the Justices seem to perceive these briefs to be among those of the highest quality that they receive.[76] There has been little examination of the relative positions of other amici filing in the Supreme Court. The few studies that have been done suggest strongly, however, that repeat players are favored over one-shotters in at least some cases.[77]

OBJECTIVE AND OUTLINE OF THIS BOOK

It is difficult to assess interest-group influence in Supreme Court litigation; the decision-making process is shrouded in mystery, and there is no obvious record of which factors may have swayed the Justices. Congress has a legislative record that allows for the examination of the testimony of invited individuals and groups. Similarly, under the Administrative Procedures Act, all comments gathered from interested individuals and groups about proposed administrative rules and regulations are published in a reporter. To determine whether these individuals and groups have influenced either Congress or the administrative agencies, we can examine the legislative or administrative record and compare it to the laws or regulations that are ultimately adopted. Both bodies usually respond to the inputs of interested groups and individuals, especially where there is a groundswell of opinion about some topic. Through the legislative and administrative record, we can create a rough blueprint of the decision-making process for Congress and the agencies. Moreover, we expect that these organizations will be representative and that they will take into account the information offered from interested outsiders about some policy position.

It is much more difficult to shed light on the decision-making process of the Supreme Court Justices. Scholarship has helped us to determine that key actors have a role to play in Supreme Court litigation, but we lack any definitive findings about the role that interest groups play in the plenary stage, that is, in the actual decision handed down by the Justices on the merits of the case. As has been noted, most studies of amicus influence have explored whether the Justices have directly cited a brief in majority, plurality, concurring, or dissenting opinions. This narrow approach may provide little insight into the Justices' use of amici arguments or data, and for this reason, I argue that a broader examination of impact must be undertaken.

This study examines the role of the interest-group community in the adjudication of privacy cases. These cases, especially those that evaluate federal and state abortion laws, bring into stark relief the role of the Supreme Court in our constitutional democracy. I have chosen to explore a relatively fluid area of law, the right to privacy, because it has few statutory or administrative underpinnings. The Justices considered this right for the first time in 1960 and recognized it only in 1965. Moreover, the Court's application of the right corresponds with the proliferation of amici briefs in the 1970s, 1980s, and 1990s. It is my assumption that this judicially created right, which hinges solely on constitutional guarantees, allows the Justices the greatest degree of flexibility in crafting decisions and, for this reason, permits interest groups to exercise maximum influence. Furthermore, interest-group participation in this area is widespread: a large number of interest groups have filed briefs in these cases, and the groups have tended to be diverse. Within this doctrinal area, I explore the role of interest groups in four issue domains: abortion, euthanasia or physician-assisted suicide, family relations, and gay and lesbian rights.

Privacy cases present the Justices with two problems. First, these cases call upon the Justices to evaluate information that is often scientific in nature and almost always outside their field of knowledge and expertise.[78] Perhaps even more important, law and science derive from two distinct methodologies. Researchers in the natural and social sciences use the empirical method and typically aim at exploring a problem from various vantage points. Their goal is to arrive at generally applicable truths about relationships or phenomena. In contrast, lawyers—and the Justices—have been trained as advocates and generally confine their inquiry to the arguments and data presented by the two opposing sides. In litigation, science is employed selectively—the goal of lawyers and expert witnesses is to use whatever data are helpful, not to present the judges or Justices with the universe of data about a particular problem. Since the issues of physician-assisted suicide, euthanasia, abortion, and to a lesser extent, gay and lesbian rights have been presented to the Court as issues that turn on scientific findings, and because the formal parties are not likely to be seen as experts on these issues, the amicus role can be assumed to be an important one. In addition, since these cases call upon the Justices to reevaluate legal theories and for the first time to apply these theories to individual actions and relationships, amici input can be assumed to be welcomed.

Second, these cases not only implicate technical issues that are typically beyond the knowledge of the Justices, they also present some of the most contentious questions in American politics. The issues underlying these cases have been the center of public debate and the subject of numerous statutes and regulations. For example, the renewed debate about abortion in the 1980s and early 1990s has provoked much public attention, with the federal, state, and local governments attempting to craft laws to regulate the abortion procedure. Similarly, during this period, some state and local legislatures acted to create a right to physician-assisted suicide. Such a right derives largely from the movement towards patient rights of the late 1980s and 1990s. And finally, the call for gay and lesbian rights was heard by a number of state and local lawmakers during this period, and these lawmakers responded by crafting laws both in support of and in opposition to these rights. These issues raise the ever-present question about the proper role of the Court in a democratic state and present the Justices with a formidable dilemma. The Justices need the data presented in the amici briefs, but in their decision-making they are expected to maintain at least a veneer of impartiality. If the Justices are perceived to be open to lobbying, especially lobbying by interest groups also active in the other branches, they may risk being seen as too partisan.

The Justices are clearly concerned about these perceptions, and at times they have complained about popular attempts to influence their decisions. For example, in his majority opinion in *Roe v. Wade*, Justice Harry Blackmun claimed that the Court's responsibility was to decide the abortion issue "free from emotion and predilection."[79] Similarly, in *Webster v. Reproductive Health Services*, Justice Antonin Scalia criticized his brethren for refusing to overturn *Roe*, saying that because of this refusal, the Justices could "look forward to at least another term with carts full of mail from the public and streets full of demonstrators urging us—their unelected and life-tenured judges who have been awarded those extraordinary, undemocratic characteristics precisely in order that we might follow the law despite the popular will—to follow the popular will."[80] Despite these complaints, this study assumes that the Justices are neither immune to nor wholly disdainful of such influence. Moreover, the right to privacy itself seems to require that the Justices be aware of the public's perceptions of some acts or relationships. The Court's 1965 decision in *Griswold v. Connecticut*, which established the right to privacy, required that the Justices consider the nation's "history and traditions" when assessing whether such a right exists. Over time, this formula has been used to confer protections only on those rights that have been embraced by the numeric majority. These cases present perhaps the ideal opportunity for democratic rule to manifest itself.

This book aims at achieving an expansive understanding of amicus influence in Supreme Court cases involving the right to privacy. As has been noted, a number of excellent studies assess impact by examining direct citations to amici briefs. These studies, however, do not provide a comprehensive picture of the amicus role, especially in privacy cases. This is especially true because, over the last thirty-five years, the Justices have become less willing to directly cite to amici briefs, especially in controversial cases. Other studies have attempted to assess influence by looking at the success scores for particular groups, that is, whether they were on the winning or losing side of cases, and others have provided case studies of particular interest groups. As Epstein has noted, these case studies have often been based upon generalizations and have not provided information that can be extrapolated to other cases or interest groups.[81] This book fills a void in our literature about decision-making by undertaking a contextual approach to assessing influence. It assesses whether the arguments and data provided by amici are adopted by the Justices in their opinions. Analysts have urged that such an approach is necessary to assess whether amici briefs influence the choices that Justices make.[82]

To assess impact, I employ two distinct methodologies. First, I provide a detailed analysis of eleven cases heard by the Court between 1960 and 1997. Two of these cases, *Poe v. Ullman* and *Griswold v. Connecticut*, resulted in the recognition of the constitutional right to privacy; four cases evaluated laws barring or regulating abortion (*Roe v. Wade, Harris v. McRae, Akron v. Akron Center for Reproductive Health*, and *Casey v. Planned Parenthood of Southeastern Pennsylvania*); three examined the issue of aid-in-dying (*Cruzan v. Director, Missouri Department of Health, Washington v. Glucksberg, Vacco v. Quill*); and two assessed family or associational rights (*Moore v. East Cleveland, Bowers v. Hardwick*). I examine the Justices' majority, plurality, concurring, and dissenting opinions in these cases and attempt to identify those instances in which the Justices have relied on arguments and data provided in an amicus brief. I then separate out those instances in which the amicus brief provides information not present in a party brief. I assume that where the Justices have employed information provided only by an amicus, they have been influenced by that amicus. The 216 amici briefs filed in these eleven cases provide a wealth of data that supplements the party briefs.

The second methodology draws upon my examination of the personal papers of Justices Black, Brennan, Douglas, Harlan, and Marshall. By studying these papers, I have attempted to discern not only how the Justices used the amici briefs in these cases but also how they viewed amici participation in a more general sense. Included in the Justices' papers are conference memoranda, draft opinions, correspondence between the Justices, and records of conference votes. This information helps to highlight the role of amici arguments in the earlier cases—*Poe*, *Griswold*, *Roe*, *Moore*, *Akron*, and *Bowers*. Moreover, the Justices' papers provide much information about the positions of all of the Justices in these cases. In their 1999 essay, Epstein and Knight strongly argue that there is a need for more research into the Justices' conference comments.[83] This book aims at helping to provide this insight.

Each of the four substantive chapters explores an issue before the Court in an attempt to discern amici influence. Chapter 2 explores the Court's creation of the right to privacy, beginning with the 1961 case *Poe v. Ullman*, in which the Justices dismissed the petitioner's claim as not presenting a justiciable controversy. This case laid the foundation for recognition of the right four years later in *Griswold v. Connecticut*, and these early cases opened the door for significant amici input in the future. Chapter 3 explores the impact of amici arguments in the abortion debate over time, beginning with its 1973 decision in *Roe v. Wade* and ending with its 1992 holding in *Casey v. Planned Parenthood of Southeastern Pennsylvania*. Chapter 4 examines the amici role in three cases involving a person's decision to hasten his or her own death. As in the abortion cases, a huge number of amici have filed in these cases, and this chapter assesses the amicus contribution to the Court's handling of these three cases. Finally, chapter 5 examines the Court's disposition of two cases involving familial or associational relations.

This book explores the following questions: first, do the amici briefs have a direct or indirect effect on how the Justices resolve these issues? Direct effect may be measured by the Justices' explicit citation to the briefs; indirect effect is discerned where the Justices employ arguments or data present only in the amici briefs. Second, do certain groups of amici have a better chance of being heard by the Justices? Are the

Justices more likely to rely on some amici than on others? Are these amici also well represented in the other branches? Most important, does amici participation promote democracy on the Court? How have changes in the Supreme Court rules altered this participation in the last two decades? This work aims at determining the extent to which amici filing makes the Court more or less receptive to the American populace.

This work proceeds on the assumption that the amici briefs provide a wealth of information either not presented by the formal parties or presented more effectively by the amici. The flexible nature of the privacy right, coupled with the Justices' lack of scientific, medical, and historical background in these cases, compels the Justices to employ this information. By seeking to uncover more subtle forms of amicus influence in a range of cases spanning more than thirty-five years, this book attempts to at develop a comprehensive understanding of the amici role in Supreme Court decision-making.

NOTES

1. Hamilton wrote that the judiciary "has no influence over either the sword or the purse; no direction either of the strength or of the wealth of the society; and can take no active resolution whatever. It may truly be said to have neither FORCE nor WILL, but merely judgment; and must ultimately depend upon the aid of the executive arm even for the efficacy of its judgments."

2. Federalist Papers No. 78.

3. For example, see Gregory A. Caldeira and John R. Wright, "Lobbying for Justice: Organized Interests, Supreme Court Nominations and the United States Senate," 42 *American Journal of Political Science* 499–523 (1998); for example, see Richard Davis, *Decisions and Images: The Supreme Court and the Press* (Englewood, NJ Press: Prentice-Hall, 1994); Barrett McGurn, *America's Court: The Supreme Court and the People* (Golden, CO: Fulcrum Publishing, 1997); William Mishler and Sheehan, "The Supreme Court as a Countermajoritarian Institution?" 88 *American Political Science Review* 87 (1994); and Helmut Norporth and Jeffrey Segal, "Popular Influence on Supreme Court Decisions," 88 *American Political Science Review* 711 (1994); Thomas Marshall, "Supreme Court and Public Support for Rights Claims," 78 *Judicature* 146 (1996); Gregory A. Caldeira and Charles E. Smith, Jr., "Campaigning for the Supreme Court: The Dynamics of Public Opinion on the Thomas Nomination," 58 *Journal of Politics* 655–681 (1996); Doris Marie Provine, *Case Selection in the United States Supreme Court* (Chicago: University of Chicago Press, 1980); Lincoln Kaplan, *The Tenth Justice: The Solicitor General and the Rule of Law* (New York: Knopf, 1987); Lee Epstein and Thomas Kobylka, *The Supreme Court and Legal Change: Abortion and the Death Penalty* (Chapel Hill: University of North Carolina Press, 1992); Rebecca Mae Salokar, *The Solicitor General: The Politics of Law* (Philadelphia: Temple University Press, 1992).

4. Alexander Bickel, *The Least Dangerous Branch: The Supreme Court at the Bar of Politics* (Indianapolis: Bobbs-Merrill, 1962).

5. See Bickel, 197; Robert A. Dahl, *A Preface to Democracy* (Chicago: University of Chicago Press, 1956), 244–249; Gregory Caldeira, "Public Opinion and the

U.S. Supreme Court: FDR's Court-Packing Plan," 81 *American Political Science Review* 1139, 1150 (1987); Barnum, 287–299.

6. Barnum, 198-201, 220, 229-37; Epstein and Knight, *The Choices Justices Make* (Washington, D.C.: Congressional Quarterly Press) 184.

7. See Jonathon Casper, "The Supreme Court and National Policy Making," 70 *American Political Science Review* 50–52 (1976); Robert J. McKeever, *Raw Judicial Power? The Supreme Court and American Society* (Manchester: Manchester University Press, 1995), 278.

8. Bickel, 19; R.L. Pacelle, "The Dynamics and Determinants of Agenda Change in the Rehnquist Court," in Epstein, *Contemplating Courts* (Washington, DC: Congressional Quarterly Press, 1995) 270–271.

9. G.A. Caldeira and J.R. Wright, "Amici Curiae before the Supreme Court: Who Participates, When, and How Much?" 52 *Journal of Politics* 782–806.

10. Lee Epstein and Jack Knight, "Mapping Out the Strategic Terrain: The Informational Role of Amicus Curiae," in Cornell W. Clayton and Howard Gillman (eds.), *Supreme Court Decision-Making and New Institutionalist Approaches* (Chicago: University of Chicago Press, 1999), 215.

11. Reagan William Simpson, *The Amicus Brief: How to Write It and Use It Effectively* (Chicago: ABA Publishing, 1998), 17, 29; Lee Epstein, "Interest Group Litigation during the Rehnquist Era," 9 *Journal of Law and Politics* (1993), 699.

12. Samuel Krislov, "The Amicus Curiae Brief: from Friendship to Advocacy," 52 *Yale Law Journal* (1963), 717.

13. Krislov, 717.

14. Krislov, 704.

15. After conducting interviews with former clerks of the Justices, Shapiro concluded that even among filers there is an elitism: he recounted that the clerks and Justices pay far more attention to those organizations with the reputation for filing briefs that are "high quality" and that provide objective analysis (21). According to Shapiro, the best-regarded amici were the Solicitor General and groups like the American Bar Association, and any briefs filed by attorneys that were well known and had appeared before the Justices (22) (Stephen M. Shapiro, "Amicus Briefs in the Supreme Court," 10 *Litigation* 21–22).

16. Casper, 63.

17. Susan Behuniak, "Friendly Fire: Amici Curiae and *Webster v. Reproductive Health Services*," 74 *Judicature* (1991), 261.

18. Zorn, 5.

19. Pacelle, 3–5.

20. Caldeira and Wright (1988), 1122.

21. Ibid.

22. In his 1998 book, *Solving the Puzzle of Interest Group Litigation* (Westport, CT: Greenwood Press, 1998), Andrew Koshner found that at least one amicus brief is filed in 93 percent of the cases heard by the Supreme Court and that amicus participation has skyrocketed since 1953, regardless of the term or issue studied. By 1993, at least one brief was filed in more than 90 percent of cases, and the average brief attracted 4.4 briefs (Koshner, 2, 7). See also, *The Supreme Court Compendium* (Washington, DC: Congressional Quarterly Press, 1995).

23. Duncan, 453.

24. The custom of allowing amici briefs arose out of the need for a mechanism to allow outside counsel to give advice either by their initiative or by request of the Court (Note, "Amici Curiae," *Harvard Law Review* 34 (1921), 773). According to Krislov, *Abbott's Dictionary of Terms and Phrases* defines an amicus curiae as "A friend of the court. A term applied to a bystander, who without having an interest

in the cause, of his own knowledge makes suggestions on a point of law or of fact for the information of the presiding judge" (Samuel Krislov, "The Amicus Brief: From Friendship to Advocacy," *Yale Law Journal* 72 (1963), 694).

25. Stephen C. Yeazell, *From Medieval Group Litigation to the Modern Class Action* (New Haven: Yale University Press, 1987), 270–271.

26. Yeazell, 268.

27. Discussed in detail in Krislov, 696–697 (1963).

28. See M. Rustad and T. Koenig, "The Supreme Court and Junk Social Science: Selective Distortion in Amici Briefs," 91 *North Carolina Law Review* (1993), 101.

29. Krislov, 704.

30. Krislov cited in Karen O'Connor and Lee Epstein, "Court Rules and Workload: A Case Study of the Rules Governing Amicus Curiae Participation," 8 *Justice System Journal* (1983), 36.

31. In its decision, the Court cited seven social science studies presented by amici that established the inherent inequality of segregated educational facilities (Rustad and Koenig, 110).

32. Pfeffer, 83, 85.

33. Caldeira and Wright (1988), 1111 (citing studies by Hakman and Puro, 1111).

34. Krislov, 720.

35. Cortner cited in Robert C. Bradley and Paul Gardner, "Underdogs, Upperdogs and the Use of the Amicus Brief: Trends and Explanations," 10 *Justice System Journal* (1985), 93.

36. Bradley and Gardner recognized that "upperdogs" had also increased their filings, but that this activity was overshadowed by that of the underdogs (93).

37. Caldeira and Wright (1990), 794.

38. For further discussion, see Thomas Morris, "States before the U.S. Supreme Court: State Attorneys General as Amicus Curiae," 70 *Judicature* (1987), 301.

39. Morris, 304. This success is due, in no small part, to the huge staffs employed by these states' Offices of Attorneys General. Throughout the 1980s, the National Association of Attorneys General and State and Local Legal Center undertook to make states' briefs of uniformly better quality and to boost states' success rates (Morris, 300; interview with Justice Harry Blackmun). These efforts met with mixed success; states did better in the area of criminal procedure than they did in civil cases (Ross, 343–344, 346).

40. Morris, 302.

41. Karen O'Connor and Lee Epstein, "The Rise of Conservative Interest Group Litigation," 45 *Journal of Politics* (1983), 479–489; Epstein, *Conservatives in Court*, 1985.

42. Ross, 346; see articles infra notes 3, 15.

43. Caldeira and Wright (1990), 795–796.

44. Lee Epstein, *Conservatives in Court*.

45. Epstein (1985); Behuniak (263, 265); Kolbert; Howard.

46. Caldeira and Wright (1990) 799–800, 804. For further discussion, see Olson (1990) 860.

47. Kevin T. McGuire, *The Supreme Court Bar: Legal Elites in the Washington Community* (Charlottesville, VA: University Press of Virginia, 1993), 76, 201.

48. Caldeira and Wright, 1990.

49. Some federal district courts, however, have expanded the amicus role and permitted "litigating amici" to participate in cases. These amici, who have their

ancestry in common law, engage in oral argument, participate in discovery, introduce evidence, and examine witnesses. In addition, litigating amici can seek the enforcement of prior decrees. These litigating amici blur the lines between amicus and formal party, and several courts have strongly criticized the powers given to these special "friends." Litigating amici appear in only a small minority of federal district court cases, and appellate courts thus far have rejected their use (see Lowman).

50. In his study, Simpson found that amici briefs were cited in 2539 opinions between 1995 and 1998 and that 428 of these cases provided three or more direct cites (Simpson, 8).

51. See Behuniak, 264.

52. For further discussion, see Donald J. Farole, Jr., *Interest Groups and Judicial Federalism: Organizational Litigation in State Judiciaries* (Westport, CT: Praeger Publishers, 1998), 4–5, 30.

53. For example, a group's leadership may decide to file a brief to rally support among members and potential members, or it may be used to mollify members concerned about group activities. Karen O'Connor found that women's rights organizations filed amici briefs because they could not fund major litigation (1980).

54. Simpson, 13–14.

55. As Joseph F. Kobylka noted in his article, the "myth of interest group invincibility in the courts," explored and supposedly dispelled by Epstein and Rowland in their 1991 article "Debunking the Myth of Interest Group Invincibility in the Courts," 85 *American Political Science Review* 205, remains alive, largely because interest groups believe they have an impact on the Court's handling of cases (Kobylka in Epstein, 112).

56. Kobylka in Epstein, 126.

57. Caldeira and Wright (1988), 1123.

58. For example, Smith contended that the petitioner's amici in the welfare case *Beno v. Shalala*, "played a significant role in preventing millions of dollars in unlawful welfare reductions" (786). In contrast, Colker contends that the briefs and opinions filed in *Webster v. Reproductive Health Services* failed to advance feminist goals (141–142, 187). See also, Anthony L. Clapes, who argues that the amici briefs filed in . . . benefited neither the court nor the software industry ("Confessions of an Amicus Curiae: Technophobia, Law and Creativity in the Digital Arts," 19 *University of Dayton Law Review* (1994), 974).

After conducting a series of interviews with former Supreme Court law clerks, Stephen Shapiro, a former deputy Solicitor General, concluded that an effective amicus brief, that is, one that had an impact on the Justices, was one that brought "something new and interesting." He noted that this could be "better research, an explanation of the connection between this case and other pending cases, an improved discussion of industry practices or economic conditions, a more penetrating analysis of the regulatory landscape, or a convincing demonstration of the impact of the case on segments apart from the immediate parties" (22).

59. McCann in Dupuis, 4.

60. Kobylka (1991); Koshner, 41. Some scholars argue, however, that litigation has much more limited impact on intragroup dynamics. For example, see Joseph Stewart, Jr., and James F. Sheffield, Jr., "Does Interest Group Litigation Matter? The Case of Black Political Mobilization in Mississippi," 49 *Journal of Politics* (1987), 781. In this article, Stewart and Sheffield contend that interest group litigation has had a negligible impact on boosting turnout for black candidates or on the election of black officials (795).

61. Hoekstra (1995), 17.

62. Laura R. Woliver, "Rhetoric and Symbols in the Pro-Life amici briefs to the *Webster* Case," presented at the 1992 Annual Meeting of the American Political Science Association, Chicago.

63. Woliver, 15.

64. Koshner, 51, 55, 68, 79, 102.

65. Supreme Court Rules 37.4 (1997 Revisions).

66. O'Connor and Epstein, *Justice System Journal* (1983). In this study, O'Connor and Epstein found that while the amicus rule formulated in 1938 and revised in 1949 initially decreased amicus participation, by the mid-1950s, the Court permitted the vast majority of motions to file (37). Similarly, in her study of abortion cases, Katherine Kolbert, attorney for the American Civil Liberties Union, found that the Court denied motions by amici to participate in only three cases, *City of Akron v. Akron Center for Reproductive Health, Inc., Thornburgh v. ACOG,* and *Webster v. Reproductive Health Services* (156). Similarly, Caldeira concluded that the Court allows amici filings because it recognizes that it needs to appear responsive and because the briefs may convey significant information about the case at hand (1990, 800).

67. *Supreme Court Rules,* 37 (2) and (3).

68. *Supreme Court Rules,* Rule 37.6.

69. *Stern et al.,* p. 4.

70. In addition to these formal rules, the Court has also adopted informal procedures to deal with amici. For example, there is a standing agreement that the Court will request the participation of some individual or organization where three or more Justices agree to extend this invitation.

71. Casper, 63.

72. O'Connor and Epstein *Justice System Journal* (1983), 42–43; G. Ivers and K. O'Connor, "Friends as Foes: The Amicus Curiae Participation and Effectiveness of the ACLU and the Americans for Effective Law Enforcement in Criminal Cases, 1969–1982," 9 *Law and Policy* (1987); Simpson, 10.

73. Bickel, 253.

74. Behuniak, 269–270; 265–267; Kolbert also examined the content of the Court's decision in *Webster* and concluded that prolife amici had an impact in this case (Kolbert, 155, 159). Acker (1993), 57; J.R. Acker, "Social Science in Supreme Court Criminal Cases and Briefs: The Actual and Potential Contribution of Social Scientists as Amici Curiae," 14 *Law and Human Behavior* (1990), 30; Rustad and Koenig, 112; Ivers and O'Connor, 172. Suzanne U. Samuels, "Interest Groups in the Supreme Court: The Impact of Amici Briefs in *"U.A.W. v. Johnson Controls,"* *Judicature* (1993); Hedman, 191; Stephen Calkins, "Supreme Court Antitrust 1991–1992: The Revenge of the Amici," *Antitrust Law Journal* (1993), 61: 269; Clapes, 906, 920, 930; Epstein and Knight in Clayton and Gillman, 225–228 (1983 Term).

75. Epstein (1989), 830; Caldeira and Wright (1988), 1115; Jeffrey A. Segal and Cheryl D. Reedy, "The Supreme Court and Sex Discrimination: The Role of the Solicitor General," *Western Political Quarterly* (1987), xx:557, 560; O'Connor *Judicature* (1983), 261; Cooper, 684.

76. McGuire (1993), 173; Segal and Reedy, 556.

77. Hedman, 204, 206. Hedman also found, however, that the Natural Resources Defense Council, the Sierra Club, the National Audubon Society, the National Wildlife Federation, the Environmental Defense Fund, and the National Association of Homebuilders, all well-known repeat players, had no discernible impact on the Court (S. Hedman, "Friends of the Court and Friends

of the Earth: Assessing the Impact of Interest Group Amici Curiae in Environmental Cases Decided by the Supreme Court," 10 *Virginia Environmental Law Journal* (1991), 187–212, 205); Acker (1993), 57–58.

78. Michael Mason. 1994. "Trial and Error." *Health* (Jan-Feb): 78; Rustad and Koenig; Acker (1990).

79. Cited in RF Nagel, *Constitutional Cultures: The Mentality and Consequences of Judicial Review* (Berkeley: University of California Press, 1989), 685.

80. Cited in Nagel, 687.

81. Epstein (1983), 688–690.

82. Epstein and Knight in Clayton and Gilman, 231.

83. Epstein and Knight call for more research into the Justices' conference comments in their article in Clayton and Gillman, 231.

2

The Right to Privacy Created: *Poe v. Ullman* and *Griswold v. Connecticut*

The right to privacy grew out of two cases heard by the U.S. Supreme Court in the early 1960s involving state anticontraceptive laws, *Poe v. Ullman* (1961) and *Griswold v. Connecticut* (1965). Before these cases, there had been no recognition of a general right to privacy under the U.S. Constitution. The Court's holdings in these cases, which relied heavily on arguments made by amici curiae, established that there was such a right, even though it was not mentioned in the text of the Constitution. Once recognized in the context of a right to use contraceptives, this right to privacy was invoked in a myriad of other circumstances.

As will be discussed in chapters 3, 4, and 5, parties and amici have attempted to broaden the protection to include abortion, aid in dying, the right to engage in consensual sodomy, and the right of an extended family to live together. Much of the the success of the parties and their amici in influencing the Court's disposition of these controversial cases can be attributed to the Court's decisions in *Poe* and *Griswold*. Amici influence in these cases is apparent in the Justices' opinions and in the personal papers of Justices Brennan, Douglas, and Harlan. The Justices' personal papers are particularly helpful in these early cases, since the collections are extensive. There are discussions about *Poe* in the collections of all three Justices, and the Brennan and Harlan collections offer important insights about the *Griswold* opinion.

HINTS OF A RIGHT TO PRIVACY: *POE V. ULLMAN*

Griswold v. Connecticut is widely recognized as the case that established a constitutional right to privacy. It was in this case that the U.S.
Supreme Court struck down a Connecticut anticontraceptive law as
violative of a married couple's right to privacy. While *Griswold* was the
first case in which a majority of the Justices recognized this right, it was
in *Poe v. Ullman*, decided by the Court in 1961, that the roots of *Griswold*
were sown. This case, often employed to demonstrate how the principles of standing and ripeness can keep courts from hearing a case, was
an important stepping-stone to *Griswold*. In *Poe v. Ullman*, a plurality of
the Court held that they could not rule on an appeal of a lower court's
dismissal of the claims of three married women who sought to
challenge the constitutionality of a Connecticut law banning the use of
contraception, because the case raised a nonjusticiable issue.[1] In the
rationale offered in the dissenting opinions, however, hints of amici
influence can be readily discerned.

The Core Issue of Justiciability for the Plurality and Concurring Justices

Writing for the plurality, Justice Frankfurter held that there was no
live controversy at issue in the case, since the three married couples
seeking access to contraception were not threatened with prosecution
under the law. Justice Frankfurter pointed out that since 1879, when the
law was promulgated, only three parties had been charged with violating it, and that these charges had been dismissed. Justice Frankfurter
contended that contraceptives were "commonly and notoriously sold
in Connecticut" and that Connecticut had followed an "undeviating
policy of nullification" of its anticontraceptive laws throughout the
more than 80 years that the law had been in existence.[2] Justice Brennan
concurred in this case, finding that the "true controversy" raised by
these laws was over the opening of birth control clinics, not the use of
contraceptives by a few married couples. According to Justice Brennan,
the Court would be compelled to consider these laws only if some party
attempted to open such a clinic, or if the state began prosecuting parties
for using contraception.[3]

The Dissents Embrace the ACLU's Argument about Marital Privacy

Justices Douglas and Harlan vigorously dissented in this case, and in
their dissents one can glimpse much of what would be the Court's
reasoning four years later in *Griswold*. In these dissents, the arguments

and data provided by amici curiae can be discerned. Justice Douglas, who wrote the majority opinion that struck down the Connecticut laws at issue four years later in *Griswold*, argued that the laws violated both the physician's First Amendment right to free speech and the married couple's right to liberty. Hinting of what was to come in *Griswold*, Justice Douglas argued that the Fifth Amendment and Fourteenth Amendment rights to liberty should be read broadly, and that the right to privacy was included within the larger "emanations of liberty."[4] Justice Douglas argued that the right to privacy had strong common law foundations and that the due process clause had to be read to encompass this right.[5] The due process clause barred states from interfering with "all that is 'implicit in the concept of ordered liberty,'" and this concept followed the standards of a free society about what is reasonable and fair.[6] Justice Douglas contended that this statute violated the due process clause because it interfered with the intimacies of the marriage relationship and invaded the "innermost sanctum of the home."[7]

Like Justice Douglas, dissenting Justice Harlan devoted significant attention to a discussion of the Fourteenth Amendment due process clause, arguing that this clause had to be read as more than just a procedural safeguard. Justice Harlan claimed that the due process clause represented the balance that the United States had struck between "liberty and the demands of organized society," and that one had to look to the purposes of the Bill of Rights to understand what was meant by "liberty."[8] Justice Douglas and Justice Harlan both focused on the uniqueness of the marital relationship: both claimed that there is nothing more private and intimate than the relationship between husband and wife and that this intimacy is central to marriage. Justice Douglas argued that the regulation interferes with the "innermost sanctum of the home,"[9] and Justice Harlan contended that the law constituted an "obnoxiously intrusive" means of regulating marriage.[10] The decisions of both Justices seem to have hinged on the fact that this law interfered with *marital* privacy, as opposed to an individual privacy. The development of this privacy argument was owed in large part to the amicus brief filed by the American Civil Liberties Union. While there were glimpses of this argument in the petitioner's brief, it was much more fully developed in the ACLU brief.

The Role of the Amici in *Poe v. Ullman*

The party briefs made only marginal contributions to the decisions reached by the plurality, concurring, and dissenting opinions. In fact, the Justices' personal papers indicate that the Justices thought the parties had done a poor job in arguing their cases. In his cert memo,

Justice Harlan criticized the "poor quality" of the petitioner's brief, noting that the brief's author had "largely forgotten the particular claims of his client."[11] Similarly, in a bench memo that followed this cert memo, one Justice agreed with Justice Harlan that "neither one of the parties gives us any help in deciding this case."[12] This Justice argued that the petitioner's jurisdictional statement, which was central to the party's standing to bring suit, was "execrable," as was its brief on the merits.[13] This Justice explained the lackadaisical approach of Connecticut by noting that the state was likely relying on a "sit-tight theory."[14] The author of this bench memo contended that the function of the memo was to "supply the lack in the parties' briefs," especially that of Connecticut.[15]

The Justices' criticisms are apparent when one examines the party briefs in this case and compares them to the opinions. There is very little development of a legal argument in the petitioner's brief. The petitioner noted simply that the anticontraceptive laws interfered with the marital relationship since they "reach[ed] into the bedroom . . . [and] affect[ed] no one else" but the husband and the wife.[16] Moreover, this brief made little contribution to the dissenters' arguments. In fact, the dissenters' focus on marital privacy, which can be discerned in both the Justices' papers and in their opinions, derived almost entirely from the amicus brief of the ACLU.

The ACLU's brief focused on the due process right to privacy and argued that the Connecticut statute interfered with an "aspect of marital conduct that is inherently private and beyond the reach of government."[17] Almost all of the ACLU's brief was devoted to a discussion of the right to privacy: the amicus recognized that this case was the first in which the Court was considering this right in this context, but argued that the right to privacy had a long and established pedigree and had been most often invoked in search and seizure cases.[18] The dissenting opinions of Justices Douglas and Harlan shared with amicus ACLU this serious concern about the ramifications of anticontraceptive laws on the right to privacy, especially marital privacy, and seem to have drawn heavily upon the legal reasoning provided in this amicus brief.

The centrality of the ACLU brief is apparent in discussions among the Justices, as well as in the dissenters' opinions. In his conference notes, Justice Douglas detailed Justice Harlan's position. He wrote that Justice Harlan argued that this was not a First Amendment case, but instead a case involving the due process right to be let alone. Justice Harlan contended that "nothing is more offensive to the concept of the right to be let alone than butting the criminal law into the privacy of the marital relationship."[19] Hinting of the central tenet upon which the *Griswold* opinion would be based, Justice Harlan argued that "all other searches pale[d] in comparison to those permissible under this Act."[20]

Similarly, in the bench memo that followed Justice Harlan's cert memo and was likely authored by Justice Douglas, the author noted that the right asserted was derived from the Fourth Amendment right to privacy in the home and had been recognized in the *Olmstead* decision establishing a right to be let alone.[21] This right to marital privacy could only be exercised by married couples and was a "human and natural" right.[22] The ACLU's brief had focused on marital privacy and the Fourth Amendment search and seizure provisions, both issues that seem to have been central to the Justices' discussions of this case.

Furthermore, even though the Justices didn't use the briefs of amici Sixty-Six Physicians and Planned Parenthood in their written opinions, the personal papers of Justices Brennan, Douglas, and Harlan strongly suggest that these briefs were read and considered. For example, the amicus brief of the Sixty-Six Physicians focused on how the law violated physicians' Fourteenth Amendment right to practice medicine and contended that the state cannot prohibit certain medical treatments unless they are "medically unsupportable or dubious."[23] In his memo, Justice Brennan argued that the right to practice medicine was "subordinate to the police power."[24] Similarly, in conference, Chief Justice Earl Warren argued that it was unlikely that the physician would be convicted for providing information about contraceptives to patients, and so the physicians probably did not have standing in this case.[25] In contrast, Justice Black argued that doctors had a First Amendment right to talk to their patients and so could not be convicted under this law.[26] In his cert memo, Justice Harlan also noted that the doctor's interest was much weaker than that of the patients.[27] Finally, in his bench memo, one Justice argued that the doctor did not have a valid claim in this litigation and that there was no "independent right to practice his profession as he [saw] fit."[28] None of these concerns was raised in the party briefs: amicus Sixty-Six Physicians alone brought these issues before the Court.

Similarly, Planned Parenthood argued that the law had no reasonable basis and interfered with public health instead of advancing it.[29] Nearly all of the Planned Parenthood brief was devoted to establishing that the anticontraceptive law had no basis in medicine, public morality, or religious belief.[30] Planned Parenthood provided only a cursory legal argument in its brief, and in this argument, the amicus contended that the statute was arbitrary and constituted an unreasonable deprivation of life, liberty, and property in violation of the Fourteenth Amendment.[31] Several Justices expressly rejected this argument, noting that it was not reasonable to conclude that there was no basis for this law and that there was nothing in the record to support the contention that all medical opinion was against the state law.[32] Furthermore, in the bench memo following Justice Harlan's cert memo, one Justice noted that "we cannot rightly say that it is silly to consider contraceptive intercourse immoral, since too many people have argued that it is immoral."[33] In conference, the Chief Justice noted that he was not convinced that there was a unanimity of medical opinion about the benefits and safety of contraception.[34] Similarly, Justice Felix Frankfurter argued that the Court could not decide for itself that 'rhythm' is no good."[35] Again, this discussion of public health appeared solely in the amicus brief.

A Lack of Information about Key Issues and a (Future) Opening for Amici

The Justices were clearly bothered by what they saw as a lack of information in this case. A number of Justices noted that the record in this case was sparse and that there had been no trial, no witnesses, no cross-examination, and no findings of fact.[36] Justice Brennan noted that he was trying to figure out the two central issues in this litigation, one of these a legal argument and the other clearly an extralegal argument. First, Justice Brennan asked about the degree to which the law interfered with liberty rights; and second, he considered what options were available to husbands and wives seeking to prevent pregnancy.[37] He puzzled over the efficacy of contraception, arguing that the Court did not have information sufficient to determine "how much better and safer [contraceptives] were than the next best [thing]."[38] He noted that "science is daily developing and improving new means of contraception which may not be illegal" and cited an article in *Time* magazine as support for this position.[39] One Justice admitted that he had done research to determine the prevalence of laws regulating contraception and had found that Connecticut was the only jurisdiction in the country and the world that banned its use by married couples.[40]

Thus, the arguments of the parties and two of the amici appear to have had very little impact on the Justices' decisions in *Poe v. Ullman*. In contrast, amicus ACLU does seem to have influenced the Court's holdings by providing an argument about marital privacy that was embraced by two of the dissenters. The Justices' papers reveal that they read and considered information present in the other two amici briefs. Moreover, these personal papers strongly hint that the Justices were beginning to recognize the need for more scientific data and may have begun to envision an expanded amicus role in this area. At several points, the Justices were clearly distressed about a lack of scientific and medical information about contraceptive use, as well as a paucity of information about the impact of Connecticut's ban on married couples. For example, Justice Brennan noted that there was nothing in the record to suggest what the medical consensus was about contraception.[41] Similarly, the Chief Justice argued that he didn't know whether there was unanimity among doctors about contraceptive use, and Justice Frankfurter contended that the Justices didn't know enough to assess the rhythm method.[42] In his personal papers, Justice Douglas kept newspaper clippings about abortion in Czechoslovakia, along with a letter from the National Council of Churches of Christ and the Rabbinical Assembly of America, with a statement by each of these groups about their position on birth control. In addition, Justice Douglas had a list of articles about contraceptive use with the handwritten comment "Voici!" next to this list.[43]

Thus, it is likely that after *Poe*, which nearly all the Justices recognized as the first substantive due process case to come before the Court in several decades, the Justices realized that they needed assistance in assessing state laws or regulations governing medical treatment. This case may have set the stage not only for recognition of the right to privacy but also for an increased willingness on the part of the Justices to use certain amici briefs for information. In this case, the Justices selectively employed the ACLU's construction of the right to marital privacy. Moreover, it was this view of privacy that was adopted by the majority in the *Griswold* litigation four years later.

THE RIGHT TO PRIVACY RECOGNIZED: *GRISWOLD V. CONNECTICUT*

In 1965, the U.S. Supreme Court was again called upon to hear a case involving a state statute that barred the use or distribution of contraceptives. Between 1961 and 1965, many states repealed their statutes that barred access to contraceptives, but the laws remained on the books in six states. Opponents of these statutes, stymied in their attempts to strike them down in the state-houses, began to look again at the courts and to consider how the problems of standing that had barred access in earlier cases might be overcome. In Connecticut, birth control advocates were instrumental in launching the Planned Parenthood Center of New Haven, which announced that its purpose was to "provide information, instruction, and medical advice to married persons as to the means of preventing conception" and to "educate married persons generally as to such means."[44] The opening of this clinic appears to have been motivated by a desire to test the Connecticut statute.

In the first few days that the Center was open, three married women were treated, received information about birth control, and were provided with a contraceptive device.[45] Almost immediately, Esther Griswold, the executive director of the Center, was arrested, along with the medical director, and convicted of violating the state law that made it a crime to assist in giving information and medical advice about how to prevent conception.[46] Griswold and the medical director were each fined $100, and the clinic was ordered closed. The convictions were affirmed by the state's highest court, and the petitioners filed a petition with the Supreme Court, contending that the Connecticut law was unconstitutional. In both their petition for certiorari and their brief on the merits, Griswold and her colleague stressed that they had standing to bring the suit and that the law violated both the free speech and due process clauses of the Constitution. The Supreme Court, now faced with two convictions under the Connecticut statute, agreed that there was standing to bring a suit challenging the law.

The Right to Marital Privacy Recognized

Writing for a seven-person majority, Justice Douglas overturned the Connecticut statute, holding that the anticontraceptive law violated married persons' right to privacy. In addition to the majority opinion penned by Justice Douglas and signed by six other Justices, there were concurring opinions by Justices Goldberg, Harlan, and White and dissents by Justices Black and Stewart. Four amicus curiae joined the petitioner doctors' brief, and no amici briefs were filed in support of the State of Connecticut. There was a remarkable amount of overlap between the party and amicus briefs, with each citing the other's briefs and providing elaboration of each other's arguments. In addition, the Justices' opinions addressed the data provided in the amicus curiae briefs and appear to have echoed, to a significant extent, the arguments advanced in the party and amicus briefs. It bears noting, however, that the party and amicus briefs did not advance novel arguments; in fact, they picked up on the Justices' concerns and hypothetical arguments advanced four years earlier in *Poe*. In the *Poe* opinions, the Justices, especially dissenting Justice Harlan, employed themes raised in the brief of *Poe* amicus ACLU; and in *Griswold*, this dialogue between the Justices, parties, and amici continued.

Interestingly, much of the *Griswold* opinions focused on the right to privacy first advanced in the dissenting opinions of Justices Douglas and Harlan in *Poe*, and little additional data was advanced in support of this right. Most of the majority, concurring, and dissenting opinions were devoted to the legal arguments, unlike the ensuing abortion decisions of the 1970s through 1990s, which turned on sociological, scientific, and medical data. Despite the fact that the *Griswold* holdings centered on legal arguments, as opposed to more overt political ones, the impact of the amici is clearly discernible. In this case, Griswold was acting together with her amici, and both were engaged in an intensive collaborative effort. The amici raised no new arguments; their function in this litigation was to second Griswold's position. Furthermore, little was raised in Griswold's brief that was not elaborated upon or seconded in the party briefs. All of the Justices addressed the party and amici briefs to a lesser or greater degree.

Amicus ACLU, so influential in the *Poe* dissents, returned in *Griswold*, again arguing that the right to privacy derives from the emanations of liberty encompassed in the Fourteenth amendment. Much of this brief sought to establish a right to marital privacy under the Fourteenth Amendment due process clause.[47] While the ACLU also advanced an equal protection argument,[48] far more attention was devoted to discussion of the impact of this law on family relations and privacy.[49] Similarly, amici Planned Parenthood and the Catholic Council on Civil Liberties (CCCL) focused on discussing the right of married couples to marital or familial privacy, and this thread ran through their briefs.[50] Amicus Adams also discussed the Fourteenth Amendment liberty right, but its focus was on how the Connecticut statute violated physicians' due process rights.[51] In their opinions, the Justices echoed this concern about the right of married couples to be free of state interference into the decision to use contraception. The majority and concurring opinions agreed that the right to marital privacy was firmly embedded in the Constitution; however, they disagreed about where this right was located.

Justice Douglas's Penumbra

Justice Douglas's majority opinion is remarkably short in length, taking up only five pages of text; in it, he devotes nearly all of his energies to establishing the right to privacy. With the exception of a brief discussion about standing and an even shorter disclaimer that the Court was not "sitting as a super-legislature to determine the wisdom, need or propriety of laws that touch on economic problems, business affairs, or social conditions,"[52] Justice Douglas's opinion set out to establish the privacy right. Perhaps anticipating what has become the most often raised criticism of his opinion, Justice Douglas focused on creating a basis for unenumerated rights. He contended that the Court has always recognized that there are rights that are not expressly set out in the Bill of Rights, and that the right to privacy is such a right.

While Justice Douglas contended that the right to marital privacy was older than the Bill of Rights itself, his decision was the first in which the Supreme Court recognized this right. The right to privacy emerged for the first time in an 1890 *Harvard Law Review* article by Samuel D. Warren and Louis D. Brandeis, but this right was articulated in a much more limited context. In this article, Warren and Brandeis contended that individuals had the right to keep certain information and images private and that they could assert this right against other individuals, specifically, journalists.[53] In his 1928 dissent in *Olmstead v. United States*,

Justice Brandeis spoke of a right to privacy, contending that this right derived from the Fourth and Fifth Amendments and created a "right to be let alone."[54] Both the Warren and Brandeis article and the *Olmstead* decision appeared several times in the Justices' papers, and while this article and decision were mentioned only briefly in the Justices' deliberations about *Poe*, they took on a larger importance in *Griswold*.[55]

Justice Douglas claimed that the specific provisions in the Constitution created "penumbras," in which may be found other, implied rights. These penumbras were, in a sense, larger than the articulated rights and provided a context for these rights. Justice Douglas claimed that the framers understood there to be a "zone of privacy" that formed the backdrop for the specific guarantees established in the Firth, Third, Fourth, Fifth, and Ninth Amendments.[56] Specifically, this zone of privacy could be glimpsed in the First Amendment right of association, the Third Amendment prohibition against the quartering of soldiers in private homes, the Fourth Amendment protection against unreasonable search and seizure, the Fifth Amendment protection against self-incrimination, and the Ninth Amendment protection of rights retained by the people. Justice Douglas claimed that these amendments established the right of individuals to be protected against governmental intrusions into the "sanctity of man's home and the privacies of life."[57]

Griswold noted that while there was no explicit mention of the right to privacy in the Constitution, "various provisions embod[ied] separate aspects of it."[58] Among these were the First Amendment freedoms of religion, speech, press, and petition, and the Third, Fourth, and Fifth Amendment protections against state interference with the private sectors of life.[59] She and amicus Adams focused on the First Amendment speech and press rights of doctors and family planning clinics.[60] Similarly, Planned Parenthood discussed the impact of the Connecticut law on physicians' Fourteenth Amendment due process rights to liberty and property, an argument echoed by Adams.[61] While Griswold's brief also noted the impact of this law on physician's rights, this argument was far less effective than the one that seems to have inspired Justice Douglas' decision, that is, that the penumbra of rights enjoyed by married couples encompassed a right to marital privacy.

The penumbral approach appears to have been articulated first in a letter from Justice Brennan to Justice Douglas, in which Justice Brennan argued that the majority holding should not base the right to marital privacy on the First Amendment right of association. Justice Brennan contended that the Court should instead read the Bill of Rights to encompass not only the articulated guarantees, but those "applications or extensions of those rights to situations unanticipated by the Framers."[62] While Justice Goldberg argued that the majority should back away from the penumbral approach to avoid attacks by Justices Black and Stewart, Justice Brennan appears to have convinced Justice Douglas to adopt this approach.[63] Justice Brennan's clear imprint on Justice Douglas is even more apparent when one considers that Justice Douglas's first draft did not even mention the right to privacy and that his early drafts struck down the Connecticut law under the first amendment right of association.[64] Justice Brennan was opposed to basing the holding on the right of association and ultimately was successful in convincing Justice Douglas to adopt the right to privacy.[65]

In his decision, Justice Douglas contended that the marital relationship clearly was within the zone of privacy, since marriage was "intimate to the degree of being sacred," and that this notion of marital privacy was "older than the Bill of Rights."[66] This vision of the marital relationship was at the heart of the petitioner's brief and the amici briefs submitted by the ACLU and the CCCL. The petitioner argued that the "home is the ultimate refuge from the outside world" and that "marital relations are the most private, the most sought to be sheltered from public gaze."[67] Similarly, CCCL noted that marital privacy was "the mainspring of human life [and] . . . feelings most close to the experience of men and women."[68] The ACLU argued that marriage and family were "the foundations of culture and the focal point around which individual lives revolve."[69]

The core of Justice Douglas's argument was that the Connecticut law intruded not only on the home, but on the marital relationship; in so doing, it had a destructive impact on this relationship. Griswold discussed at length the detrimental effects of this law, and a number of these ill effects were elaborated upon by the amici. For example, she and amicus ACLU noted that this law forced married couples to choose between abstinence and ill health or death.[70] Griswold and her amici also warned that this law encouraged abortion and sterilization.[71] Moreover, like Justice Douglas, they were concerned about the effects this law had upon family relations.[72]

Furthermore, Justice Douglas warned that in forbidding the *use* of contraceptives, the state was insinuating itself into the marital bedroom. Justice Douglas's warning was ominous: "Would we allow police to search the sacred precincts of marital bedrooms for telltale signs of use of contraceptives?"[73] This is one of the most frequently quoted passages of Justice Douglas' opinion. There is evidence that other Justices were also deeply concerned about the possibility that the marital bedroom would be subject to intensive searches.[74] As has been noted, the specter of such invasions was first raised in the Justices' conference discussions in *Poe*, but it was elaborated upon by Griswold and her amici in this case. Griswold contended that the "hand of the government was reaching in not only to the home, but into the bedroom" and that the laws would authorize the state to search the bathroom closet for evidence of the "instruments of crime."[75] This image was also invoked in the amicus briefs of the ACLU, which contended that "couples want legislators as well as policemen out of their bedrooms,"[76] and by the CCCL, which contended that the state had "no competence, no power, and no jurisdiction in the bedrooms of agreeing spouses."[77] Similarly, Planned Parenthood argued that the law "reache[d] the marital bed of every Connecticut couple."[78] Both Griswold and amicus Planned Parenthood argued that the state law allowed police wide-ranging authority to investigate contraceptive use. Griswold warned that the law permitted police to "question close friends or servants about contraceptive use," and amicus Planned Parenthood noted that there would be both "inquisitorial and physical invasion by police and courts into marital intimacies" as a result of this law.[79]

The Concurring Opinions

Seven justices agreed to strike down the law at issue in *Griswold*; however, there was significant disagreement about the basis for this holding. While Justice Douglas's majority opinion relied solely upon the right to privacy, the concurring opinions of Justices Goldberg, Harlan, and White employed alternative bases. The concurrence of Justice Goldberg, which was joined by Chief Justice Warren and Justice Brennan, invalidated the anticontraception statute on the basis of the Ninth Amendment, contending that the right of marital privacy was a fundamental right, even if the framers did not enumerate it. Relying upon both case law and history, Justice Goldberg contended that the framers did not intend that the Bill of Rights would be exhaustive. According to Justice Goldberg, the inclusion of the Ninth Amendment ensured that the basic and fundamental rights would be guaranteed, even if they were not delineated in the text of the Constitution.[80]

To determine whether a right was fundamental, Justice Goldberg employed the test used by the Justices to determine which of the Bill of Rights were incorporated to apply to the states under the Fourteenth Amendment. He contended that a fundamental right was one that was rooted in the traditions and conscience of the people and could not be denied without violating the fundamental principles of liberty and justice that were at the base of our civil and political institutions.[81] Justice Goldberg concluded that the right to marital privacy was one such fundamental right and that the state could not interfere with this right unless it showed that it had an interest that was compelling. Like Justice Douglas, Justice Goldberg accepted the view of marriage articulated by both the petitioner and its amici. Justice Goldberg contended that marital privacy was a fundamental right and should be accorded the highest constitutional protection, because this right was "as old and as fundamental as our entire civilization."[82] Like Justice Douglas, the petitioner, and the amici, Justice Goldberg asserted that the marital relationship and home were realms that states could not enter.[83]

The concurrences of Justices Harlan and White both relied upon the Fourteenth Amendment's due process clause to strike down the Connecticut statute and, like Justice Goldberg, contended that the right to marital privacy was a fundamental right. Moreover, this heightened protection for married couples is implicit in the arguments of Justices Brennan, Douglas, and others. In letters to each other and in conference discussions, these Justices contended that the marital relationship was entitled to the greatest degree of protection.[84] Griswold only briefly mentioned the Fourteenth Amendment due process clause in grounding their right to marital privacy,[85] but the amici focused their energies on this clause. Justice Harlan's brief concurrence explored the impact of the statute on those values that were implicit in ordered liberty. There is a clear parallel between Justice Harlan's views and the argument advanced by the ACLU that marriage and family are the foundations of our culture and that the Fourteenth Amendment due process clause protects individuals against states.[86]

Of all the Justices, Justice White was most willing to explore the impact of the Connecticut law on married couples. Interestingly, his willingness to move beyond a strictly legal argument allowed him to more fully employ the briefs of Griswold and the amici. Like the other Justices who struck down this law, Justice White argued that the law interfered with the marital relationship, but he also noted that this law should be struck down because of its impact on "disadvantaged citizens." Justice White may have been influenced by Justice Brennan's concurrence in *Poe*, which briefly noted that the law might have a differential impact on the indigent and undereducated. Planned Parenthood also sounded this theme in its *Griswold* brief, contending that the impact of the law would be felt mostly by these groups, since they would be most likely to utilize family planning clinics, which the law barred.[87] Griswold also briefly noted this disparate impact, arguing that the law discriminated against low-income individuals.[88] In addition, Justice White argued that the law was much too broad and that the state's rationale, that the law discouraged extramarital and premarital sex, was out of proportion to an absolute ban on contraceptives.[89] He hinted that there were instances where the state could not bar family planning, among these, where the woman's life or health would be endangered by pregnancy. In this discussion of the impact of the law on married couples' life and health, Justice White was closely in step with the briefs of Adams and Planned Parenthood, which provided extensive information about the physical and psychological benefits of birth control.[90]

In addition, Justice White concluded that the articulated justification for the law, that the state sought to prevent extramarital and premarital affairs, was not advanced by the law since many couples could use nonprescription contraception. Justice White questioned why the state would limit the application of the law to birth control clinics and not engage in broader enforcement, an argument that was present in Griswold's brief. Furthermore, Justice White argued that the law was overbroad.[91] In this argument, he was joined not only by the petitioner, but by amici Adams and Planned Parenthood, who contended that the state could employ narrower alternatives to meet its goal of discouraging extramarital and premarital affairs.[92]

The Dissenting Opinions: No Basis for a Constitutional Right (but Amici Influence!)

Unlike the majority opinion of Justice Douglas, the concurrences employed settled case law to strike down the Connecticut statute and provided a test for evaluating other state laws that interfered with the right to marital privacy. In their opinions, these two dissenters responded to many of the concerns of the amici; while they used these briefs negatively, that is, they expressly rejected them, the influence of the amici is clearly apparent. The dissents of both Justices Black and Stewart emphasized that there was no constitutional basis for overturning the Connecticut statute, and neither justice recognized a general right of privacy in the Constitution. Justice Black contended that the majority and concurring opinions were using privacy instead of strict scrutiny and warned that privacy was an ambiguous concept that could be either expanded or shrunken in meaning.[93] Justice Black specifically criticized Justice Goldberg's attempt to use the Ninth Amendment to strike down laws that either violated fundamental principles of liberty and justice or were contrary to the traditions and conscience of the people. He contended that it was impossible for a court to determine which traditions were rooted in the conscience of the American people and claimed that in making this determination, judges and justices would inevitably fall back on their own notions of liberty and justice. According to Justice Black, there was "no machinery with which to take a Gallup poll," nor was there "a gadget which the court can use to determine what traditions are rooted in the conscience of people."[94] For this reason, Justice Black argued, decisions about "natural justice" had to be left in the hands of the legislatures.[95] Conference discussions reveal that Justice Potter Stewart also believed that the petitioners should seek relief in the Connecticut legislature.[96]

This reference to Gallup polls and public opinion likely was a response to the briefs submitted by Griswold and by amici Adams and

Planned Parenthood. Griswold provided an extensive discussion of how the statute did not "conform with the majority view" on contraception and argued that objective measures of this view that could be found in public opinion, medical practice, religious views, and federal, state, and local laws.[97] Planned Parenthood argued that a thorough discussion of societal views, such as was offered in the petitioner and amici briefs, would enable the Court to assess the "full development and present place" of contraception in American life, an assessment required by *Brown v. Board of Education*.[98] The Planned Parenthood brief included extensive appendixes in support of its position that there was widespread support for contraception in American society. Interestingly, this discussion also was in tune with the concerns voiced by the Justices in the Brennan, Douglas, and Harlan papers about the views of the populace and the medical community about contraception.

According to Planned Parenthood, the anticontraception law was inconsistent with various governmental laws and programs in place to encourage family planning.[99] In addition, Planned Parenthood contended that all religions recognized the moral right and obligation of couples to limit propagation.[100] Furthermore, Planned Parenthood provided extensive discussion about contemporary community views on contraception, arguing that Gallup polls and the statements of national leaders indicated strong support for family planning.[101] Similarly, Adams noted that there was consensus among the populace that contraception was permissible.[102] Both Planned Parenthood and Adams argued that the prohibition against contraception was at odds with established medical practice, which saw contraception as an important guarantor of physical and psychological health.[103] The state rejected this view of medical practice, contending that there was disagreement in the medical community about the "benefits and costs" of contraception.[104] Probably without knowing it, the parties and the amici were responding to the concerns earlier voiced by the Justices in their notes to each other and in conference deliberations about *Poe v. Ullman*, wherein they discussed the paucity of information about medical and popular views of contraception.

Similarly, Justice Black may have been responding to party and amici arguments about public opinion when he concluded that majority sentiment was irrelevant to the Court's decision-making process. Similarly, he may have had these briefs in mind when he entered into an extensive discussion of the role of courts in a constitutional democracy. Much of his dissent is devoted to this discussion, and he argued that the Justices penning the majority and concurring opinions struck down the law because they believed that it was "unreasonable, unwise, arbitrary, capricious and irrational," rather than because it violated any specific constitutional provision. In making this determination, Justice Black claimed that his brethren were assuming not a judicial role but a legislative one, and in so doing, were blurring the separation of powers. Justices Black and Douglas were continuing a long-running feud about the place of the Court in the democracy, with Justice Douglas arguing that the court was not "sitting as a superlegislature"[105] and Justice Black implying that the majority was in fact assuming such a role.

The Role of Amici in *Griswold v. Connecticut* and Party and Amici Coordination

In *Griswold*, the amici were better at anticipating the Justices' concerns than they were in *Poe*, with many of their arguments being either explicitly or implicitly addressed in the majority, concurring, and dissenting opinions. The amici took few chances in this case: they almost always addressed arguments that had been advanced in Griswold's brief, and they usually provided additional data to support these arguments. All of the amici focused on the due process clause of the Fourteenth Amendment, arguing either that married couples had a right to privacy or that doctors had a due process right to provide information about contraception. The amici who focused on marital privacy were successful: *Griswold* established that there was a right to privacy held by married couples that warranted heightened constitutional protection. The amicus asserting physician rights, however, was not successful; here, as in *Poe*, the Justices were resistant to conferring additional constitutional protections upon doctors.[106]

The ACLU penned what was probably the most influential amicus brief in this case, and its brief mirrored the one that it had submitted in *Poe*. The ACLU was successful in influencing dissenters in *Poe*, and in *Griswold* it saw its views become part of the majority opinion. Furthermore, its arguments became the center of discussions among the Justices in conference deliberations.[107] To a far greater extent than either of the parties, the ACLU appears to have anticipated the Justices' concerns in *Griswold* and focused its energy on grounding the privacy right. While Griswold devoted relatively little space to this right (13 out of 96 pages), almost all of the ACLU brief centered on it. The other briefs, particularly that of Planned Parenthood, also appear to have helped the Justices to decide this case. Planned Parenthood provided an assessment of the societal view of contraception and discussed the detrimental impact of this statute on married couples. The CCCL impressed upon the Justices the need for heightened protection of the marital relationship. Finally, Adams provided the Justices with a more extensive discussion of the medical consensus on birth control, arguing that a ban on prescription contraception undermined health and well-being. It bears noting that these discussions provided information that the Justices had noted was missing in the *Poe* litigation.

What is perhaps most striking about interest-group participation in this case is the great degree to which the amicus effort appears to have been coordinated. The amici cited each other repeatedly: Adams cited Planned Parenthood five times,[108] Planned Parenthood cited Adams three times,[109] and the ACLU cited Planned Parenthood once.[110] Furthermore, the amici effort appears to have been coordinated with that of the petitioner Griswold. Griswold clearly knew what was in these briefs and approved of the arguments and data employed by amici. She repeatedly cited to the amici briefs, especially to the brief of Planned Parenthood. In the petitioner brief, there were six cites to Planned Parenthood and one cite to the Adams brief.[111] Perhaps even more important, the amicus briefs raised no arguments that were not present in this brief. There was considerable overlap in these briefs, and while the amici provided elaboration of Griswold's position, they were merely seconding this position. It is perhaps not surprising that Griswold's brief was so comprehensive. There were no page limitations of the party briefs in the 1964 Term, and her brief was nearly 100 pages long. When the page limitation was introduced in 1980 and the parties had to limit their briefs on the merits to 50 pages, the ability of parties to include everything, including the kitchen sink, was also limited.[112] It is perhaps not surprising that the role of the amici was altered with this procedural change. In fact, while amici participated with parties in the cases that came after this, there was never again the almost perfect correspondence between party and amici arguments that was apparent in this case. In the two 1997 physician assistance in dying cases discussed in chapter 4, there was a large degree of correspondence between the party and amici briefs, but in these cases, amici either quietly raised new issues or elaborated on points raised only briefly in party briefs. It was only in *Griswold* and in *Moore v. City of East Cleveland*, discussed in chapter 5, that amici raised *no* new issues.

THE LEGACY OF THE POE AND GRISWOLD DECISIONS: ESTABLISHING THE RIGHT TO PRIVACY AND CREATING OPPORTUNITIES FOR AN EXPANDED AMICUS ROLE

Griswold was a landmark case for several reasons. It was in this case that the Court for the first time recognized a general right to privacy. While state courts had been finding privacy rights in tort law since the early 1900s, these rights were actionable in a relatively narrow range of cases involving the press.[113] In *Griswold*, the Justices expanded the privacy right far beyond this limited application. Furthermore, while the majority claimed that it was based solely on privacy analysis and eschewed any suggestion that it relied on the Fourteenth Amendment due process clause, this case actually turned on the application of substantive due process. The Court's willingness to employ a much more expansive interpretation of the right to privacy, coupled with its implicit use of substantive due process, have created significant opportunities for interest-group participation in later cases involving the privacy right.

The right to privacy is not mentioned in the text of the U.S. Constitution; to find a constitutional right to privacy, the Justices had to rely upon both explicit clauses in the Constitution and Bill of Rights and an implicit understanding of the larger subtext of this document. Justice Douglas' majority opinion tied the privacy right to the First, Third, Fourth, Fifth, and Ninth Amendments, finding that they created a penumbra under which privacy could be located; the concurring opinion of Justice Goldberg found the privacy right squarely within the Ninth Amendment; and the concurrences of Justices Harlan and White relied on the Fourteenth Amendment due process clause. Moreover, the majority and concurring opinions all relied upon natural law principles to understand these specific constitutional protections. The Justices attempted to uncover the larger principles upon which the Constitution was based, and they argued that these principles protected even those rights that were not explicitly enumerated in the text. By relying on natural law, the Justices expanded the scope of the Constitution far beyond the specific protections in the Bill of Rights.

While a number of scholars have traced the use of natural law back to some of the earliest Supreme Court cases,[114] this was the first decision in which the Justices used specific provisions in the Constitution to justify an expansion of their role. Justice Douglas's penumbra can only be understood if one is able to discover the larger meanings of the specific constitutional provisions invoked. This development allowed the Justices to look beyond the constitutional text to a larger subtext and to consider not only constitutional principles but also a broader understanding of individual rights. While such penumbral reasoning may not have been novel,[115] this was the first case in which the Court expressly embraced its use. *Griswold* called upon judges to be not only technicians, strictly applying legal principles, but artisans as well. By employing penumbral reasoning, judges were called upon to understand not only the written text but also the broader meanings of this text.

This enlarged role, and the broader understanding of rights that underlay it, ultimately compelled the Justices to look beyond the narrow legal questions presented in privacy cases and to invite broader participation by not only formal litigants, but interest groups as well.

Over time, these parties would consider whether privacy analysis should be employed in an ever-expanding universe of cases and would argue about whether the larger meanings of the Constitution guarded against governmental interference. *Griswold* obviously introduced a huge degree of uncertainty into constitutional adjudication and compelled the Justices to move beyond the case law in interpreting the Bill of Rights. It was this heightened uncertainty, coupled with the Justices' need to rely on arguments and information that was not strictly legal, that opened the door to an expanded amicus role.

Furthermore, the interest-group role was altered by the Justices' reliance on the due process clause of the Fourteenth Amendment. Justice Douglas's majority opinion was careful to eschew any reliance on this clause; however, the concurrences and dissents hinged on this provision. Much of the commentary surrounding *Griswold* centers upon the implicit use of the clause. Under the Fourteenth Amendment, individuals are entitled to due process before the state governments may take their life, liberty, or property. For more than 100 years, the Justices have disagreed about the scope of the due process clause. Some have argued that this provision guarantees only procedural protections: that is, it mandates that a certain process be followed before one can be deprived of their rights. Other Justices have contended that this clause should be read more broadly as guaranteeing not only procedural fairness but substantive fairness, as well. At the heart of substantive due process is the understanding that there are certain unenumerated rights that must be protected against governmental encroachment. These substantive due process rights are fundamental, and a state may interfere with these rights only where there is a compelling reason for doing so.

While the Justices have embraced the use of substantive due process in a number of instances throughout the twentieth century, Justice Douglas contended that he was not employing this approach in *Griswold*. His position in the ongoing debate about incorporation of the Bill of Rights to apply to the states, and his position that the Fourteenth Amendment due process clause mandated only the incorporation of specific provisions of the Constitution, may have compelled him to base his *Griswold* opinion on specific clauses and to reject an alternative approach based on the more amorphous conception of fundamental fairness.[116] In spite of this attempt to ground privacy on specific protections, the concept of fairness employed in this case can only be understood in light of a broad interpretation of the purposes and intents of the Constitution and Bill of Rights. For example, the zone of privacy adopted by Justice Douglas can be understood only in the context of the marital relationship. This privacy interest is relational and does not exist outside of the association between husband and wife. One must understand the contours of the marital relationship to appreciate the scope of the privacy right. Similarly, one must use a broader context to understand the right recognized by Justice Goldberg in his concurrence. Justice Goldberg's opinion hinged upon the Ninth Amendment, but used the language of fundamental rights to determine which rights the people retain. Citing *Snyder* and *Gitlow*, Justice Goldberg found that the due process clause of the Fourteenth Amendment protected those liberties that were "so rooted in the traditions and conscience of the people as to be ranked as fundamental."[117] He used the discourse about incorporation to find that to determine which rights are fundamental, Justices must look to the traditions and conscience of the people and assess whether the right "cannot be denied without violating those fundamental principles of liberty and justice that lie at the base of all our civil and political institutions."[118] Similarly, the concurrences of Justices Harlan and White employed substantive due process, with its inquiry into whether a right is fundamental, to strike down the Connecticut law.

Thus, in reaching their decisions, the majority and concurring opinions relied not only on the explicit provisions in the Bill of Rights, but on broader notions of fairness. As groups sought to extend the privacy right discovered in *Griswold*, the Justices were repeatedly faced with a number of questions raised by the *Griswold* holding. First, is the right to privacy a fundamental right? This is a critically important question, because fundamental rights are deserving of the greatest degree of constitutional protection, but it is a question that is left unanswered by the majority. If privacy is a fundamental right, then states may only interfere with this right if there is a compelling state interest and the state action is narrowly tailored to advance this interest. Few regulations will survive this rigorous inquiry. If, however, privacy is not a fundamental right, states will be permitted to regulate this right if they can demonstrate that there is merely some legitimate state interest and that the regulation is rationally related to this interest. There is a presumption of constitutionality in cases where there is no fundamental right at play, and for this reason, the question of whether privacy is a fundamental right is critically important.

As a society, we have accepted, with relative equanimity, that rights explicitly created in the Constitution are deserving of heightened protection. We are in significant disagreement, however, about whether there are fundamental unenumerated rights and about how much protection to afford these rights. The *Griswold* decision was based upon a fundamental unenumerated right, the right to privacy, and it quickly became apparent that this right was a controversial one. Even locating the right to contraception *within* the Constitution, by relying on the due process clause of the Fourteenth Amendment, has not diminished the controversy surrounding this case.

Substantive due process calls upon Justices to employ notions of fairness in ascertaining which rights are fundamental. The Court's 1937 decision in *Palko v. Connecticut* established that a fundamental right was one that was either deeply rooted in our nation's history and traditions or implicit in the concept of ordered liberty so that neither liberty nor justice would exist if it was sacrificed.[119] This approach has been problematic since it assumes that our history and traditions, and our notions of liberty and justice, lead to one inexorable set of truths about individual rights. I am arguing here that Griswold and its progeny are on shaky ground not only because they relied on the right to privacy, which is not expressly recognized in the Constitution, but because this case and those that followed called upon the Justices to revisit the contentious issue of fundamental rights. Some analysts contend that the Justices who sought to strike down the anticontraception law in *Griswold* should have grounded their decision on a less controversial clause, like the liberty component of the due process clause or the equal protection clause.[120] Analysts often make the same argument about the abortion right—that privacy is too tenuous to support this right. These commentators may be overlooking one critical fact: both due process and equal protection are based upon some notion of fairness, and we as a society are not in agreement about what is fair with regard to controversial issues like abortion, euthanasia, and gay rights.

Thus, much of the debate about whether there existed a privacy right, and about the contours of this right, was apparent in the *Griswold* opinions. The Justices were sharply divided about whether the Constitution created a right to privacy and where such a right could be located. Moreover, the majority opinion did not establish a standard for evaluating laws that ran afoul of the right to privacy. Perhaps most troubling, the opinion failed to state whether the privacy right was a fundamental right, deserving of the protections of strict scrutiny. These omissions and ambiguities were problematic, since the Justices created a right to privacy that could be broadly invoked to challenge not only anticontraceptive laws, but other laws as well. The tremendous potential of this privacy right quickly became apparent, as cases were brought challenging laws that regulated or prohibited not only contraceptives, but also abortion, assistance in dying, familial relations, and homosexual activities. While the Court quickly dispatched the question of whether states had a legitimate purpose in barring the use of contraceptives, it ran into much more difficulty in assessing states' purposes in criminalizing abortion, euthanasia, and homosexual activities. *Griswold* provided little guidance to courts in evaluating the states' purposes or in assessing the effects of these statutes. This decision failed to establish whether the right to privacy was a fundamental one, to be accorded the greatest degree of protection, or whether this right was less than fundamental, and one that states could regulate for less than compelling reasons.

Griswold recognized a right to privacy, but its legacy has been contradictory and unclear. A majority of the populace appears to have been strongly supportive of the notion of marital privacy, but to find this right, the Justices had to rely upon a broad interpretation of the Bill of Rights, along with natural law principles of fairness.[121] The Justices penning the majority and concurring opinions relied upon their understanding of our nation's traditions and history, and the concurring opinions of Justices Goldberg and Harlan emphatically argued that the right to privacy was mandated by the basic values that underlay the founding of the republic. Over time, litigants have attempted to use *Griswold* to establish that the right to privacy adheres to a broad range of activities. They have sought to employ fundamental rights analysis to make their arguments, claiming that our traditions and history bar the regulation of a number of activities, including gay and lesbian sexual activities, the use of abortion, and physician assistance in dying. In their decisions, the Justices have been unwilling or unable to correct some of the deficiencies apparent in *Griswold*, and there has been little development of privacy law. Moreover, later cases have failed to definitively establish whether privacy is a fundamental right, although a majority of the Justices appear to have accepted that it is not, since they have allowed states more flexibility in regulating abortion, euthanasia, and gay and lesbian rights.

Furthermore, the Justices have failed to articulate a standard for evaluating the right to privacy. Little attention has been paid to the development of privacy jurisprudence, with the Justices largely ignoring legal doctrine and instead focusing on the medical and social scientific data presented in these cases. While *Griswold* focused on the creation of legal doctrine governing privacy, few of the subsequent cases are concerned with this doctrine. The one facet of legal doctrine that the Justices have been concerned about has been whether a state regulation is supported by our nation's history and tradition, and they have signaled that this is an issue that can be understood only in light of historical evidence. This focus derives from the Court's ongoing debate about fundamental rights and allows significant opportunities for amici to influence the Court. Many of the cases that followed *Griswold* turned on the historical record or on the traditions of the American people to assess whether a state regulation could stand. Interest groups likely appreciated this emphasis on history and tradition, because they probably believed that they could provide much needed information to the Justices. Similarly, the Court's focus on basic fairness, so apparent in Justice Douglas's penumbral approach, likely opened the door to amici who wanted to assure that the Justices had all the medical, social science, and scientific data that they might need to evaluate any case at their threshold. Thus, the Court's focus on "fairness" and on the history and traditions of the American people has allowed interest groups to play a significant role in the adjudication of a wide range of privacy cases. The following chapters discuss how the Court has employed the data present in amici curiae briefs, and how its selective use of certain data and reliance on certain groups has made the Court less, rather than more, democratic.[122]

NOTES

1. The U.S. Supreme Court had also dismissed an earlier case challenging the same Connecticut law, *Tileston v. Ullman* (1943) 318 U.S. 44, holding that doctors could not raise patient rights.

2. 367 U.S. 502–504. Some commentators have since disputed the Court's finding that the statutes were not being enforced. See Mary L. Dudziak, "Just Say No: Birth Control in the Connecticut Supreme Court before *Griswold v. Connecticut*," 75 *Iowa Law Review* 915–939, 917 (1990).

3. 367 U.S. 509.

4. 367 U.S. 517.

5. 367 U.S. 521–522.

6. 367 U.S. 518-19, note 9.

7. 367 U.S. 519, 21.

8. 367 U.S. 542, 44.

9. 367 U.S. 521.

10. 367 U.S. 554–555.

11. Harlan Papers, Harlan cert memo, file box 117, p. 1.

12. Harlan Papers, Bench memo, file box 117, p. 1. It is very difficult to determine who penned this brief, since there is no author. It is very likely that the brief came from Justice Harlan himself, since the pattern seems to be that an "unauthored" memo belongs to the Justice in whose collection it is found.

13. Harlan Papers, Bench memo, file box 117, p. 1.

14. Harlan Papers, Bench memo, file box 117, p. 1.

15. Harlan Papers, Bench memo, file box 117, p. 1.

16. Petitioners' brief in *Poe v. Ullman*, 28.

17. Amicus brief of the American Civil Liberties Union in *Poe*, 5.

18. Amicus brief of ACLU in *Poe*, 7–10.

19. Douglas Papers, Conference notes on *Poe*, file box 1248, 3/3/61.

20. Douglas Papers, Conference notes on *Poe*, file box 1248, 3/3/61.

21. Harlan Papers, Bench memo, file box 117, p. 10.

22. Harlan Papers, Bench memo, file box 117, pp. 5, 13, 14, 21.

23. Amicus brief of Sixty-Six Physicians in *Poe v. Ullman*, 11.

24. Brennan Papers, file box 55 (b), p. 7.

25. Douglas Papers, Conference Notes, file box 1248, 3/3/61.

26. Harlan Papers, Cert memo, file box 117.

27. Harlan Papers, Cert memo, file box 117, p. 19.

28. Harlan Papers, Bench memo, file box 117, p. 19.

29. Amicus brief of Planned Parenthood in *Poe v. Ullman*, 11, 14.

30. Amicus brief of Planned Parenthood, 15–42. Amicus Planned Parenthood also provides extensive appendixes that provide detailed bibliographies

for scientific and medical articles on contraception, along with commentary on the stances taken on contraception by the major religious denominations in the United States and a discussion of the legal status of contraception in the states and territories (appendixes A-G).

31. Amicus brief of Planned Parenthood, 45–49.

32. Brennan Papers, Memo from Brennan, file box 55 (b), p. 8.

33. Harlan Papers, Bench memo, file box 117, p. 20.

34. Douglas Papers, Conference notes, file box 1248, 3/3/61.

35. Douglas Papers, Conference notes, file box 1248, 3/3/61.

36. Brennan Papers, Memo from Brennan, file box 55 (a), pp. 4–5.

37. Brennan Papers, Memo from Brennan, file box 55 (a), pp. 5–7.

38. Brennan Papers, Memo from Brennan, file box 55 (a), p. 7.

39. Brennan Papers, Memo from Brennan, file box 55 (a), p. 7.

40. Harlan Papers, Bench memo, file 117, p. 16.

41. Brennan Papers, Memo from Brennan, file box 55 (b), p. 8.

42. Douglas Papers, Conference notes, file box 1248, 3/3/61.

43. Douglas Papers, Clippings file, file 1248.

44. Petitioners' brief in *Griswold v. Connecticut*, 4.

45. Petitioners' brief in *Griswold v. Connecticut*, 8.

46. Section 53-32 of the Connecticut General Statutes stated that "any person who uses any drug, medicinal article or instrument for purpose of preventing conception shall be fined not less than $50 or imprisoned not less than 60 days nor more than one year or be both fined and imprisoned," and Section 54-196 made it a crime to "assist, abet, counsel, cause, hire or command another to commit any offense" in the code, and stated that an accessory should be subject to the same penalties that she would be if she were the principal offender.

47. ACLU brief in *Griswold*, 6–8, 9–10.

48. ACLU, 14–6.

49. ACLU, 8, 11–13.

50. CCCL, 7, 11–4; pp. 7, 9–10, 12–13.

51. Adams et al., 9, 13.

52. 381 U.S. 482.

53. Samuel D. Warren and Louis D. Brandeis, "The Right to Privacy," 4 *Harvard Law Review* 193–220 (1890).

54. 277 U.S. 438, 478 (1928).

55. See letter from Justice Brennan to Justice Douglas, Brennan Papers, file box 130, 4/24/65; Conference notes in Douglas Papers, file box 1347.

56. 381 U.S. 484.

57. Justice Douglas citing to *Boyd*, 381 U.S. 484.

58. Petitioner, 79.

59. Petitioner, 80-82.

60. Petitioner, 69; Adams et al., 22, 24, 14–15.

61. Planned Parenthood, 14–16, 24; Adams et al., Motion, 2–3, amicus brief, 9, 11–12.

62. Letter from Justice Brennan to Justice Douglas, Brennan Papers, file box 130, 4/24/65.

63. Letter from Justice Goldberg to Justice Brennan, Brennan Papers, file box 130, 4/27/65.

64. Bernard Schwartz, *The Unpublished Opinions of the Warren Court* (New York: Oxford University Press, 1985), 228–229.

65. See Letter from Justice Brennan to Justice Douglas, Brennan Papers, file box 130, 4/24/65; Notes from conference, Douglas Papers, file box 1347.

66. 381 U.S. 486.
67. Petitioner, 86.
68. CCCL, 13 (citing Pope Paul VI's remarks on birth control in 1964).
69. ACLU, 7.
70. Petitioner, 62; ACLU, 14, Planned Parenthood, 11–12.
71. Petitioner, 67–70, Planned Parenthood, 20.
72. 381 U.S. 485; Petitioner, 65; ACLU, 8, 12–13; Planned Parenthood, 9.
73. 381 U.S. 486.
74. See Douglas Papers, file box 1347 (in Douglas' notes, he contends that enforcement of the law would result in a "shocking invasion of privacy, as the intimacies of the marital relationship were spread upon the record of a criminal proceeding through the testimony of the accused's [sic] friends, servants, neighbors—or perhaps through the accused's confession of his (or her) crime"); Douglas Papers, file box 1347 (letter from Justice White to Justice Douglas, wherein Justice White contends that the Fourth Amendment is implicated by this law since the law would authorize a search for an intrauterine coil).
75. Petitioner, 87.
76. ACLU, 8–9.
77. CCCL, 14.
78. Page 12.
79. Petitioner, 87; Planned Parenthood, 13.
80. 381 U.S. 488–489.
81. 381 U.S. 493.
82. 381 U.S. 496.
83. 381 U.S. 495.
84. In a letter to Justice Douglas, Justice Brennan argued that "it is plain that, in our civilization, the marital relationship above all else is endowed with privacy" (Brennan Papers, file box 130, 4/24/65). Similarly, in his notes, Justice Douglas contended that the Connecticut law "intruded deeply into the privacy which the institutions of home and family require in order to survive" (Douglas Papers, file box 1347), and in Douglas's conference notes, Justice Thomas Clark is said to have argued that there is a "right to marry, to have a home, [and] to have children," and Justice Arthur Goldberg is said to have contended that "if one can form a club, he can join wife [sic] and live with her" (Douglas Papers, file box 1347).
85. Petitioner, 83–84, 90.
86. ACLU, 6.
87. Page 21.
88. Petitioner, 71. In a letter to Justice Douglas, Justice White also offered a tongue-in-cheek analysis, arguing that the case raised Eighth Amendment concerns since there was "an obvious addiction to sex involved and it [was] cruel and unusual punishment to deprive one of it or to permit it only at the cost of having children" (Douglas Papers, file 1347).
89. 381 U.S. 503.
90. Adams et al., 1,3,5,8; pp. 14–16, 17.
91. 381 U.S. 506.
92. Petitioner, 72; Adams et al., 16; p. 21.
93. 381 U.S. 509.
94. 381 U.S. 519.
95. 381 U.S. 512.
96. Douglas Papers, file box 1347, notes from Conference.
97. Petitioner, 48–60.

98. Planned Parenthood, 25.

99. Pages 25–28; Appendix 1A.

100. Pages 33–35; Appendix 1C.

101. Pages 34–38; Appendix 1D.

102. Adams et al., 1.

103. Pages 28–32; Appendix 1B; Adams et al., 2 Motion, 1,3,5 Brief.

104. Respondent, 21–24.

105. 381 U.S. 482.

106. In fact, while the Justices' personal papers suggest that this was a key issue in the *Poe* litigation, by the time the Court heard *Griswold*, it was a minor question. Only the Chief Justice referred to the physicians' First Amendment rights in conference deliberations, noting that these rights did not justify invalidating the law (Douglas Papers, file box 1347, Conference notes).

107. Douglas Papers, file box 1347, Conference notes.

108. Adams et al., 1, 17, 18.

109. Planned Parenthood, 15, 22, 28.

110. ACLU, 13.

111. Petitioners brief, 41, 42, 43, 46, 52, 64.

112. According to Rule 34.3 in *Supreme Court Practice*, "[a] brief on the merits shall be as short as possible, but, in any event, shall not exceed 50 pages in length" [Robert L. Stern, Eugene Gressman, and Stephen M. Shapiro, *Supreme Court Practice* (Washington, DC: Bureau of National Affairs, Inc., 1986 edition, p. 547].

113. Allen, 687.

114. For example, several commentators have pointed to the Court's 1798 decision in *Calder v. Bull* as an example of natural law jurisprudence. For example, see G. Sidney Buchanan, "The Right to Privacy: Past, Present, and Future," 16 Ohio Northern University Law Review (1989): 403–510, 407; William Wayne Justice, "Recognizing the 9th Amendment's Role in Constitutional Interpretation," 74 Texas Law Review (196): 1241–1244, 1241; and Thomas B. McAffee, "A Critical Guide to the 9th Amendment," 69 Temple Law Review (1996): 61–94, 91.

115. Several analysts claim that penumbral reasoning has had a long and productive history, beginning with opinions by Justice Oliver Wendell Holmes and continuing today. For example, see Glenn H. Reynolds, "Penumbral Reasoning on the Right," 140 *University of Pennsylvania Law Review* (1992): 1333–1348, 1346).

116. Nadine Strossen, "The Right to Be Let Alone: Constitutional Privacy in *Griswold*, *Roe*, and *Bowers*," in Eastland, 91.

117. 381 U.S. 487.

118. 381 U.S. 493.

119. *Palko v. Connecticut* 302 U.S. 319, 325, 326 (1937).

120. For example, see Bruce Fein, "*Griswold v. Connecticut*: Wayward Decision-Making in the Supreme Court," 16 *Northern Ohio University Law Review* (1989): 551–560, 551; Janet L. Dolgin, "The Family in Tradition: From *Griswold* to *Eisenstadt* and Beyond," 82 *Georgetown Law Journal* (1994): 1519–1571, 1521–1522; Lackland H. Bloom, Jr., "The Legacy of *Griswold*," 16 *Northern Ohio University Law Review* (1989): 511–544, 528–529; Richard D. Mohr, "Mr. Justice Douglas at Sodom: Gays and Privacy," 18 *Columbia Human Rights Law Review* (1986–1987): 43–110, 44, 108; Cathy A. Harris, "Outing Privacy Litigation," 65 *George Washington Law Review* (1997): 248–xx, 272–273; Catherine Grevers Schmidt, "Where Privacy Fails: Equal Protection and the Abortion Rights of Minors," 68 *New York University Law Review* (1993): 597–638, 599; Grey, 380.

121. In the preface to their book, Ellen Alderman and Caroline Kennedy claim that most people believe that there is a general right to privacy even though it is not expressly mentioned in the Constitution [*The Right to Privacy* (New York: Alfred A. Knopf, 1995), xiii].

122. Some commentators, among them Stephen Schnably, have contended that the privacy right should be used as "a vehicle for applying democratic norms"; however, as this book will suggest, this right has been shown to advance the views of a select population (Schnably, 870).

3

Amici Curiae and the Abortion Debate

Griswold v. Connecticut opened the door to many other cases where litigants alleged that a federal, state, or municipal law violated their right to privacy. Abortion laws were the first to come under fire, and in 1973 the Supreme Court ruled that restrictive abortion laws in Georgia and Texas ran afoul of the privacy right. In the aftermath of this decision in *Roe v. Wade*, Congress and thirty-four state legislatures passed new abortion laws. In the two decades that followed *Roe*, the Supreme Court heard twenty-one cases involving challenges to these new laws.[1] In many of these cases, the Court was the subject of intense interest group lobbying, as individuals and groups filed amici curiae briefs to provide the Justices with alternative legal theories as well as historical, sociological, scientific, and medical information. This chapter focuses on four critically important cases heard by the Court in the two decades following the *Roe* decision. In addition to *Roe*, this chapter examines amici participation in *Harris v. McRae*, the first case that called upon the Court to evaluate post-*Roe* limitations on access to abortion, *City of Akron v. Akron Center for Reproductive Services*, which involved a city ordinance that imposed stringent regulations on the abortion procedure; and *Casey v. Planned Parenthood of Southeastern Pennsylvania*, which upheld the validity of *Roe* while at the same time transforming the abortion right.

Eighty-seven briefs were filed in these four cases: nineteen briefs were filed in *Roe* and its companion case, *Doe v. Bolton*; eleven briefs filed in *Harris v. McRae*; twenty-two briefs filed in *Akron v. Akron Center for Reproductive Services*; and thirty-five briefs were filed in *Casey v. Planned Parenthood of Southeastern Pennsylvania*. This chapter explores the extent to which the Supreme Court employed the legal arguments and extralegal data presented in these briefs. Beginning with *Roe*, the Supreme Court has constructed abortion as primarily a medical issue, rather than a gender issue or broader civil liberties question; because of this, in cases heard after *Roe*, the Justices have been deluged with medical and scientific information about the abortion procedure, pregnancy, and childbirth. It would seem that these cases presented the amici with their best opportunities for influencing the Justices because they were able to provide the data that the Justices needed to place the cases in a larger context of medical care and public health. Interestingly, as this chapter demonstrates, the Justices relied heavily on certain friends who provided not only this medical and scientific information, but alternative legal arguments as well. Moreover, concerns about basic fairness, so much a part of *Griswold*, underlay much of the debate in all four cases and provided the amici with significant opportunities to influence the Justices.

THE RIGHT TO PRIVACY APPLIED TO ABORTION LAWS: *ROE V. WADE*

In 1971, the Supreme Court heard two cases that challenged state laws that sharply limited access to abortion. These two cases, *Roe v. Wade* and *Doe v. Bolton*, were reargued in late 1972, and in January 1973 the Court struck down the abortion laws as violative of privacy rights. At issue in *Roe v. Wade* was a Texas law that barred abortion except where the life of the woman was in jeopardy.[2] *Doe v. Bolton* challenged a Georgia statute that restricted abortion to cases where the health of the woman was at risk, where the pregnancy resulted from rape or incest, or where the fetus had a "grave and irremediable mental or physical defect."[3] The district courts that had heard the *Roe* and *Doe* cases had struck down the laws, finding that the right to privacy encompassed the right to choose abortion. Neither court, however, provided the plaintiffs injunctive relief, and the holdings went unimplemented.

This section considers the impact of both *Roe* and *Doe* amici on the *Roe v. Wade* opinions. My assumption is that the Justices read these cases in tandem and considered all the amici briefs when deciding each case. Nineteen amici briefs were filed in the two cases. The amici weighed in on a range of issues, among them, the case law governing due process, equal protection and the right to privacy, the history of abortion laws, the impact of abortion laws on women, the issue of fetal rights, and the medical practice of abortion. The influence of amici on Justice Blackmun's majority opinion is apparent in a number of areas—in particular, in the discussion of the historical background of abortion laws, the abortion procedure, and the issue of fetal rights. Justice Blackmun's willingness to go beyond the legal arguments and caselaw likely accounts for the discernible impact of the amici briefs. It bears noting, however, that this is one of the few cases in this book in which the opinion derives from sources largely outside of the party and amici briefs.

Direct Cites to Amici Briefs

Roe is one of the few cases in this study in which the Justices extensively employed direct citation of amici briefs. There are eight direct citations to amici briefs, and all are in Justice Blackmun's majority opinion. All these cites refer to "the amici" in general; only two expressly name the amicus, and both amici are identified only in footnotes. The first direct cite is to amicus American Ethical Union, which he cites in his discussion about the disagreement among organized religions about whether life begins at conception.[4] The second direct cite is to the brief of the National Right to Life Committee (NRLC), which he cites for the proposition that some believe that life begins at conception.[5] The other six direct cites referred to the briefs without naming them; Blackmun noted the briefs in his discussion of state interests in using abortion bans to limit illicit sexual relations,[6] to regulate the medical practice of abortion,[7] and to protect fetal life.[8] Justice Blackmun also cited the briefs of the amici when he noted that some believed that the abortion right should be absolute,[9] and that some thought that life began at conception[10] and that fetuses had constitutional rights.[11] This pattern of direct citation is much different from that we see in the other cases examined in this book. In *Roe*, there is much more direct citation than in the other cases: in an opinion of 25 pages, there are 8 cites. As discussed later in this chapter, this is striking, given the reluctance of later Courts to cite to the briefs in much longer opinions. It is also significant that the Justices—in particular, Justice Blackmun—made explicit mention of the amici, but were very reluctant to identify the amici to whom they referred.

Indirect Use of Amici Briefs

The influence of the amici on Justice Blackmun's opinion is apparent not only in his direct cites to their briefs but, also perhaps more significantly, in his indirect reliance upon them. Justice Blackmun's implicit use of the amici briefs is apparent in a number of areas; however, it is in his discussions about the common law "quickening" distinction, the position of professional organizations, and the burdens imposed on women by the abortion laws that this influence is most profound.[12] More subtle amici influence can also be discerned in Justice Blackmun's discussion of the state's interest in maternal health and fetal life.

Quickening Distinction

Much of Justice Blackmun's majority opinion focused on the history of abortion laws, and the amici provided little information about ancient attitudes, the Hippocratic Oath, or English and American statutory law governing abortion, all facets of the Justice's opinion that likely derived from independent research at the Mayo Clinic's Medical Library in the summer of 1972. There was substantial overlap, however, between Justice Blackmun's decision and the amici briefs in the discussion of the common law basis of abortion and, in particular, of the quickening distinction. While Roe noted only that medical and legal standards regarding abortion were based upon the common law distinction between "quick" and "unquick" fetuses,[13] it was the amici that provided extensive discussion of this point. At common law, and in the law of the early American states, the legality of abortion was dependent upon whether the fetus was "quick," that is, far enough along in its development that the woman could sense its presence. Typically, women with fetuses that were not yet quick could have abortions, but there was a penalty for aborting a quickened fetus. Justice Blackmun focused on this common law distinction and used it to draw conclusions about the state's interest in adopting abortion laws.

Amici on both sides of this case noted the quickening distinction; a discussion of this distinction was incorporated into the briefs of amicus American College of Obstetricians and Gynecologists (ACOG), Certain Physicians of the American College of Obstetricians and Gynecologists (Certain), the National Legal Program on Problems of the Poor (NLP), the NRLC, New Women Lawyers (NWL), the California Committee to Legalize Abortions (CCLA), and Texas Diocesan Attorneys (TDA).[14] Moreover, these briefs appear to have provided information that was used by Justice Blackmun. For example, in discussing the common law and Lord Coke's position that the abortion of an unquickened fetus was neither a misdemeanor nor a felony, Justice Blackmun may have drawn on the briefs of the NLP[15] and ACOG.[16] Justice Blackmun may also have integrated information about Lord Bracton and Blackstone that was provided by various amici.[17]

The history of abortion regulation was a key component of Justice Blackmun's decision. He argued that this history provided "insight . . . [that enabled the Court to determine] state purposes and interests" in adopting abortion bans.[18] The amici appear to have highlighted for

Justice Blackmun the key components of the common law history of abortion regulations. For the remainder of his study of history, Justice Blackmun likely relied on other sources, including, perhaps, the extensive list of sources provided in the appendixes and supplements provided by amici ACOG and Planned Parenthood of America.[19]

Position of Professional Organizations about Abortion Laws

Moreover, in his examination of abortion laws, Justice Blackmun included a discussion of the positions of the American Medical Association (AMA), the American Public Health Association (APHA), and the American Bar Association (ABA) on this issue. Roe noted only that national medical organizations had issued statements supporting some elective abortions,[20] but amici provided a wealth of data about the changing positions of the AMA and ABA, much of which appears to have been employed by Justice Blackmun. For example, in his opinion, Justice Blackmun discussed the shift in the AMA's position on abortion in the late 1960s and early 1970s.[21] In particular, Blackmun detailed the resolution adopted by the AMA House of Delegates, which significantly liberalized access to abortion. He stated that this resolution was based on the understanding that abortion was a medical procedure and that doctors should not be restrained by state laws that significantly curtail their ability to make medical judgments.[22] This discussion of the ACOG and AMA positions was provided by ACOG, the NLP, Planned Parenthood, and the American Association of University Women (AAUW); ACOG provided extensive appendixes that detailed its policy statements, along with a summary of data on the implementation of revised abortion statutes.[23]

Similarly, ACOG and Planned Parenthood appear to have played an important role in equipping Justice Blackmun with information about the evolving position of the American Bar Association on abortion. Again, petitioner Roe provided only a cursory discussion of this issue, noting simply that the ABA had passed a Uniform Abortion Act.[24] It was ACOG and Planned Parenthood that provided extensive discussion of the ABA's position on abortion and, in particular, the Uniform Abortion Act. In its brief, ACOG and Planned Parenthood provided the most recent versions of proposals by the ABA Commissioners on Uniform State Laws and gave the Justices information about the Uniform Abortion Act adopted by the Commissioners and approved by the ABA in February 1972.[25] This Uniform Act allowed for the termination of pregnancies up to twenty weeks, and beyond this point in cases of rape and incest or where the physician determines that continuing the pregnancy will impair the physical or mental health of the woman. Justice Blackmun contended that this Uniform Act was part of a "trend towards the liberalization of abortion law, especially in the first trimester,"[26] a point made by the AAUW in its brief.[27]

Privacy, Due Process, and the Burdens Imposed on Women by Abortion Laws

Most of Justice Blackmun's relatively short opinion was devoted to a discussion of the medical aspects of abortion. He devoted little attention in the opinion to a discussion of the legal basis for the right to privacy. In fact, less than three pages are devoted to this discussion, and of these pages, less than two are devoted to the legal precedent that established a right to access abortion under the privacy right.[28] This passing reference to the privacy right may reflect a reticence about striking down the laws on these grounds. In a Memo to the Conference dated May 18, 1972, Justice Blackmun proposed invalidating the laws on the basis of vagueness, and noted that the Justice was anxious to avoid the more complicated Ninth Amendment issues in this litigation.[29] In his majority opinion, Justice Blackmun did employ privacy, but his analysis is relatively superficial, and he relied heavily on case law dating from the 1891 decision in *Union Pacific R. Co. v. Botsford* and the 1937 decision in *Palko v. Connecticut*.[30]

The other Justices writing opinions eschewed any reliance on privacy and instead focused on the liberty component of the Fourteenth Amendment due process clause. For example, Justice Stewart's concurrence was based almost entirely on the due process right, and he linked the caselaw governing marriage and family life to this right.[31] Similarly, in his concurrence, Justice Douglas argued that the abortion right had roots in the *Boyd v. United States*, an 1886 case involving the Fourth Amendment search and seizure provision, and that his *Griswold* decision was central to this right.[32] Justice Douglas had penned seven drafts of the *Roe* decision,[33] and nearly all of his seven-page opinion focused on the legal precedent establishing a due process right to access abortion. Justice Douglas's focus on liberty seems to have derived in large part from comments by Justice Brennan to Douglas's initial drafts. In these comments, Justice Brennan argued for a broad reading of the privacy right, contending that it includes not only freedom from bodily restraint, but also the right to make the "basic decisions of one's life" and the right to "autonomous control over the development and experience of one's intellect, interests, tastes and personality."[34] Similarly, Chief Justice Burger likely would have relied solely on the legal argument in reaching his decision. While he did not discuss either the liberty or the privacy right, he noted that he thought the Court had relied too heavily on "various scientific and medical data in reaching its conclusion."[35] In a Memo to the Conference penned in May 1972, the Chief Justice criticized the quality of the parties and joked that on reargument he would propose that the Court "appoint amici for both sides."[36] The dissents of Justices White and Rehnquist also focused on the legal right and argued fiercely that the majority had stepped far outside settled privacy jurisprudence in establishing an abortion right.[37]

Thus, the Justices employed both due process liberty and privacy in justifying their decisions. Both the parties and their amici focused on the case law in this area, and independent amici influence cannot be readily discerned. In providing the *rationale* for employing liberty and privacy rights, however, the amici appear to have had a profound impact. Much of this discussion focused on the burdens that restrictive abortion laws imposed on women, and the Justices relied heavily on a select group of amici in this part of the discussion. For example, Justice Blackmun argued that the right to privacy was broad enough to encompass the abortion decision and that denying this right would result in severe detriment to women seeking abortions. He catalogued the harms that befell women who were forced, against their will, to carry a pregnancy to term. Justice Blackmun noted that these women often suffered a "distressful life and future, psychological harm, [harm to their] mental and physical health, distress regarding the unborn child, and the stigma [that attached to] unwed motherhood."[38] Similarly, Justice Douglas argued that women had to bear the "pain, higher mortality rates, and aftereffects of childbirth" and often had to "abandon their educational plans, [suffer a] loss of income, forgo the satisfaction of their careers, and [endure a further taxing] of the mental and physical health in childcare, [as well as] . . . social stigma."[39] Justice Douglas also noted that one's "health" should be defined broadly, to encompass concerns about these hardships.[40]

In discussing the burdens placed on women by unwanted pregnancy, Justices Blackmun and Douglas likely relied upon the briefs of ACOG , the American Ethical Union (AEU), NWL, State Communities Aid Association (SCAA), and AAUW, who all provided extensive information about the detrimental effects of pregnancy on women's well-being.[41] Most of Roe's discussion was limited to a discussion of how this pregnancy had affected her,[42] but the amici briefs discussed the burdens placed on women more generally. For example, the brief of AAUW contended that "[compelled] pregnancy severely limits a woman's liberty" and catalogued the hardships that would befall a woman who was not able to terminate an unwanted pregnancy.[43] The AAUW provided extensive discussion of the effect of "compulsory pregnancy" on women's educations, careers, mental and physical health, economic status, and relationships with family members, including the unwanted child.[44] In addition, Roe and several amici included appendixes with extensive bibliographies that detailed the social and medical impact of unwanted pregnancy.[45]

It bears noting that party and amicus influence seems to have been absent in the most important aspect of this decision, that is, the creation of the trimester framework. Justice Blackmun asserted that women did have the right to choose abortion, but that at different points in the pregnancy, the state's interest in maternal health and fetal life could place significant limitations on this right. Neither the formal parties nor the amici recommended this framework. In fact, the closest that one could say amici came to the trimester framework was in their discussions of the Uniform Abortion Act, which permitted abortion without any categorical restrictions up to twenty weeks. This is interesting, suggesting the role that external reports may play in U.S. Supreme Court litigation. I come back to this point in chapter 4, when I discuss the impact of the Report of the New York State Task Force on Death and Dying on the Court's disposition of the two physician-assisted-dying cases, *Washington v. Glucksberg* and *Vacco v. Quill*.

State Interest in Barring Abortion

In addition to exploring the right to privacy and the liberty interests at play in this litigation, the parties, amici, and Justices focused on the state's articulated interests in maternal and fetal life. In this area, the role of amici was perhaps even more subtle, although probably not less important than in the other areas discussed. Justice Blackmun's trimester framework hinged on two questions: first, whether abortion posed a greater risk to the woman's health than carrying the pregnancy to term; and second, whether the fetus had become viable. Both of these issues, maternal health and fetal life, were central to the states' purported rationales in adopting abortion bans. Justice Blackmun devoted significant energy to discussing these interests and concluded that the interests did not justify an absolute ban in the first trimester, but grew substantially as the pregnancy advanced and ultimately became compelling at some point in the second and third trimesters.[46] From Conference Memoranda and correspondence between the Justices, it appears that Justice Blackmun supported drawing the line at fetal viability. Both Justices were affected by amici and party arguments about maternal health, and Justice Blackmun cited the "Petitioners and their amici" as support for the position that abortion in early pregnancy had become relatively safe.[47] Other Justices, most notably, Justice Brennan, opposed this distinction, contending that it "focused on the fetus rather than the woman" and was inconsistent with the interests articulated by the states. He argued that the "cutoff" point should be derived from assessing when the dangers to women's health were greater from abortion than from pregnancy and childbirth.[48]

In addition to this direct citation, the Justices indirectly relied on the briefs of the parties and their amici in discussing maternal health. The

Petitioners in both *Roe* and *Doe* focused on the medical implications of abortion and concluded that abortion was safer than childbirth.[49] In their discussion, the Petitioners explicitly relied on the analysis of amici ACOG and Planned Parenthood, noting that "abortion is an accepted medical procedure for terminating pregnancy and that amici medical organizations recognize the acceptability" of this procedure.[50] Moreover, the cooperation between the Petitioners and their amici is even more striking given the facts that much of the Petitioners' discussion of the medical aspects of abortion mirrors that of amicus ACOG and that the structure and content of these briefs are identical.[51] Justice Blackmun appears to have relied on this joint analysis, along with a discussion provided in Planned Parenthood's supplemental brief. In this brief, Planned Parenthood set out the "background facts" for this litigation, focusing on the impact of laws liberalizing abortion on maternal and infant mortality, the differential treatment of poor and nonwhite women, and the number of freestanding abortion clinics.[52] The Justices wholly ignored respondent amici arguments that abortion was unsafe or could result in serious complications.[53]

Furthermore, as in their discussion of the impact of abortion laws on maternal health, the parties and their amici had profound disagreements about the nature of the state's interest in fetal life. Again, the impact of amici on the Justices was subtle in this area; in fact, some amici may have had a negative impact on the Justices, that is, they may have swayed the Justices to vote against their position. The respondents and their amici devoted much of their briefs to discussing the "humanness" of the fetus and to arguing that the fetus is a human being entitled to the state's protection.[54] The respondents and their amici also argued that fetuses had a right to life under the Fifth and presumably Fourteenth Amendments and that the equal protection clause protected fetuses.[55] These arguments that life begins at conception and that the fetus has rights protected under American law were countered almost entirely by the Petitioners' amici, who devoted considerable energy to arguing that the question of when life begins is a philosophical and religious question.[56] This argument was made forcefully by NWL, which devoted a portion of its brief to discussing the disagreements among religions about when life begins.

Ultimately, Justice Blackmun sided with Roe's and Doe's amici on both issues. Justice Blackmun explicitly cited the briefs of the NRLC, AEU, and amici in general in concluding that there was "disagreement among those trained in medicine, philosophy and theology" about this issue.[57] Justice Blackmun also accepted the view of the Petitioners and their amici on the issue of whether fetuses were persons within the meaning of the U.S. Constitution. He concluded that while the Constitution did not define "person," the application of the Fifth and Fourteenth Amendments, along with federal and state common law and statutory law, strongly suggested that fetuses were not protected.[58] He looked at many of the areas of the law discussed by the Petitioners and their amici,[59] among them, tort and property law, and concluded that fetuses were not covered under these laws. This selective use of some amici arguments and data and the rejection of others was apparent in *Roe*, as it was in later cases.[60]

Cooperation among Amici

There was significant cooperation among the parties and the amici and between amici in *Roe v. Wade*. Most of this cooperation, however, was on the side of the Petitioners. The Petitioners invited the Court to examine the amici briefs filed on their behalf[61] and relied heavily on the briefs of amici ACOG , Planned Parenthood, the ABA, and New Women Lawyers. In fact, the Petitioners cited the ACOG brief repeatedly and employed much of the same data and arguments that appeared in the amici's *Doe* and *Roe* briefs.[62] Similarly, the Petitioners' amici referred to Doe's and Roe's briefs,[63] as well as to the briefs of other "friends."[64] In particular, a number of amici cited the policies or briefs of ACOG , the AMA, and the ABA.[65] It bears noting that the Petitioners and their amici made positive use of each other's briefs and did not note their opponents' briefs.

In contrast, the respondent made only one mention of an amicus brief, and it was amicus AMA, which supported its opponents.[66] Similarly, with the exception of one statement by the NRLC applauding the state's interpretation of medical science,[67] the only cites to the state's amici were negative cites of Roe's or Doe's briefs or the briefs of opposing amici. In fact, the entire brief of the NRLC seems to have been devoted to targeting and attacking the briefs of *Roe* and *Doe*. It is very likely that like their adversaries, the states and their amici, recognized that some amici, notably the AMA and the ABA, could potentially affect the outcome of the litigation. For this reason, the respondents and their amici targeted these amici for criticism, as the petitioners had targeted them for praise.[68]

Cooperation among parties and amici was apparent not only in direct cites to each other but in their "parceling out"of the issues in this case. Several briefs stated that the amicus chose to concentrate on only one issue in the litigation and referred the reader to other amicus briefs for discussion of other issues. This division of labor is slightly more pronounced among the *Roe* amici. For example, four amici briefs filed in support of *Roe* and *Doe* stated that their briefs concentrated on one aspect of the debate.[69] In contrast, one respondent amicus brief notes that it so confined itself. Moreover, amici coordination was also apparent in the sharing of data, and the use of similar, and sometimes identical, language in the briefs. One would assume that parties to a case would rely on many of the same resources in writing their briefs. But the parties and some amici went much further—they actually used the same wording. In some places, whole blocks and even pages of texts were identical. For example, in discussing the problem of contraceptive failure, the briefs of *Roe* and amicus ACOG are identical for several pages.[70] Similarly, the entire section on the "medical nature of abortion," which encompassed between six and eight pages, appears verbatim in both the *Roe* and ACOG briefs.[71] Amici on the other side of the debate also employed each other's writings. Much of the information about the medical complications of abortion present in the brief of Certain Physicians, Professors and Fellows of the American College of Obstetrics and Gynecology is also present in the brief of Sassone: here, two pages of text are identical.[72]

In summary, there was substantial cooperation and competition among amici in the *Roe v. Wade* litigation. A number of amici drew directly on the briefs of other friends, while at the same time hotly disputing claims of other amici in major substantive areas. The briefs that the Supreme Court saw were an amalgam of many organizations and reflected the pooling of resources and the shared construction of legal arguments. It is often difficult to sort out the data and arguments provided by the formal parties from those encompassed in the amici briefs. Perhaps in part because of this coordinated effort, the impact of amicus arguments was muted.

Conclusions about *Roe*

An examination of the party and amici briefs reveals that there was significant overlap between these briefs with regard to some of the most important issues in the *Roe* litigation. The party briefs, and especially the brief of Jane Roe, provided extensive discussion of a number of subjects: among these, the right to privacy and the state interests in maternal health and fetal rights. In these areas, the amici role was limited to merely seconding the arguments in Roe's brief. These topics appear to have been very important, especially to Justice Blackmun, who expressly noted the impact of the amici in his discussion of all of these issues. More interestingly, the amici not only seconded the petitioners' arguments, they elaborated on points raised only briefly by the parties, specifically, the quickening distinction, the position of medical and legal organizations on the abortion issue, and the burdens imposed on women by unwanted pregnancy. The amici appear to have had an important role in helping the Justices to consider these issues. For example, Justice Blackmun's majority holding hinged on the historical basis for abortion laws, including the quickening distinction, and the position of the AMA and ABA on this medical procedure. Similarly, Justices Blackmun and Douglas appear to have been strongly influenced by the discussion of the burdens borne by women who must bring an unwanted pregnancy to term.

There is a great deal of overlap between party and amici briefs in *Roe*, and for this reason, it is difficult to assess interest-group influence in this case. This overlap is largely the result of the fact that the party briefs are quite lengthy: Roe's brief is 145 pages and Texas's brief is 58 pages. This ability to discuss all of the topics at play in the litigation relegated the amici to what was essentially a "me, too!" position. None of the data or arguments that the Justices found central to this case was presented by the amici alone: all of them were at least hinted at by the parties. While the amici's impact was on issues not attributable to them alone, *Roe* is nonetheless an important case because of what it portended for future amici roles, particularly in the abortion domain. Amici in *Roe* were not all equal on the playing field: the Justices demonstrated that they were willing to accept the arguments and data presented by some amici and to reject those provided by others. This is apparent both in the Justices' direct cites and in their indirect reliance upon these briefs. Furthermore, the *Roe* litigation suggests that the patterns of conflict and cooperation among formal parties and their amici that characterize later cases are being established as early as 1973.

THE FIRST CHALLENGE TO THE ABORTION RIGHT: HARRIS V. MCRAE

Immediately following *Roe*, there was intense activity in both Congress and the state legislatures aimed at reversing the holding or limiting its impact. At issue in *Harris v. McRae* was a rider to the federal appropriations bills for fiscal years 1977, 1978, and 1979 that barred the use of federal funds to reimburse Medicaid abortions. The rider, known as the Hyde Amendment, took different forms each of these years; the most restrictive form limited the use of Medicaid funds for abortions "except where the life of the mother would be endangered if the fetus were carried to term."[73] Most of the legislative debate about the Hyde Amendment centered on the question of whether Congress could refuse to fund abortions that were "medically necessary," though not needed to save the life of the woman. The District Court for the Eastern District of New York struck down the Hyde Amendment, finding that it violated the equal protection clause of the Fifth Amendment and the free exercise clause of the First Amendment.[74]

Writing for a 5-4 majority, Justice Potter Stewart overturned the district court's decision, holding that the Hyde amendment violated neither the equal protection nor the due process guarantee.[75] In evaluating the equal protection claim, Justice Stewart contended that the Hyde Amendment had to be evaluated under the rational relationship test, a test that was readily met by demonstrating that Congress had enacted the amendment to advance a legitimate state interest, here, protecting and promoting fetal life.[76] Justice Stewart dispensed with the due process claim by contending that the "right to privacy" established in Roe did not create an affirmative obligation on the part of the government to ensure that women be provided with abortion services. Instead, Justice Stewart argued, it required only that government not interfere with the decision by creating obstacles.[77] Similarly, the concurring opinion of Justice Byron White focused on the due process clause. Justice White argued that Roe struck down only "coercive interference" with the abortion decision and that they Hyde Amendment did not constitute such interference.[78]

The dissenting opinions of Justices William Brennan, Thurgood Marshall, and John Paul Stevens also focused on the due process and establishment clause claims. The dissents all argued, however, that the Hyde Amendment should be struck down because it violated these provisions. The dissenters all contended that the amendment violated the right to privacy established in Roe, since it effectively eliminated access to abortion services for poor women. The dissents also argued that indigency was a "suspect class" and that the amendment could be upheld only if it served some "compelling state interest" and was the least restrictive means for serving this interest. Much of the debate among the Justices centered on their reading of the due process and equal protection provisions. There was far less discussion of the impact that the decision would have on women and their families than there had been in Roe v. Wade. Similarly, there was less discussion of the historical underpinnings of the right to privacy or the equal protection guarantees. Moreover, the importance of the abortion decision for women's rights and for fetal rights, which was central to the Roe decisions, was far less visible in Harris. Justices Stewart, Brennan, and Marshall all alluded to Roe, and one can discern that this case is part of a larger debate, but there is little discussion of this larger debate.[79] This case was one that was addressed largely in isolation from the other abortion cases decided by the Court.[80] It is almost as if the Hyde Amendment, which was adopted by Congress only three years after the Court's decision in Roe, was unimportant. This lukewarm approach to the Hyde Amendment was apparent not only in the Justices' opinions, but in the interest-group participation in this case.

Direct and Indirect Reliance on Briefs

There was less interest-group activity in *Harris v. McRae* than there was in *Roe v. Wade*, *Akron v. Akron Center for Reproductive Health*, or *Planned Parenthood of Southeastern Pennsylvania v. Casey*, the other three cases considered in this chapter. Only eleven amici curiae briefs were filed in this case—the fewest for any case under consideration in this study—and the impact of the amici is least apparent in this case. There were no direct cites to amici briefs in this case, and even indirect reliance is scant. Unlike the other cases, the Justices in *Harris* largely ignored both the issue of basic fairness, implicit in the penumbral approach to privacy articulated in *Griswold*, and the examination of history and traditions, so central to fundamental rights jurisprudence. In fact, the only areas in which amici influence can be glimpsed is in the dissenters' discussion of the due process clause and in their assessment of the impact of the amendment upon indigent women, both of which skirt the issue of fairness.

Specifically, amici appear to have helped to provide data for the dissenters' argument that the Hyde Amendment coerced indigent women to bear children that they would not have borne by choice and, for this reason, undermined women's liberty and privacy rights. For example, Justice Brennan contended that these women didn't really have a choice and that the Amendment was coercive "by design and effect."[81] Justices Blackmun and Stevens echoed this argument, claiming that the majority and concurring opinions were largely out of touch with reality.[82] This argument that the Hyde Amendment provided poor women with an illusory choice is one that was made by the respondents[83] and seconded by NOW and the State of New York. In its brief, NOW argued that Hyde provided women with several grim alternatives: either find funds in their meager incomes to pay for a legal abortion, submit to a cheaper, illegal abortion, self-abort, or continue their life-threatening abortion to term.[84] New York also noted that Hyde restricted the availability of abortion services and eliminated any real alternatives to childbirth.[85] This correspondence between amici arguments and the dissenting opinions suggest that the Justices were influenced in writing their opinions by the amici's characterization of the "choice" offered to poor women under the Hyde Amendment.

In several other areas, amici made arguments apart from those made by the respondent that seem to have influenced the Justices. First, in his discussion of suspect classifications under the equal protection clause, Justice Marshall drew upon the views of the National Council of Churches of Christ. In its brief, the National Council argued that footnote 4 of *U.S. v. Carolene Products* decision, which laid out the criteria for a suspect classification, was operative in this case. According to

Justice Marshall, under *Carolene Products*, indigency was a suspect classification because it "seriously curtails the operation of political processes ordinarily relied upon to protect minorities."[86] In its amicus brief, the Council had noted that the *Carolene Products* framework was operative in *Harris* and that strict scrutiny should be applied, since poverty had impeded the exercise of the fundamental right to choose abortion and the amendment discriminated against a "discrete, easily identifiable and traditionally disenfranchised segment" of society.[87] The respondent only briefly noted the *Carolene Products* decision in noting an Eighth Circuit decision handed down that Term.[88] Extensive discussion of this case appeared only in the brief of the Council, and it is likely that Justice Marshall was influenced by amicus and integrated the discussion into his dissenting opinion.

Second, Justices Marshall and Brennan appear to have integrated the language of several amici about the relative "powerlessness" of indigent women affected by the Hyde Amendment. Both Justices asserted that these women were in a position of "powerlessness," and were unable to protect themselves against encroachments upon their right to privacy.[89] This discourse about "powerlessness" was provided only by the Association of Legal Aid Attorneys of the City of New York (Legal Aid) and National Organization for Women (NOW) in their amici briefs: Legal Aid asserted that the amendment would "increase powerlessness,"[90] and NOW contended that the group of affected women were "powerless, disadvantaged and starkly defined."[91] The issue of powerlessness was discussed only in these amici briefs; it did not appear in the party briefs. Finally, Justice Brennan's claim that the Hyde Amendment was an attempt to override the Court's decision in *Roe v. Wade*[92] was an argument only made by amici. The National Council of Churches of Christ in the U.S.A. (NCCC), Legal Aid, and the State of New York et al. all contended that the purpose and effect of the Hyde Amendment was to undermine *Roe*.[93] Unlike the respondent, which argued that the Amendment was part of a larger religious movement aimed at undermining the abortion right, the amici made a broader and far less subtle argument. They contended that the primary effect of the Hyde Amendment was to overrule *Roe* and force women to carry their fetuses to term.

Cooperation and Conflict Among Amici

There was some cooperation among the amici in *Harris*, but to a far less degree than in the other abortion cases under consideration. In only two instances did an amicus cite to another's brief,[94] and only once did a formal party cite an amicus.[95] Unlike the groups in *Roe*, these amici did not divide up the issues in the litigation, but in some instances cooperation between the parties and their amici is apparent. For example, the amici seconded McRae's arguments about the religion clauses.[96] Similarly, the amici seconded Harris's arguments about whether the Hyde Amendment effectively foreclosed meaningful choice for poor women and violated the equal protection clause and about whether fiscal concerns could be used to justify the amendment. In addition, the amicus NCCC provided elaboration of reference to *U.S. v. Carolene Products* by the respondents.

Cooperation between the parties and their amici and among the amici was far less common in this case. While the groups in *Roe* sharply disagreed about the central issues in the case, amici in *Harris* did not. Only the Coalition for Human Justice and the Bergen-Passaic Health Systems Agency sharply disagreed about the impact of this amendment on the poor.[97] Moreover, most of the arguments and data presented by the amici was ignored. Very few amici were heard in this case, and only the dissenters made use of amici arguments or data.

Conclusions about *Harris*

The impact of the amici briefs on the Court's decision in *Harris v. McRae* was very limited, and only four of the eleven groups filing briefs appear to have been heard: New York State, Legal Aid, NOW, and the NCCC. All of these amici had significant organizational strengths. New York State, a governmental entity, was seen by the Justices as being highly professional; Legal Aid was a professional organization; and NOW and the NCCC were institutions with significant resources.

Only dissenting Justices Brennan and Marshall employed amici arguments and data. To a significant extent, the Justices appear to have "fought out" the Hyde Amendment among themselves. Most of the debate about strict scrutiny and rational relation centered on the Justices' different views of these levels of constitutional analysis; there may have been little room for the amici to maneuver in this debate. Unlike the Court's decision in *Griswold* or *Roe*, in *Harris*, the Justices didn't focus on fundamental rights analysis or on issues of basic fairness, and few technical or scientific issues were at play here. Furthermore, the extensive discussion of the impact of these laws on women's health or fetal rights, so apparent in the cases that came before and after *Harris*, were not present here. To some extent, this case stands alone—there was less interest in this litigation among interest groups, and the amici made only marginal contributions to the Supreme Court's decision. There were only passing references to the abortion cases that had come before it. As in the other case that generated little amici interest, *Moore v. City of East Cleveland*, which is discussed in chapter 5, the

Justices relied to a significant extent on the legal issues at play in this litigation, and amici played a much less significant role.

A RE-VIEWING OF THE ABORTION RIGHT AND ROE V. WADE: *CITY OF AKRON V. AKRON CENTER FOR REPRODUCTIVE HEALTH, INC. ET AL.*

In the 1983 case *City of Akron v. Akron Center for Reproductive Health*, the Supreme Court for the first time since *Roe v. Wade* considered a broad anti-abortion statute that regulated abortions in the first and second trimesters. This case turned on the question of which constitutional framework should be employed to evaluate abortion regulations. At issue in this case was a municipal ordinance that had five components: it mandated that second trimester abortions be performed in hospitals and not clinics; it required parental consent for minors' abortions; it regulated the informed consent procedure; it imposed a twenty-four-hour waiting period between the informed consent and the procedure; and it regulated the disposal of the abortus.[98] *Akron* was the first of several broad anti-abortion statutes to come to the Court in the 1980s and early 1990s. *Akron* also was the first case to be heard by the Court that squarely raised the question of whether the trimester framework was workable. In the decade between *Roe* and *Akron*, many perceived that medical advances had begun to weaken the framework by making early second trimester abortions safer. Much of the debate in *Akron* centered on the role of medical and scientific knowledge in the abortion debate. In *Akron*, the argument among the parties and their amici was largely extralegal and required the Justices to weigh medical and scientific evidence about the abortion procedure. Perhaps for this reason, it is not surprising that amici played an important role.

Writing for a 6-3 majority, Justice Lewis Powell invalidated all of the provisions of the ordinance and found that the ordinance violated women's right to access abortion services and that there was no compelling state interest in the ordinance. Much of Justice Powell's decision focused on the specific provisions at issue in this case. Justice Powell devoted little space to discussion of the proof framework to be used in abortion cases or to the continued viability of *Roe v. Wade*. In contrast, in her dissenting opinion, which was joined by Justices Rehnquist and White, Justice Sandra Day O'Connor focused almost exclusively on the *Roe* decision and said little about the specific provisions of the *Akron* ordinance. Most of Justice O'Connor's dissent was devoted to discussion of the trimester approach and the proof framework at issue in abortion cases.

There was significant interest-group activity in *Akron*, which presented the largest number of amici briefs ever filed in an abortion case. A range of medical and scientific organizations, along with civil rights and religious groups, filed the twenty-one amici briefs in this case. Most amici focused the proper proof framework to be employed. Those writing in support of petitioner Akron argued that the less-stringent rational relationship test could be used to evaluate abortion regulations that did not unduly burden the woman's decision. The rational relationship test is highly deferential to legislatures and requires only that the challenged law bear some rational relationship to a legitimate state interest. On the other hand, those groups and individuals filing in support of respondent Akron Center for Reproductive Health contended that the strict scrutiny test be used. This test is employed where a law has an impact on a fundamental right, and it presumes that the law is invalid. To withstand strict scrutiny, the governmental entity must show that the law serves some compelling state interest and is narrowly tailored to achieve that interest. Since this case presented the strongest challenge to *Roe* thus far, perhaps it is not surprising that many amici discussed the *Roe* decision. A significant number of amici argued either that *Roe* was wrongly decided and should be overturned or that *Roe* was good law and governed the disposition of *Akron*.

Direct Cites to Amici Briefs

Akron involved issues that were much more technical and required more scientific and medical knowledge than had the *Harris* case. In fact, *Akron* is much closer to *Roe*, since both cases involved statutes that regulated the abortion procedure itself. One might have expected that the Court would *directly* rely on amici briefs in *Akron*, as it did in *Roe*. After all, the Court was considering regulations that involved a medical procedure, and various amici provided extensive information about the impact of the regulations on the abortion procedure. Despite this technical focus, there are only two direct citations to amici briefs, and only one to a brief filed in this case.[99] This one direct cite, however, was very important. In this one cite, Justice Sandra Day O'Connor explicitly adopted the undue burden standard that had been articulated by the Solicitor General in the amicus brief filed by the United States.[100] Moreover, despite the paucity of direct cites in this lengthy holding (Justice opinion was 33 pages; Justice O'Connor's was 23 pages), there is evidence of significant indirect amici influence.

Indirect Reliance on Amici Briefs

A number of amicus briefs provided information that was not provided by the City of Akron or the Clinic but that appears in the majority and dissenting opinions. Both Justices Powell and O'Connor appear to have relied on the arguments and data provided by amici, but it bears noting that some amici were much better heard by the Justices. As in both *Roe* and *Harris*, the Justices relied upon groups with known medical or scientific expertise to provide them with much needed information. This influence is apparent in three areas: in the Justices' assessment of the validity of the *Roe* decision; in their discussions about the proper proof framework to be used in abortion cases; and in their handling of the specific provisions of the *Akron* ordinance.

The Justices Reconsider Roe v. Wade

Akron presented the first direct challenge to *Roe*, and in this decision, the Justices expressly reconsidered the scope of the abortion right. The majority and dissenting opinions were in sharp disagreement about the continuing validity of the trimester framework; the influence of some amici, most notably, the United States and several professional organizations, is apparent in the Justices' discussions. In his majority opinion, Justice Powell noted that *Roe* had been under significant pressure and that a number of state legislatures had passed laws limiting the abortion right. He also noted that in the decade since *Roe* had been handed down, the Court had been sharply criticized for reaching the wrong decision.[101] Despite this state response, Justice Powell reaffirmed *Roe*, reiterating that there is a fundamental right to abortion and that abortion regulations must be evaluated under the stringent strict scrutiny framework.[102] He held that the state was prohibited from regulating first trimester abortions and that regulations affecting second and third trimester abortions would be subjected to strict scrutiny, that is, they would have to be narrowly tailored to meet a compelling state interest. This argument that abortion regulations be evaluated under strict scrutiny was articulated in both Clinic and amici briefs. In adopting strict scrutiny, Justice Powell echoed the arguments of not only the clinic, but also amici American Public Health Association (APHA), California Women Lawyers (CWL), Certain Law Professors (Professors), National Abortion Federation (NAF), NOW, and Planned Parenthood. All of these amici warned that abortion regulations had to be closely scrutinized because of their impact on a fundamental right.[103] Perhaps even more significant, in rejecting the rational relation test as incompatible with a fundamental right like abortion, Justice Powell employed the same argument advanced by amicus Certain Law Professors, which warned that strict scrutiny had to be used in this case, because in the words of both the Justice and this amicus, a "more relaxed standard" would undermine this fundamental right and would conflict with precedents.[104]

The influence of amici on Justice O'Connor's discussion of the proof framework is even more striking. Much of her dissent focused on the

undue burden standard and the issue of deference to legislative judgment. In reaching her conclusions, Justice O'Connor appears to have
been strongly influenced by the arguments of the Solicitor General. Her
only direct cite to an amicus brief was to the brief of the United States;
in this cite, she revealed that she had accepted the Solicitor General's
view that a regulation has to impose an undue burden before strict
scrutiny can be employed.[105] The United States very clearly offered the
undue burden test in its amicus brief, and Justice O'Connor directly
attributed this test to the Department of Justice.[106] She accepted the
argument of the United States that state regulations infringe on
women's right to privacy only if they constitute an undue burden[107] and
that women's rights have to be balanced against state interests[108] even
in the first trimester.

In this direct cite, Justice O'Connor also explicitly accepted the Solicitor General's view that legislative deference was appropriate in abortion cases.[109] The U.S. focused on both the undue burden standard and
the principle of legislative deference, and these concerns were central
to Justice O'Connor's opinion. For example, the U.S. contended that
federal courts should defer to the state legislatures because they have
"superior fact-finding capabilities" and are better able to "fine-tune and
redirect" abortion policy.[110] These parallels between the U.S.' brief and
Justice O'Connor's opinion, coupled with her direct citation to this
brief, strongly suggest that she was powerfully influenced by this
amicus.[111]

The Nature of the State Interest

Like its decision in *Roe*, the Court's *Akron* decision turned on the
Justices' understanding of the nature of the state's interest in regulating
abortion. Not surprisingly, Justice Powell carved out a much narrower
role for states in this area, while Justice O'Connor allowed the states
much greater latitude. While their approaches to abortion regulation
differed, both Justices appear to have been strongly influenced by the
medical and scientific groups that participated as amici. Indeed, both
Justices looked to medical judgment and advances in scientific technology as a way of determining the scope of the state interest in the
regulation of abortion.

Justice Powell retained not only *Roe*'s trimester framework, but its
focus on the role of the physician in effectuating the abortion right. In
Akron, as in *Roe*, the Supreme Court recognized the central role played
by the physician, contending that "the full vindication of the woman's
fundamental right necessarily requires that her physician be given 'the
room he needs to make his best medical judgment.'"[112] Powell argued
that regulations that restricted second trimester abortions were constitutional only if they had some "medical basis" and were part of "ac-

cepted medical practice."[113] Thus, the majority asserted, the role of the physician and the standards of medical practice were critical to determining whether the abortion regulations were to be upheld.

A flurry of correspondence occurred between Justices Powell, Blackmun, and Brennan about whether the Court should note that not all doctors are "competent, conscientious and ethical," and that there is significant variation among abortion clinics. Justice Powell initially took notice of the varying quality of physician and clinic care, but Justice Blackmun and Brennan convinced him to strike it from his opinion.[114] Justice Powell's initial concern may have been sparked by the briefs of several amici, who discussed what they called "clinic abuses" and detailed the ways in which pregnant women were coerced into having abortions by clinic staff concerned about making a profit.[115]

In relying on medical practice and the physician's judgment, the majority was likely influenced by the arguments of several professional organizations that filed as amici. The briefs of ACOG , the APHA, and Professors all focused on the role of the physician in the abortion decision, and all contended that the abortion regulations departed from accepted medical practice. Most of ACOG's brief focused on the impact of the *Akron* regulations on the physician's ability to exercise his or her medical judgment, and Justice Powell appears to have accepted its arguments.

Notably, Justice Powell directly cited ACOG's *Standards for Obstetric-Gynecologic Services*, included in the brief's appendix, as support for his position that the states could regulate second trimester, but not first trimester abortions on the basis of maternal health.[116] In addition to this direct cite to ACOG standards, Justice Powell employed several critical arguments offered by ACOG. Perhaps most significantly, Justice Powell's opinion echoed the ACOG argument that the regulations presented "a serious obstacle to sound medical practice"[117] and that the state should not be substituting its judgment for the physician's medical judgment.[118] In its brief, ACOG strongly criticized the state for adopting these regulations and argued that many of the regulations, among these, the informed consent and hospitalization provisions, ran counter to established medical practice.[119] In addition, the arguments of the APHA, that the *Akron* statute treated abortion differently from other medical procedures and that "the physician's judgment is a strong safeguard of maternal health"[120] were incorporated into the majority opinion, as was the brief of the Professors, which contended that the *Akron* regulations "constrain[ed] the physician's exercise of his/her medical judgment."[121]

Justice Powell appears to have accepted the argument made by a number of amici that the state's interest in maternal health had to be evaluated on the basis of whether the regulations were supported by established medical practice and whether they permitted physicians to exercise their professional judgment. Moreover, Justice Powell was likely influenced by the arguments of a number of amici that the state's interest in maternal health did not justify the serious burdens that these regulations placed on access to abortion. Justice Powell's conclusion that the *Akron* ordinance "imposed a heavy and unnecessary burden on women's access" to abortion[122] was supported by the arguments and data provided by amici APHA,[123] Committee for Abortion Rights and Against Sterilization Abuse (CARASA),[124] NAF,[125] and NOW.[126]

Like Justice Powell, Justice O'Connor also appears to have been influenced by amici arguments about the nature of the state interest in this case. While Justice O'Connor rejected the trimester framework established in *Roe*, she continued to focus on the two state interests that helped to define the trimester approach, that is, maternal health and fetal life. She contended that these interests were present throughout the pregnancy and did not depend upon the particular trimester.[127] Justice O'Connor's opinion echoed the amicus brief of the United States and the brief of the City of Akron that first trimester regulations were permissible.[128] Moreover, Justice O'Connor argued that the medical and scientific technology had advanced to such a point that the trimester approach had become unworkable. Drawing on data provided by amicus ACOG, Justice O'Connor contended that the lines that once separated the trimesters had been blurred by advances in obstetrics, gynecology, and neonatology and that these advances placed *Roe* on a "collision course with itself."[129] Justice O'Connor claimed that technology had made abortion safer than pregnancy beyond the second trimester, but had enabled fetuses to become viable earlier than the third trimester. The underlying logic of *Roe*, which was that the state interest in maternal health became compelling at the point at which pregnancy was safer than abortion, no longer existed. Similarly, the state interest in potential life could no longer be confined to the third trimester, since fetuses would be viable before then.

As evidence of these advances in technology, Justice O'Connor relied on ACOG 's Obstetrics-Gynecology Standards,[130] as well as the arguments that the organization offered in its amicus brief. In this brief, ACOG noted that medical science had made abortion safer than childbirth beyond the first trimester.[131] Instead of using this evidence to bar the abortion regulation in *Akron*, however, Justice O'Connor used it to permit the regulation. For Justice O'Connor the steady advancements in technology highlighted the need for a different analytical framework for understanding the abortion right.[132] Justice O'Connor thus employed ACOG's data, but rejected its larger argument.

An Assessment of the Regulations at Issue in Akron

While Justice O'Connor's dissenting opinion focused on the undue burden standard and a traditional separation of powers argument, Justice Powell's majority decision focused on the individual provisions of the *Akron* ordinance. Justice Powell's reliance on amici arguments and data was apparent in this area, as it had been in his discussion about the state interest. While he did not directly cite any amicus brief, he did employ data that was provided *only* by amici.

Hospitalization Provision. Justice Powell noted that twenty-three states had provisions that require that second trimester abortions be performed in hospitals, but he struck down this provision, as he did the others.[133] In rejecting the hospitalization requirement, Justice Powell contended that outpatient clinics performing these abortions could do so as safely as full-service hospitals.[134] In reaching this conclusion, Justice Powell relied heavily on the APHA Recommendation Guide and ACOG standards.[135] While the Akron Center for Reproductive Health simply noted that abortions could be performed at least as safely in clinics as in hospitals,[136] the amici provided extensive support for this position. For example, the APHA Recommendation Guide noted by Justice Powell was discussed at length in the amici briefs of the APHA itself and the NAF.[137] Similarly, the ACOG Obstetrics-Gynecology Standards cited by the majority were discussed at length in the brief of ACOG.[138]

Justice Powell was concerned not only about the relative safety of abortions performed in clinics and hospitals but about the effects of the *Akron* regulations on women. This concern about impact, reminiscent of the majority holdings in *Griswold* and *Roe*, enabled the Justices to consider the underlying fairness of the regulations. Of greatest concern to Justice Powell was the fact that abortions performed in hospitals were twice as costly as clinic abortions and that very few hospitals performed abortions in the City of Akron.[139] In discussing the impact of the hospitalization requirement, Justice Powell indirectly relied on amici. A number of amici discussed the burdens imposed by this requirement, and it is likely that Justice Powell was aware of these arguments. Professional groups, in particular, appear to have been heard by Justice Powell. For example, ACOG and the APHA provided lengthy discussions of the impact of the requirement on access to abortion. In its brief, ACOG noted that relatively few hospitals perform second trimester abortions[140] and contended that the requirement interfered with the physician's ability to exercise his best medical judgment in determining where the abortion should take place.[141] Similarly, the APHA noted that only two hospitals performed any second trimester abortions in 1977 and that only nine abortions were performed in these hospitals in

1977.[142] Much of the APHA brief was concerned with this requirement and provided the Court with extensive evidence of the negative impact of the requirement on women's health.

Other amici argued that the hospitalization requirement made abortions less accessible and more costly,[143] as did the Clinic,[144] but it bears noting that the Clinic and almost all of the amici recognized that ACOG and the APHA were the "experts" in this area. For example, the Clinic used the ACOG Manual of Standards, the APHA Recommended Program Guide for Abortion Services, and the standards of the Planned Parenthood Federation of America as support for its position that the medical community has found early second trimester clinic abortions to be acceptable.[145] Similarly, NOW cited the policy positions of ACOG and the APHA as support for its position that abortion methods could be safely used outside of hospitals.[146] ACOG and the APHA focused on the hospitalization requirement in their briefs, and they appear to have gotten a good return on their investment: Justice Powell's evaluation of this provision appears to have been strongly influenced by these two briefs.

Informed Consent Provision. Like the hospitalization requirement, the informed consent provision of the *Akron* law prompted the Justices to rely on the arguments and data provided largely by amici. The informed consent provision required that physicians read an extensive statement to prospective patients that discussed the risks of the abortion procedure and described the anatomical and physiological characteristics of the embryo or fetus. Justice Powell rejected the informed consent provision, finding that the City had gone beyond the permissible limits established by the Court in earlier cases. Justice Powell contended that the informed consent provision was not intended to inform women, but to withhold their consent. Moreover, Justice Powell argued, the detailed statement describing the anatomical and physiological characteristics of the fetus would at best be based on "speculation by the physician."[147] Similarly, the statement that abortion is a "major surgical procedure" and the long list of possible physical and psychological complications were misleading and did not truly inform the woman about the real risks of the procedure.[148] It appears that Justice Blackmun was quite concerned about this misinformation and, in a letter to Justice Powell, urged that the Court strike down this "inaccurate" informed consent provision.[149]

The amici provided ample evidence to the Court to help the Justices evaluate the informed consent provision, and Justice Powell relied heavily on these arguments and data. Most significantly, Justice Powell contended that the "facts" provided in the informed consent statement were based on speculation,[150] echoing the positions of ACOG, NAF, and

Planned Parenthood, who contended that the descriptions were untrue and without scientific validity.[151] Furthermore, Justice Powell's description of the statement of possible complications from abortion as a "parade of horribles" paralleled the description provided in the brief of Certain Religious Organizations.[152]

Justice O'Connor was also influenced by amici in her assessment of the informed consent provision. She noted that the provision, which requires all physicians to read a detailed statement, may have violated physicians' First Amendment free speech rights, but that this claim had not been raised by either of the parties.[153] The Clinic only briefly touched on the first amendment rights of physicians,[154] but amici extensively discussed these rights. For example, the brief of Certain Religious Organizations discussed this right at length,[155] as did Planned Parenthood.[156] This point was also raised, though briefly, by ACOG.[157]

Parental Consent. The amici also appear to have influenced the Court's handling of the parental consent provision. Justice Powell struck down this provision, which required that the parents of women under the age of 18 be informed that their minor daughters sought abortions and that the parents of women under the age of 16 consent to these abortions. Justice Powell struck down this provision because it did not provide a "by-pass" procedure for mature minors or those whose best interests necessitated that their parents not play a part in the decision-making process.[158] This point about the lack of alternatives for mature minors or minors for whom abortion was in the "best interest"[159] was not only made by the Clinic, but elaborated upon by ACOG and NAF. Both groups argued that the *Akron* provision constituted an "absolute veto" of the minor's decision[160] and that it failed to provide a "quick and confidential procedure" for mature minors or those for whom parental involvement would be harmful.[161]

Physician Counseling. The *Akron* ordinance required not only that a detailed informed consent be read to the patient, but that a physician be the person who read the statement and provided counseling. Justice Powell struck down this requirement, principally because he found that the requirement interfered with the physician's medical judgment by requiring that he or she employ this consent regardless of the patient's circumstances.[162] As in the discussion of the hospitalization and informed consent requirements, the impact of amici on Justice Powell's handling of the physician counseling provision is striking. Most notably, in focusing on the physician-patient relationship, Justice Powell embraced the arguments of ACOG , the American Psychological Association (APA), Planned Parenthood, the NAF, CWL, and NOW, all of whom argued that the provision would undermine the relationship.[163]

Moreover, Justice Powell explicitly endorsed the counseling guidelines of the NAF and APHA, which were included in the briefs.[164] In rejecting the physician-only requirement, he employed ACOG's standards, and he looked to APHA and NAF standards as support for his decision that trained counselors can provide counseling.[165] The impact of the brief of amicus American Psychological Association, which detailed the role to be played by non-physicians in abortion counseling, is also apparent.[166]

Waiting Period and Disposal of Fetal Remains. The Justices spent far less time discussing the waiting period and disposal provisions than they did the informed consent, physician counseling, and parental consent provisions. In evaluating the 24-hour waiting period requirement and disposal provision, however, the Justices were influenced by many of the same amici who informed their judgment with regard to the other provisions. In particular, Justice Powell was strongly influenced by the data and arguments provided by ACOG, and he noted that ACOG recommendations advised that clinics allow "sufficient time for reflection prior to making an informed decision." Consistent with the views of this amicus, Justice Powell contended that the physician would advise the patient to defer the abortion if such a wait were in the patient's best interest.[167] Similarly, Justice Powell appears to have employed the arguments of the American College of Pathologists in discussing the disposal provision. Like this amicus, Justice Powell argued that the provision, which required that fetal remains be disposed of in a "humane and sanitary manner," was unclear and that this "uncertainty [was] fatal because of the criminal liability" that violators assumed.[168]

Certain groups were heard by the Justices in *Akron*—their arguments were employed and their data relied upon. What becomes apparent, however, is that a large number of groups were not heard by the Court—the Court didn't mention them by name and didn't use their arguments or data. Nearly all groups who were heard were professional or medical organizations. Justices Powell and O'Connor paid attention to groups that provided abortion services, most notably, ACOG, the APHA, the NAF, and Planned Parenthood. Justice Powell also heard several professional organizations—he accepted some of the arguments used by California Women Lawyers, Certain Law Professors, and the National Organization for Women. Also loudly heard was the U.S. Department of Justice.

These groups had expertise and were likely viewed by the Court as moderate groups; in fact, their arguments were based on precedent and did not require that the Court overturn settled case law, most notably *Roe v. Wade*. The groups that were not heard tended not to be professional or medical organizations and often called for the overturning of

Roe. For example, the Justices relied little, if at all, on the arguments or data provided by Americans United for Life, Feminists for Life, the Legal Defense Fund for Unborn Children, United Families Foundation, and Women Exploited, or Womankind.[169]

Cooperation and Conflict among Amici

A wide variety of groups filed briefs in *Akron*, and they used very different tactics. Nearly all of the briefs filed in support of the City of Akron were penned by single groups, while multiple groups filed almost all of the briefs in support of the Clinic. With the exception of the amicus brief filed by the United States, the petitioner amici briefs were all filed by groups that are prolife, and nearly all of these were single-issue groups and concerned exclusively with the abortion issue. All of these prolife briefs were highly critical of the *Roe* decision and urged the Court to go beyond the issues in *Akron* to directly address the legitimacy of *Roe*. In contrast, almost all of the briefs filed in support of the Clinic were filed by professional groups, and many of these were multiple-issue groups. They were active outside of the abortion debate and worked on issues that were largely independent of the abortion issue. In *Akron*, perhaps more than any other case in this book, there was a pretty clear lineup: on one side of the case, the amici were single-issue, somewhat radical citizen groups who filed individual briefs; and on the other side, the amici were multiple-issue, mostly moderate professional groups, who signed on with other organizations.

Furthermore, the pattern of amici coordination discerned by Susan Behuniak in her excellent study of the *Webster* litigation was apparent in the 1983 *Akron* case. In *Akron*, as in *Webster*, the groups filing in support of the abortion restrictions did not coordinate their briefs. These groups filed individual briefs, even though some of the briefs were redundant. For example, the briefs of three City of Akron amici, Feminists for Life, United Families Foundation, and Womankind, Inc., appear to have shared data and discussed many of the same issues at great length.[170] Despite the fact that these briefs are overlapping, the amici did not choose to join together to file one brief—instead, they filed three individual briefs.

On the other hand, the Clinic's amici coordinated their activities. These groups were much more likely to divide the issues among themselves and to write about only a few of the issues in this case. For example, the American Psychological Association focused only on the informed consent provision,[171] the American Public Health Association discussed in detail the second trimester hospitalization requirement,[172] and the National Abortion Federation wrote exclusively about the proof framework to be used in abortion cases.[173] In addition, a number of amici explicitly deferred to the expertise of other amici. The American Public Health Association noted that it was in full agreement with the arguments made by amici National Abortion Federation and Planned Parenthood about second trimester hospitalization requirements.[174] The APHA also relied on the ACOG's *Manual of Standards on the Abortion Procedure* in discussing the impact of restrictive abortion laws on women's health.[175] Similarly, NAF deferred to the expertise of ACOG and Planned Parenthood in discussing the safety of second trimester abortions.[176]

The same pattern of party-amici cooperation discerned in *Roe* and *Harris* was apparent in *Akron*, as well. In a number of instances, the parties briefly raised an issue that was elaborated upon by an amici. It bears noting, however, that the party briefs were considerably shorter in *Akron* than they had been in *Roe* and *Harris*, and so the ability of the parties to raise every possible argument, or all the arguments discussed in the amici briefs, was much reduced. For example, the petitioners' and the respondents' briefs in *Roe* were 145 and 58 pages long, respectively. In *Harris*, the petitioners' and respondents' briefs were 39 pages and 187 pages long, respectively. In contrast, in *Akron*, heard after the Court imposed a 50-page limit on party briefs, the page lengths were only 50 pages for both the petitioner and respondent.

In addition to coordinating their activities, some amici demonstrated that they were fully aware of the briefs filed by other, sometimes unfriendly amici. A number of amici devoted a significant portion of their briefs to responding to the amicus brief of the United States. The Department of Justice filed a brief in favor of the *Akron* law, recommending that the Court employ a deferential standard in assessing abortion laws. The briefs of the California Women Lawyers,[177] Certain Religious Organizations,[178] Certain Law Professors,[179] and the National Association for the Advancement of Colored People[180] were sharply critical of the United States' brief and devoted a considerable amount of space to criticizing it.[181]

Conclusions about *Akron*

There was significant amici influence on the Justices' opinions in *Akron v. Akron Center for Reproductive Health*; however, this study strongly suggests that the Justices were very selective about which amici they heard. Some groups, particularly professional organizations or groups with special expertise, were successful in Court; their arguments and data were employed by the Justices even if the Justices didn't directly cite their amici briefs. Among the most successful were the United States, ACOG, APHA, NOW, Planned Parenthood, the NAF, the American Psychological Association, Certain Law Professors, California Women Lawyers, Certain Religious Organizations, and the American College of Pathologists. Perhaps most significantly, dissenting Justice O'Connor employed much of the Solicitor General's brief, and her opinion mirrored this brief with regard to the discussions about the undue burden standard and the need for deference to legislative judgment. This is important, since this issue comes to the fore again in the *Webster* and *Casey* decisions heard in 1989 and 1992.

This study suggests that interest-group participation in abortion litigation had begun expanding by 1983. Many more groups filed in *Akron* than had filed in *Harris* or *Roe*, and this pattern of widening participation continued in the *Webster* and *Casey* cases. *Akron* was a critically important case, because it shed light on the sharp disagreement among the Justices about the continuing validity of *Roe v. Wade*. The majority reaffirmed *Roe* and contended that the *Akron* statute, along with any other statutes, could be assessed by using the trimester approach. On the other hand, the dissent contended that the *Roe* framework was not workable and that advances in science and medicine would make it even less workable in the future.[182] Since so much of the *Akron* decision, and of the abortion cases in general, have been based on the Justices' understanding of the scientific and medical literature about abortion, it is perhaps understandable that amici providing this information would have a significant role in the decision-making process. Furthermore, the Justices' concern about fairness, so apparent in the earlier cases, provided interest groups with an opening to provide information to the Justices about the impact of the municipal law on women's access to abortion. The Court's continuing focus on basic fairness and its attention to the history and traditions of the American people, provided another significant opening for amici influence less than a decade later, in *Planned Parenthood of Southeastern Pennsylvania v. Casey*.

THE FINAL CHALLENGE TO *ROE V. WADE*: PLANNED PARENTHOOD OF SOUTHEASTERN PENNSYLVANIA V. CASEY

Following the Supreme Court's 1989 decision in *Webster v. Reproductive Health Services*,[183] a flurry of activity occurred in the state legislatures aimed at creating anti-abortion laws that would pass muster under the plurality's undue burden standard. In 1988 and 1989, the Pennsylvania legislature amended its Abortion Control Act to regulate access to abortion throughout pregnancy. Among those provisions challenged by Planned Parenthood of Southeastern Pennsylvania were the provisions mandating spousal notification, informed consent, a 24-hour waiting period, informed parental consent, and extensive record keeping. A number of these provisions had been considered by the Court during the 1970s and 1980s and had been struck down as violative of the right to privacy, but the Court's decision in *Webster* was perceived by many as opening the door to reconsideration of the restrictions.

The U.S. Supreme Court granted cert in this case to consider the law in light of the *Webster* decision and to settle conflicts that had arisen among the circuits about the proper standard to use in evaluating abortion laws. Ultimately, the Justices were unable to reach agreement about the standard to use in this case, and as in the *Webster* and *Thornburgh v. ACOG*[184] cases, the Court issued a plurality decision. Its decision in *Casey* affirmed the Circuit Court's ruling that had upheld all of the provisions except for the spousal notification provision. Seven of the Justices penned an opinion in this case: the plurality decision was written by Justices O'Connor, Kennedy, and Souter; and the Chief Justice and Justices Blackmun, Stevens, and Scalia each wrote opinions that concurred in part and dissented in part from the plurality holding.

The Justices' opinions focused on three basic issues: they once again considered the nature of the right at issue in *Roe v. Wade* and, in particular, whether this right was fundamental; they also attempted to understand the place of *Roe* in abortion jurisprudence; and finally, they considered the specific provisions of the Pennsylvania law. For the first time since *Roe*, the Justices seriously deliberated about whether abortion is a fundamental right, and they closely considered the traditions and history of anti-abortion laws. More than half of Justice Blackmun's *Roe* decision had been devoted to a discussion of the history of these laws, and this history was also a central concern for all of the Justices in *Casey*. Ever since the Court decided *Palko v. Connecticut*, the Justices have defined a fundamental right as one that is rooted in the nation's history and traditions. In *Roe*, Justice Blackmun found that there was no basis in our nation's history or traditions for restrictive abortion laws, since these laws had been promulgated only relatively recently and since the United States had always had a strong commitment to the principles of bodily integrity and liberty. For Justice Blackmun, there was no question that the right to abortion was a fundamental right. Cases decided after *Roe*, however, were less than clear about whether abortion was a fundamental right, deserving of strict scrutiny, and in *Casey*, the Court pointedly considered this question. Perhaps predictably, the Justices were split on this question. The plurality argued that this liberty interest did constitute a fundamental right, as did the Justices Blackmun and Stevens. In contrast, Chief Justice Rehnquist and Justice Scalia rejected this view of the abortion right, arguing instead that the right to choose abortion was not a fundamental right since proscriptions against abortion were rooted in our nation's history and traditions. The Justices were also split about whether *Roe* should be governed by the principle of stare decisis. Chief Justice Rehnquist and Justice Scalia vigorously maintained that *Roe* had been wrongly decided and that the Court could and should overturn the decision. The plurality holding of Justices O'Connor, Kennedy, and Souter rejected this view, as did the opinions of Justices Blackmun and Stevens. The plurality focused on the principle of stare decisis and argued that the Court should be extremely careful about overruling prior decisions since such an action threatened the Court's stability and legitimacy.

Finally, the Justices sharply disagreed about whether the Pennsylvania law was constitutional. The plurality upheld all of the provisions except for the spousal notification section, while the Chief Justice and Justice Scalia upheld every provision and Justices Blackmun and Stevens struck down all of these provisions. The Justices' opinions integrated elements of both the litigants' briefs and the amici briefs. In fact, nearly all of the arguments in the holdings were arguments that had been made by the parties and their amici, and the Justices confined themselves to these arguments. A large number of individuals and groups filed amicus curiae briefs in this case, and there was even more coordination and cooperation between the parties and their amici than there had been in any of the other cases under consideration in this study.

Direct Cites to Amicus Briefs

Significant interest-group activity occurred in *Planned Parenthood of Southeastern Pennsylvania v. Casey*. Thirty-five individuals and groups filed amici briefs in this case, and only one abortion case, *Webster*, had more amici.[185] Nonetheless, amici influence is very difficult to trace in this case since the amici almost always seconded or expanded on arguments or data provided in the party briefs. Interestingly, there was virtually no direct citation to amici briefs in the Justices' opinions. The plurality opinion cited the amicus brief of the United States only once, in the first paragraph of its decision, when the Justices noted that

> Liberty finds no refuge in a jurisprudence of doubt. Yet 19 years after our holding that the Constitution protects a woman's right to terminate her pregnancy in its early stages, that definition of liberty is still questioned. Joining the respondents as *amicus curiae*, the United States, as it has done in five other cases in the last decade, again asks us to overrule *Roe*.[186]

Justice Blackmun noted the arguments of the United States twice, when he criticized its use of the rational relation standard.[187] And finally, the plurality signaled that it had read the amici briefs, when it noted that both the "Respondent and its *amici* would deny that women have come

to rely upon the *Roe* decision."[188] Strangely, in a decision that was more
than ninety pages long, these four cites were the only references to
thirty-five amici briefs that had been filed. That is remarkable, given
that the Justices appear to have been aware of amici arguments and to
have incorporated elements of these arguments into their decisions.

Indirect Reliance on the Amici Briefs

While there are very few direct cites in this case, there is ample
evidence of indirect amici influence. This influence is difficult to detect,
since the party and amici briefs mirrored each other to a great extent.
In fact, the pattern apparent in *Akron* and the physician-assisted suicide
cases discussed in chapter 4, where the party raised an issue and left it
to the amicus to elaborate, was clear in this case as well. The influence
of amici arguments and data is most apparent in three areas: first, the
Justices' discussions of the nature of the liberty interest at stake in the
abortion debate; second, the future of *Roe v. Wade*; and third, the individual provisions of the Pennsylvania law.

Nature of the Liberty Interest at Stake in the Abortion Debate
The majority holding in *Roe v. Wade* established that the right to
choose abortion was a fundamental right, since it derived from
individuals' right to bodily integrity and was based on the history and
traditions of the American people. In *Casey*, the Court once again
considered the nature of the abortion right, and the plurality, along with
Justice Blackmun, reasserted that the abortion right derived from the
wider right to control one's bodily integrity and reproduction. In reaching their decisions, Justices O'Connor, Kennedy, and Souter[189] and
Justice Blackmun[190] echoed the arguments made by petitioner Planned
Parenthood and amicus ACOG about the nature of the abortion right.[191]
Much of the debate in *Casey* centered on the proper proof framework to
be used in evaluating abortion regulations. If the abortion right was a
fundamental right, that is, deeply rooted in our nation's history and
traditions, these regulations would have to be evaluated under the strict
scrutiny model and would be permissible only if they were narrowly
tailored to achieve a compelling state interest. The *Casey* litigants and
their amici disagreed sharply about the historical record governing
abortion. As in *Roe*, the state and its amici argued that many states had
abortion laws in place since the mid 1800s, and that proscriptions
against abortion were rooted in English common law.[192] In contrast,
Planned Parenthood and its amici contended that Justice Blackmun's
assessment in *Roe* of the historical record was accurate and that abortion
laws were not were not rooted in the nation's history or traditions.[193]
Moreover, they argued that recent findings in the historical record lent

even greater support to this conclusion. The disagreement among the parties and their amici about the historical record was apparent in the Justices' handling of this issue. The plurality opinion adopted the view of Planned Parenthood and amicus "250 Historians," finding that the state laws in place in 1868 did not "mark the outer limits" of the privacy right.[194] While the plurality did not attempt to determine that point in history that was to serve as the guide, it appears to have been strongly influenced by the brief of 250 Historians, which provided a detailed discussion of the practice of abortion during the colonial era and early to mid-nineteenth century.[195] Based on this record, amicus 250 Historians concluded that "for much of our nation's history, abortion was tolerated and not illegal."[196] Conversely, the opinions of Chief Justice Rehnquist and Justice Scalia accepted the view of Pennsylvania and its amici that abortion bans were deeply rooted and dated much further back than the mid-nineteenth century. For example, Chief Justice Rehnquist pointed to the common law view that abortions performed after quickening were to be criminalized,[197] and Justice Scalia noted that "longstanding traditions in American society" permitted abortion to be prohibited.[198] Similar views had been expressed not only by Pennsylvania,[199] but by amicus United States, who found that the privacy right was not deeply rooted in our nation's history,[200] and by a number of amici, who offered analyses of the historical record that were at odds with that provided by Planned Parenthood and its amici.[201] Significantly, certain American State Legislators urged the Justices to reject the brief of "250 Historians," contending that this amicus had distorted the historical record by failing to recognize that anti-abortion laws had existed at common law.[202] The Academy of Medical Ethics also announced that it had found evidence of indictments or convictions under anti-abortion laws going back 800 years and argued that this evidence supported the position that anti-abortion laws were deeply rooted.[203]

It bears noting that, in the discussion about the historical record, the roles of the parties and their amici were clear: the parties raised the issue of the historical record but left it to their amici to provide elaboration and documentation. Planned Parenthood's only discussion of this issue appeared in its reply brief,[204] and Pennsylvania's noted simply that the *Roe* decision was inconsistent with the historical proscription against abortion.[205] It was the amici who provided the expansive historical background about abortion regulations provided in this case, and the Justices appear to have relied upon this background in reaching their own views of the historical foundations of abortion laws in the United States.

The Application of Roe v. Wade

In addition to relying on the amici for information about the historical record, the Justices also used these briefs to reconsider the *Roe* decision.

Throughout the 1980s and early 1990s, there was increasing pressure on the Court to reconsider and, ultimately, to overrule *Roe v. Wade*. In the 1989 decision, the Justices held that the Missouri abortion law at issue in *Webster* did not offer an opportunity to rule on the continuing legitimacy of *Roe*. *Casey* was widely seen as the case that would provide the Court with a forum and a fact pattern for overruling *Roe v. Wade*.

Stare Decisis. In deciding to retain *Roe*, the *Casey* plurality discussed the principle of stare decisis at length and appears to have been influenced to a significant degree by the arguments of Planned Parenthood and its amici. First, the Justices in the plurality asserted that *Roe* was still "workable" and that there had been no doctrinal change, erosion of constitutional principle, developments that were at odds with the decision, or changes in the factual assumptions of the decision.[206] In its reasoning, the plurality was echoing the arguments made by amici ACOG, the Alan Guttmacher Institute, Representative Don Edwards, and the State of New York that *Roe*'s doctrinal footings remained firm, and that the right to make decisions about one's intimate relationships, family, and reproductive decisions, established in a line of cases decided before *Roe*, remained in place.[207]

The plurality also asserted that *Roe* had to be retained because it was ingrained in the social fabric of the nation and American women had come to rely upon it. The Justices held that people had organized their intimate relationships and "made choices that define their views of themselves and their places in society" based on the *Roe* holding.[208] Moreover, the plurality asserted that *Roe* had helped women to make decisions about their reproduction, and thus had facilitated women's ability to participate equally in the economic and social realms.[209] This argument that *Roe* be upheld because women had come to rely upon the abortion right is present in a number of amicus briefs, as well as briefly in Planned Parenthood's briefs. For example, Planned Parenthood stated that millions of women had exercised their right to choose abortion in the twenty years since *Roe* was decided,[210] and amici Don Edwards, New York, and 178 Organizations provided substantial elaboration of this point.[211] Similarly, the Court's assertion that *Roe* had enabled women to contribute equally to the social and economic life of the nation mirrored the arguments made by both Planned Parenthood and and amicus New York.[212]

The plurality opinion and the opinions of Justices Blackmun and Stevens focused on the effects that overruling *Roe* would have on the Court's legitimacy and authority. These Justices contended that the Court needed to rely on its past decisions since they provided stability and continuity over time. Moreover, the Justices argued that the costs of overruling past decisions like *Roe* were significant and would cause the populace to lose confidence in the Court's ability to render decisions free from political pressures.[213] This argument was made briefly by the petitioners, but again was expanded upon by amici Don Edwards, 178 Organizations, the NAACP, and New York, who furnished detailed information about the significant social costs that would be incurred if *Roe* were overturned.[214] This concern about basic fairness was reminiscent of the Justices' earlier discussions of fairness that were so much a part of the fundamental rights framework articulated in *Griswold* and *Roe*.

Chief Justice Rehnquist and Justice Scalia also relied on the legal arguments offered by the litigants and their amici about the principle of stare decisis. Both of their opinions asserted that the principle of stare decisis did not save the *Roe* decision and that the Court should take the opportunity in this case to overrule the decision. Justice Scalia argued that *Roe* had no legitimacy, since it had been wrongly decided.[215] In reaching this decision, he echoed the arguments made briefly by Pennsylvania and then repeated by the United States, Representative Hyde, National Right to Life, and the Knights of Columbus.[216] Similarly, the Chief Justice argued that *Roe* should be rejected because it had resulted in a "confused state of abortion jurisprudence."[217] The United States also reached this conclusion, as did the Catholic Conference and National Right to Life.[218]

In discussing *Roe* and the principle of stare decisis and in particular the history of abortion law, the Justices' decisions drew upon the arguments made by the litigants and their amici. When the Justices shifted gears and began discussing the proper proof framework to be used in *Casey*, however, they did not rely extensively on the legal arguments provided in these briefs. There is little correspondence between the Court's opinions and the litigant and amicus briefs in this case. Instead, the Justices appear to have drawn exclusively on their already established positions in the abortion debate. The influence of the United States, so apparent in the *Akron* case, continued to be manifest in this case. It was the United States' undue burden standard, presented in *Akron*, that replaced the *Roe* trimester framework in *Casey*. Furthermore, the litigants and amici likely recognized the futility of arguing in favor of or against the trimester approach; ironically, ACOG, which filed in support of Planned Parenthood, wrote off the trimester approach, noting that the abortion right was not "dependent on the trimesters of pregnancy."[219] Similarly, in a likely attempt to appeal to Justice O'Connor, who had voiced concerns about the impact of advances in medical technology on the trimester approach, Amicus American Academy of Medical Ethics noted that these advances were central to the resolution of the abortion controversy.[220]

Applying the Undue Burden Framework to the Pennsylvania Law

At issue in *Casey* were five provisions of the Abortion Control Act: a spousal notification requirement, an informed consent provision, 24-hour waiting period provision, an informed parental consent requirement, and a record-keeping provision. The Third Circuit had upheld all of these provisions except the spousal notification requirement. The plurality in *Casey* upheld this lower court decision, finding that the spousal notification law unduly burdened women's right to choose abortion, but that the other provisions did not. The litigants and their amici appear to have had an impact on the Justices' handling of the spousal notification requirement, but not on the other requirements, perhaps because similar provisions had already been examined by the Justices in other cases.

Spousal Notification. In *Casey*, the Court was presented for the first time with a spousal notification requirement. While the Court had considered, and rejected, a spousal consent requirement in *Planned Parenthood of Central Missouri v. Danforth*,[221] the *Casey* provision was the first that required notification, as opposed to consent. In its handling of this requirement, the plurality appears to have relied upon the arguments and data of the petitioners and amici in its discussion of this requirement. For example, the plurality echoed the brief of the petitioner when it noted that most women in well-functioning marriages would discuss whether they should have abortions, but that women in dysfunctional and violent relationships might not be able to exercise their right to abortion if they were forced to discuss this issue with their spouses.[222]

The amici were loudly heard in the plurality's discussion of the statutory exception for women who reported to governmental authorities that they had suffered physical or sexual abuse. The plurality wholly accepted amici arguments that this exception was too narrow and did not allow the "millions of women [who] suffer physical and psychological abuse" to avoid discussion their abortion decision with their abusers.[223] The plurality noted that a number of situations were not accounted for in the abortion law, among them cases where women were exposed to sexual or psychological abuse or where their children or other significant parties were abused.[224] In making this argument, the Justices relied heavily on the amici briefs of the Pennsylvania Coalition, the American Psychological Association, and ACOG, who all argued that the exceptions were insufficient to protect women against being subjected to serious and undue burdens on their right to choose abortion.[225]

Moreover, the plurality opinion and that of Justice Blackmun noted that the spousal notification provision was based on the stereotype that women are subordinate to men, and that the provision conferred upon husbands too great a degree of authority over their wives.[226] Justice Blackmun also noted that the spousal notification law did not recognize the "unique role of women in the decision-making process."[227] In arguing that this provision was based on stereotypical notions about men and women, the Justices echoed the arguments made by Planned Parenthood and expanded upon by amici APA, 250 American Historians, and the Rutherford Institute.[228]

The Justices who upheld the spousal notification provision likewise relied on the briefs, notably that of Pennsylvania and its amici. In his opinion, Chief Justice Rehnquist accepted the state's argument that the spousal notification requirement advanced its interests in ensuring procreation within marriage, in advancing the integrity of the marital bond, and in protecting potential life.[229] In making this argument, the Chief Justice appears to have employed the arguments of Pennsylvania, which were seconded by amici Feminists for Life, National Legal Foundation, the Rutherford Institute, and the State of Utah, who all contended that Pennsylvania could take steps to protect and promote marital integrity and prenatal life.[230] Similarly, Chief Justice Rehnquist adopted the view articulated by Pennsylvania and amicus State of Utah that Planned Parenthood had not provided any evidence to show how many women would be negatively affected by the spousal notification provision and that the provision should be upheld because, in the vast majority of instances, it did not unduly burden women's choices.[231]

Informed Consent, 24-Hour Waiting Period, Record-keeping Provision, and Informed Parental Consent Provisions. A strong correspondence exists between the plurality's arguments and those of the litigants and amici on the issue of informed consent; however, for the Justices, these were not novel arguments. For example, Justice O'Connor's dissent in *Akron* had incorporated a number of these arguments, and similarly, the arguments of Justices Blackmun and Stevens about informed consent in *Casey* mirrored their opinions in *Akron*. Specifically, both Justices Blackmun and Stevens contended that the informed consent provision should be struck down because they singled out abortion for different treatment, did not provide women with full information about the relative risks of abortion and childbirth, and did not help women to make informed decisions about abortion.[232] As in the Justices' discussion of the undue burden standard, the impact of amici on the Justices' view of informed consent appears to have been long lasting. The Justices relied upon a conception of this issue that had been forged by the parties and their amici in earlier cases, perhaps most notably in *Akron*. The difference between *Akron* and *Casey* was that the informed consent standard was rejected under the strict scrutiny approach embraced in *Akron*, but upheld under the *Casey* undue burden standard.

Furthermore, the parties and their amici were largely silent on the remaining provisions in *Casey*, probably because they saw them as largely settled by the time this case reached the Court. For example, the record-keeping provision had been upheld in the 1976 *Danforth* case, and the right of states to require parental consent had been established relatively early in the abortion debate in the 1983 case, *Planned Parenthood Assn. of Kansas City v. Ashcroft*.[233] Perhaps it is not surprising that the parties and amici devoted so much attention to this issue and that the Justices relied so heavily upon the information provided in these briefs, since this was the one novel provision of the state law.

Coordination and Conflict among Amici

The groups and individuals filing amicus briefs in *Casey* concentrated on a wide range of topics, but there was a considerable degree of coordination among them. Very few arguments advanced by the amici were not present in the party briefs. In many ways, the party and amici briefs coalesced—as a unit, they raised the same issues. For example, the parties and their amici wrote about the historical foundations of abortion laws and discussed at length the principle of stare decisis. All agreed that *Roe* was at issue in this case and presented proof frameworks that either supported or supplanted this decision. In addition, all the briefs discussed the effects of the spousal notification and informed consent provisions, but few briefs considered the 24-hour, record-keeping, and informed parental consent provisions. The pattern of amici cooperation and coordination that was apparent in *Roe* and *Akron* was even more pronounced here. The parties raised issues, sometimes superficially, and left it to the amici to expand upon them.

In addition to this pattern of coordination, there was significant conflict among amici and the parties about key issues, and this disagreement was apparent in the Justices' opinions. For example, the parties and their amici clashed over the question of whether the historical record and traditions surrounding abortion laws justified treating the abortion right as a fundamental right. This disagreement is apparent in the conflict between the plurality opinion and the opinions of the Chief Justice and Justice Scalia. Similarly, the amici and the parties disagreed about whether *Roe* should be reaffirmed, with some arguing that the fabric of American society was dependent upon a reaffirmance and others arguing that the case should be overturned because it was wrongly decided. Again, the plurality relied upon the principle of stare decisis, while the Chief Justice and Justice Scalia argued fiercely that *Roe* should be overturned. The parties and amici also clashed over the issue of which test should be used to evaluate abortion regulations. The plurality opinion voted in favor of the undue burden standard, Justice Blackmun firmly supported the trimester approach, and Chief Justice Rehnquist and Justice Scalia adopted the rational relation standard. Finally, the parties and amici disagreed about the effects of spousal notification on women and families, and of the informed consent provision on physicians. The plurality struck down both provisions, as did Justices Stevens and Blackmun, and the Chief Justice and Justice Scalia upheld the provisions.

The cooperation and conflict between the parties and the amici and among the amici can be discerned not only in their briefs, but also in the degree to which they cited each other. The parties both cited to the briefs of their amici, but Planned Parenthood cited these briefs much more heavily and accorded much more weight to certain briefs than to others. The Solicitor General's brief garnered the largest number of party cites, far exceeding any other amici. Planned Parenthood cited the brief of the United States twelve times in an attempt to minimize the impact of this amicus, who was likely perceived to be most influential.[234] In addition to its cites to the United States, Planned Parenthood cited other opposing amici with relatively high frequency. There are cites to amici American Academy of Medical Ethics,[235] American Association of Prolife Obstetricians and Gynecologists (AAPOG),[236] Feminists for Life,[237] the National Legal Foundation,[238] the Rutherford Institute,[239] and the U.S. Catholic Conference.[240] Planned Parenthood cited friendly briefs seven times, highlighting the arguments or data of amici ACOG,[241] 250 American Historians,[242] Certain Members of Congress,[243] 167 Distinguished Scientists and Physicians,[244] NAACP,[245] and City of New York.[246] In contrast, Pennsylvania only cited to amici twice: once to its ally, the United States,[247] and the other time to its opponent, ACOG.[248]

The amici also cited to each other, but the pattern was opposite to what it had been among the parties. Only one of Planned Parenthood's amici, Don Edward, cited to another amicus; not surprisingly, it was to the United States.[249] In contrast, ten of Pennsylvania's amici cited the briefs of other amici, and in most instances, these were *negative* cites, that is, they criticized the arguments or data provided in another amicus brief. For example, amicus American Academy of Medical Ethics repeatedly criticized the Historians' Brief,[250] as did Certain State Legislators.[251] The United States took shots at ACOG, as did the AAPOG and Hyde.[252] Amici Hyde and The National Right to Life Committee (NRLC) fiercely criticized the brief of Don Edwards,[253] and the NRLC, United States, and University Faculty of Life (UFL), argued against the City of New York's brief.[254] The United States, and UFL also critiqued the brief of the NAACP.[255] In addition, the

NRLC and Life Issues Institute (LII) downplayed the briefs of 178 Organizations.[256] Finally, the United States sought to undermine the arguments of the APA and the Pennsylvania Coalition.[257]

In addition to criticizing their opponents' amici briefs, Pennsylvania's amici also sought to strengthen their allies' briefs. The United States and the State of Utah urged the Court to adopt the arguments of the United States.[258] Certain State Legislators, the United States, and UFL highlighted the brief of the American Academy of Medical Ethics.[259] Both the United States and Hyde cited with approval the brief of Certain American State Legislators.[260] Hyde also supported the briefs of Catholics United for Life, the Southern Center for Law and Ethics, and the National Right to Life Committee.[261] Finally, Life Issues Institute (LII) cited the brief filed by ally American Victims of Abortion in *Bray v. Alexandra.*[262]

Thus, the parties and amici cited to each other. They were quite aware of the arguments being made in the amici briefs, and they were anxious to put a "spin" on the briefs of the amici, ostensibly for the Justices' benefit. Planned Parenthood was more likely to cite to their opponents' amici than was Pennsylvania, and Planned Parenthood clearly recognized the potential influence that the Solicitor General's brief might have on the Justices. In contrast, Pennsylvania tended to use their amici to criticize the briefs of its opponent's amici, although the state's amici also cited their friends with favor.

Conclusions about *Casey*

The influence of amici on the Court's opinions is more subtle in this case than in most others under examination in this study. There were only four direct cites to amici briefs in this case, and all four were used negatively. For example, the plurality noted that amicus United States had been badgering the Court to overturn *Roe* and had filed an amicus brief in the last five cases aimed at achieving this result. In addition, the plurality criticized respondent Pennsylvania and its amici, noting that they would "deny that women have come to rely on the *Roe* decision." Similarly, Justice Blackmun criticized the United States for adopting the rational relation standard to evaluate abortion laws and argued that this standard was not sufficiently protective of reproductive rights. In addition, Justice Blackmun argued that the United States had acknowledged at oral argument that sectarian concerns like those at issue in this case were not valid state interests.

Amicus influence is perhaps most difficult to discern because of the overlap between party and amici briefs. The primary function of the amici in *Casey* appears to have been to elaborate on arguments raised briefly in party briefs. There were few instances in which the amici provided arguments that were novel; in fact, the only evidence that the Justices had accepted arguments that the amici alone raised was in Justice Stevens' discussion of the parallels between the state's interest in fetal life and its interest in potential immigrants, an argument made by America21, and in the plurality's discussion of the impact of spousal notification on women in abusive marital relationships, an argument made solely by the APA, ACOG, and the Pennsylvania Coalition.

It is very likely that the impact of these briefs was more profound when they "seconded" and expanded upon a point made only briefly by the parties than it was when amici presented novel arguments and data. For example, amici influence is very apparent in the Justices' discussion of the historical foundations of abortion laws, where Planned Parenthood briefly noted the need for more historical analysis and then 250 Historians provided an extensive discussion of this history. Similarly, in their discussion of stare decisis, amici Don Edwards, the NAACP, New York State, and 178 Organizations provided what seems to have been a welcome elaboration of the role of *Roe* in the larger polity. Amici U.S., Hyde, NRLC, and Knights of Columbus also added significantly to the discussions of the Chief Justice and Justice Scalia about how *Roe* was wrongly decided and should be overturned, a point made only briefly by Pennsylvania. In addition, amici APA and 250 Historians likely helped to influence the plurality by significantly expanding Planned Parenthood's point that women and men have much different roles to play in the abortion debate. And finally, amici Feminists for Life, National Legal Foundation, the Rutherford Institute, and the State of Utah elaborated on Pennsylvania's argument about the salutary effects of the notification requirement on marital integrity, a discussion that appears to have intrigued the Chief Justice and Justice Scalia.

The patterns of party and amici coordination and conflict noted in *Akron* were apparent in *Casey* as well. The parties and their amici believed that the amici briefs of certain friends and enemies had the potential to influence the Justices, and they made a determined effort either to highlight or to undermine these briefs. In particular, Planned Parenthood believed that the United States would have an important role to play and devoted much space in its brief and reply brief to criticizing the Solicitor General's argument. This effort may have been successful; the only times the Solicitor General's brief and oral argument are mentioned by the Justices, they are placed in a negative light. This case underlines the great degree to which the party and amici effort was likely a collaborative effort. By 1992, the prochoice and prolife movements had become adept at employing these briefs to coordinate their efforts. It is quite possible that they had begun to realize the importance of placing the briefs of their own amici and their enemies' amici in a larger context for the Justices.

CONCLUDING REMARKS
ABOUT ABORTION CASES

These four abortion cases were decided over a twenty-year span and raised distinct legal questions. *Roe* called upon the Court to consider the application of the right to privacy to abortion bans. In *Harris*, the Justices considered whether a rider to a federal appropriations bill that barred the use of Medicaid funds for abortions violated the right to privacy. Both *Akron* and *Casey* forced the Justices to consider the *Roe* trimester framework and the application of *Roe* to increasingly restrictive abortion laws. Amici played an important role in these cases, by providing the Justices with an expanded discussion of points only briefly raised by the parties, by bringing their recognized expertise and knowledge to the bar, and by identifying those amici who they thought would be most influential.

Relatively few direct cites of amici briefs appear in any of these four cases: in *Roe*, Justice Blackmun cited to amici eight times, but only named two amici; in *Harris*, there were no direct cites; in *Akron*, Justice O'Connor cited only to the United States; and in *Casey*, the plurality cited to the U.S. twice, as did Justice Blackmun. This paucity of direct cites is interesting for at least two reasons. First, these are relatively long decisions: *Roe* is 25 pages long, *Harris* takes up 33 pages, *Akron* is 56 pages, and *Casey* is 92 pages. Second, the amici appear to have provided the Justices with information that they needed and employed.

The failure of the Justices to directly cite the briefs of amici is surprising when one considers the extent to which they relied on these briefs. In *Roe*, Justice Blackmun relied extensively on information provided by ACOG, the National Legal Program, Planned Parenthood, the AMA, the ABA, and New Women Lawyers. In particular, the amici briefs were used to discuss the quickening distinction, the role of professional organizations, the burdens imposed upon women by unwanted pregnancy, and the state's interests in maternal health and fetal life. In *Harris*, there was less amici influence, but still, the voices of amici can be detected in discussions about the nature of the due process right at issue and the effect of the Hyde Amendment on indigent women. In particular, amici Council, NOW, Legal Aid, and New York State were heard by the Justices.

The *Akron* Court relied extensively on the United States, which provided the undue burden standard employed by Justice O'Connor in her dissenting opinion. In addition, both Justice O'Connor and Justice

Powell, who penned the majority opinion, relied on amici ACOG , PP, APA, NAF, the American College of Pathologists, APHA, NOW, Certain, and California Women Lawyers. Finally, in *Casey*, the Justices employed the briefs of ACOG, Edwards, New York, 178, the APA, and the United States. Moreover, among the amici in all four cases, certain friends were also regarded as experts: in all four cases, ACOG and the United States were given significant deference.

The impact of amici is most clear in discussions about the scientific and medical issues at play. Amici briefs were also employed, however, when the Justices chose to discuss the impact of abortion laws on women and when they delved into the historical background of these laws. Amici briefs were not employed as frequently when the Justices reconsidered some question or issue it had already examined: the *Casey* opinion suggests that the Justices may be more likely to rely on positions they have crafted in earlier cases than they are to evaluate the issue anew.

These four cases also suggest that amici and their parties tend to work together. With the exception of *Harris*, where there was little evidence of either cooperation or conflict among parties and amici or between amici, the participants functioned as a unit in these cases. There was a coalescing of issues in the briefs, and it was unusual for an amicus to explore an issue that had not at least been touched upon by either the formal parties or some other amici. The parties tended to cite the briefs of prominent amici, as did the amici, and for this reason, a large number of cites to ACOG and the United States appeared in these amici briefs.

One may also discern a pattern in the amici briefs that were ignored in these cases. The Justices tended to not employ arguments that were outside of the mainstream. Perhaps for this reason, arguments about the constitutional rights of embryos and fetuses or about the Eighth Amendment cruel and unusual punishment clause, the Thirteenth Amendment involuntary servitude prohibition, or the First Amendment religion clauses were ignored. In addition, the Justices chose sides in conflicts among amici. For example, when faced with the choice of whether to accept the arguments of groups like the AMA, ACOG, the APHA, and NAF over those of the American Association of Prolife Obstetricians and Gynecologists, Physicians for Life, or Certain Physicians of ACOG, the Justices always chose the more mainstream organizations.

The abortion cases provide some of the most striking evidence of amici influence, but this evidence must be tempered by two facts. First, the Justices rarely provided a direct cite to the amici briefs, even where they were relying upon information contained almost entirely in these briefs. Second, in *Roe*, *Akron*, and *Casey*, the amici and parties discussed much of the same information and made many of the same arguments.

In all four cases, the arguments and data in the amici briefs showed up, often in abbreviated form, in the party briefs. For this reason, it is more difficult to find the "smoking gun" of amici influence in these cases. It is interesting to consider, however, that this pattern may have had several purposes. It may be that the parties and amici believed that the seconding of party arguments by the amici would strengthen these arguments, or conversely, they may have feared that the Justices would not consider amici arguments and data that were present solely in these briefs. It is conceivable that the participants may have concluded that the heightened awareness and public criticism of the Court's abortion decisions would make the Justices more vulnerable to charges that they were deciding cases on the basis of politics, not law, and for this reason, they may have suspected that the Justices would pay less heed to arguments made solely by amici.

By the time *Casey* was considered, the parties and their amici were likely sensitive to the Justices' concerns about how the Court would be perceived in its handling of this controversial issue. In fact, the Justices in this case closely adhered to the principle that underlies the adversary system, that is, that courts should consider only those arguments and data that are presented to them in case briefs. In *Casey*, the parties and their friends provided the Justices with all of the information that was needed to decide the novel questions before them: nearly every aspect of the plurality, concurring, and dissenting opinions can be traced to a party or amicus brief. This reliance is striking, particularly when one considers that in *Roe*, Justice Blackmun was very willing to engage in his own independent research and that vast portions of his decision are not traceable to either party or amici briefs.

NOTES

1. Six of these cases involved public funding for abortion services (*Beal v. Doe* 432 U.S. 438 (1977), *Maher v. Doe* 432 U.S. 464 (1977), *Poelker v. Doe* 432 U.S. 59 (1977), *Harris v. McRae* 448 U.S. 297 (1980), *Bowen v. Kendrick* 487 U.S. 589 (1988), *Rust v. Sullivan* 500 U.S. 377 (1991)). Two cases involved the sale or advertisement of abortion services or contraceptives (*Carey v. Population Services International* 431 U.S. 678 (1977), *Bigelow v. Virginia* 421 U.S. 809 (1975)). Five cases assessed parental consent or notification laws (*Bellotti v. Baird* 428 U.S. 132 (1976), *Bellotti v. Baird* (*Bellotti II*) 443 U.S. 622 (1979), *H.L. v. Matheson* 450 U.S. 398 (1981), *Hodgson v. Minnesota* 497 U.S. 417 (1990), *Ohio v. Akron Center for Reproductive Health* 497 U.S. 502 (1990)). In two cases, the Court was called upon to evaluate informed consent statutes (*Planned Parenthood of Central Missouri v. Danforth* 428 U.S. 552 (1976), *Thornburgh v. ACOG* 476 U.S. 747 (1986). Six other cases involved comprehensive abortion control laws that regulated where abortions were performed, established waiting periods, mandated informed consent, and regulated how the fetus was to be treated (*Colautti v. Franklin* 439 U.S. 379 (1979), *Akron v. Akron Center for Reproductive Health* 462 U.S. 416 (1983), *Planned Parenthood*

Association of Kansas City v. Ashcroft 462 U.S. 476 (1983), *Simopoulos v. Virginia* 462 U.S. 506 (1983), *Webster v. Reproductive Health Services* 492 U.S. 490 (1989), and *Planned Parenthood of Southeastern Pennsylvania v. Casey* 500 U.S. 833 (1992)).

2. Texas Penal Code article 1191 at 429 (1961) read: "If any person shall designedly administer to a pregnant woman or knowingly procure to be administered with her consent any drug or medicine, or shall use towards her any violence or means whatever externally or internally applied, and thereby procure an abortion, he shall be confined in the penitentiary not less than two nor more than five years; if it be done without her consent, the punishment shall be doubled. By 'abortion' is meant that the life of the fetus or embryo shall be destroyed in the woman's womb or that a premature birth thereof be caused." Texas Penal Code article 1196 at 436 (1961) continued: "Nothing in this chapter applies to an abortion procured or attempted by medical advice for the purpose of saving the life of the mother."

3. Georgia Code section 26-1201 read: "Except as otherwise provided in Section 26-1202, a person commits criminal abortion when he administers any medicine, drug or other substance whatever to any woman or when he uses any instrument or other means whatever upon any woman with intent to produce a miscarriage or abortion." Section 1202 provided certain exceptions: "(a) Section 26-1201 shall not apply to an abortion performed by a physician duly licensed to practice medicine and surgery pursuant to Chapter 84-9 or 84-12 or the Code of Georgia of 1933, as amended, based on his best clinical judgment that an abortion is necessary because (1) A continuation of the pregnancy would endanger the life of the pregnant woman or would seriously and permanently injure her health; or (2) The fetus would very likely be born with a grave, permanent and irremediable mental or physical defect; or (3) The pregnancy resulted from forcible or statutory rape."

The Georgia statute had a list of other requirements, among these, that the decision to abort be assented to by a panel of other doctors and that the abortion take place in a hospital that was accredited by the Joint Commission on American Hospitals (JCAH).

4. 93 S.Ct. 705.

5. 93 S.Ct. 730.

6. 93 S.Ct. 724.

7. 93 S.Ct. 725.

8. 93 S.Ct. 725.

9. 93 S.Ct. 727 (two cites).

10. 93 S.Ct. 730 (two cites).

11. 93 S.Ct. 728.

12. In the opening section of his opinion, Justice Blackmun demonstrated that he was aware of the content of the amicus briefs in this case by noting that the abortion debate touches on several other issues, including population growth, poverty, and race. The Petitioner's brief mentioned these issues, noting that "the question of abortion potentially and actually affects virtually every person in the United States" (Petitioner's brief, 91), but the Petitioner left the elaboration of the issues to the amici, who discussed them, sometimes at great length, in their briefs. For example, a number of organizations debated whether the state has an interest in regulating abortion as a means for controlling population growth (CCLA, 26, NLP in *Roe*, 18-9, PP, 41). Similarly, amici briefs detailed the impact of abortion laws on poverty (NLP in *Roe*, 22-8, 29, NLP in *Doe*, 22-51, ACOG in *Doe*, 63, State, 8-9) and racial equality (NLP in *Roe*, 22-9, 37, NLP in *Doe*, 22-51, ACOG in *Doe*, 63, State, 5-7). Justice Blackmun stated that

while he was aware of these related issues, he sought to dispose of these cases "free of emotion and predilection," and to do this, that he would focus on the medical aspects of abortion and on the medical-legal history of abortion statutes (93 S.Ct. 709). Justice Blackmun was clearly aware of the furor the *Roe* holding would likely unleash. In a Conference Memorandum written just before the opinion was handed down, Justice Blackmun proposed that the Court dispatch a written announcement of the decision to the press. As a justification for this unprecedented practice, Justice Blackmun explained that he "anticipate[d] the headlines that [would] be produced when the abortion decisions [were] announced (In this announcement, Justice Blackmun wrote that "we have endeavored, too, to note the change in attitudes over the last century of professional bodies such as the AMA, the APHA, the ABA, and indeed the changing attitudes among the citizens of the country") (Conference Memorandum from Justice Blackmun, 1/16/73, Marshall Papers, file 98). Justice Brennan responded to the Memo by praising Justice Blackmun's work on the abortion decisions, but noting that he had "very definite reservations" about releasing the memo to the press (Letter from Justice Brennan to Justice Blackmun, 1/17/73, Marshall Papers, file 98).

13. Petitioner, 34.

14. ACOG in *Roe*, 14; Certain, 17, 30; NLP in *Roe*, 15, 18; NLP in *Doe*, 15; NRLC, 25; NWL, 44, 52; CCLA, 26; Texas, 25.

15. NLP in *Roe*, 15.

16. ACOG -*Roe*, 14; NLP, 15;CCLA, 26.

17. 93 S.Ct. 718-9; NWL, 46; NLP, 18, Certain Physicians, 17, 29-30; NRLC, 25; Texas Attorneys, 25. Justice Blackmun ignored the discussions of Certain and the NRLC, which focused on the fact that abortion of a quick fetus was always murder (NRLC, 25) and that medical science has obliterated the quickening distinction, which had always been based on "maternal sensitivity [rather than] fetal competence" (Certain, 17, 29, 30).

18. 93 S.Ct. 715. Discussion of the history of abortion laws took up nine pages of Justice Blackmun's 25-page opinion.

19. Justice Blackmun may also have made use of some of the articles and letters sent to the Court by various individuals. For example, see Letter to Justice Brennan from Richard A. Schwartz, M.D., discussing the policy issues related to abortion laws and the Letter to Chief Justice Warren (sic) from James E. Trosko, Ph.D., including his article, "Abortion: A Matter of Human Rights or Human Needs?" Both of these letters also included extensive appendixes (Letter to Justice Brennan, Brennan Papers, file 281; Letter to Chief Justice Warren, Brennan Papers, file 281).

20. Petitioner, 40-1.

21. 93 S.Ct. 721-722.

22. 93 S.Ct. 722.

23. ACOG in *Doe*, 52, 74-8; NLP in *Roe*, 35; PP, 10-1; AAUW, 21.

24. Petitioner, 2.

25. ACOG in *Doe*, supplemental brief; PP, 10.

26. 93 S.Ct. 724, fn 41.

27. AAUW, 23.

28. 93 S.Ct. 726-8.

29. Conference Memorandum from Justice Blackmun, 5/18/72, Brennan Papers, file 281.

30. 93 S.Ct. 727. Schwartz has noted that the conference discussions and communications among the Justices reveal that Justice Blackmun was the least firm of those who sought to invalidate the laws, and that Justice Brennan urged

him to write an opinion striking down the laws on constitutional grounds (Schwartz (1988), 144). It also bears noting that Bernard Schwartz's analysis of the conference votes in *Roe* reveals that in some votes, Justice Blackmun actually upheld the laws (Schwartz (1988), pp. 86-7). Strossen has argued that Justice Blackmun disposed of the constitutional questions in *Roe* "in a fairly off-handed fashion" (Strossen in Eastland, xv).

31. 93 S.Ct. 733-5. Eva Rubin has argued that Justice Powell believed that the right to privacy was tenuous as it applied to abortion and that he sought an alternative rationale for striking down the laws (Rubin, 127).

32. 93 S.Ct. 756.

33. Schwartz (1988), p. 87.

34. See Schwartz (1988), 88-9; 93 S.Ct. 756-9.

35. 93 S.Ct. 755.

36. Conference Memorandum from Chief Justice Burger, 5/31/72, Brennan Papers, file 281.

37. 93 S.Ct. 736-7, 763.

38. 93 S.Ct. 727.

39. 93 S.Ct. 759.

40. 93 S.Ct. 760.

41. ACOG in *Doe*, supplementary appendix; AEU, 21-3; NWL, 24; State, 2, appendix A; AAUW, 24-33.

42. Petitioner in *Roe*, 9, 73, 91.

43. AAUW, 24-33. NWL argued that women with unwanted pregnancies would be forced to face unemployment, the termination of their educations, and poverty (NWL, 17-23). Similarly, Petitioner *Roe* contended that the contested laws compelled the woman to "serve as an incubator for months and then as an unwilling mother for years" (Petitioner - *Roe*, 106).

44. AAUW, 24-33.

45. See Petitioner, supplementary appendix to brief (includes ACOG and AMA Position Statements as well as studies of the effects of abortion practices); ACOG in *Doe*, supplementary appendix to brief; State, 2a-6a, "Report from the City of New York Health Services Administration on the effects of the liberalized abortion law on maternal mortality and the incidence of late term abortions."

46. 93 S.Ct. 731-2.

47. 93 S.Ct. 725.

48. Letter from Justice Brennan to Justice Blackmun 12/13/72, Brennan Papers, file 281.

49. Petitioner in *Roe*, 115. The *Roe* Petitioners provided extensive information about the "medical nature of abortion," and concluded that while abortion had been more dangerous than childbirth in the 1800s, when the laws were adopted, it was now much safer (pp. 20-33). The *Doe* Petitioners reached the same conclusions about the relative risk of harm from abortion and childbirth (pp. 12, 26) and further contended that the abortion bans placed women's health and lives at risk since illegal abortions were much more dangerous than legal abortions (pp. 12, 26-7).

50. Petitioner in *Roe*, 98.

51. See ACOG in *Doe*, 7-14; Petitioner in *Roe*, 19-23.

52. PP, supplemental brief, 7-9. Amici NLP, NWP and CCLA also provided brief discussions of the risk of abortion to maternal health, but these provided no information that was not already in the more extensive ACOG and Planned Parenthood material NLP in *Doe*, 14-7, NWL, 10; CCLA, 25.

53. Certain, 33-5, 46-55; Sassone in *Roe* and *Doe*, 14-21, 25-51.

54. Respondent in *Roe*, 9, 31-49; NRLC, 19-20, see also 3, 21-2; Certain, 8-26; Sassone in *Roe* and *Doe*, 11-3; TDA, 64-5, 70; Women for Life, 9-11.

55. Respondent in *Roe*, 56; Respondent in *Doe*, 37-9, 41; Americans United for Life, 7-9; Buckley, i-iii, 4-5; NRLC, 42-3; TDA, 46-9, 53, 76, 84-6.

56. AEU, 31-2; NWL, 7, 51-3; NLP in *Roe*, 19; PP, 11, 29.

57. 93 S.Ct. 725 n45, 730.

58. 93 S.Ct. 729.

59. Petitioner in *Roe*, 120; AEU, 25-7; NLP, 19; PP, 26-7.

60. Furthermore, the Justices ignored many arguments made by the parties and their amici. For example, the Court rejected arguments about the due process rights of physicians to provide abortions as a means of safeguarding their patients' health. The Petitioner and many of its amici made this argument, contending that the laws were vague and did not provide adequate notice to physicians about when abortion was a permissible option (Petitioner in *Doe*, 14-5, 28-9, 44-6; Petitioner in *Roe*, 110, 121, 141-3; ACOG in *Doe*, 23-5, 37, 51; ACOG in *Roe*, 4-5, 10-3; NLP in *Doe*, 45; PP, 11). Similarly, the Justices ignored Petitioner and amici arguments about how abortion laws denied access to health care (Petitioner in *Roe*, 98 n84) and violated the right to travel (Petitioner in *Doe*, 14,42), the Eighth Amendment cruel and unusual punishment prohibition (NWL, 7, 24-8), and the equal protection clause (Petitioner in *Doe*, 15, 46; ACOG in *Doe*, 56-63, 67; NLP in *Doe*, 7, 22-38, 48; NWL, 6-7, 25-7, 32; State, 4-9).

61. Petitioner in *Roe*, 52.

62. See ACOG brief in *Doe*, 7-8, 18-9 and Petitioner's brief in *Roe*, 44-7; also direct cites to amici briefs in *Roe* Petitioner's brief, p. 3, p. 98 fn 84 (Planned Parenthood); to the policies of the AMA and ACOG regarding elective abortions (40-1); and to "amici medical organizations" (p. 98); to New Women Lawyers (118); and to the ABA's Uniform Abortion Act (2).

63. AEU referred to the *Doe* Petitioner's brief, noting that the delays that resulted from the cumbersome Georgia procedure created hazards to women's health (citing *Doe* Petitioner's brief, 10-1, AEU p. 21); and the *Roe* Petitioner's brief for the principle that there was no reason to limit abortion services to accredited hospitals (citing *Roe* Petitioner's brief, 18-9, AEU p. 23).

64. In addition, ACOG took notice of the brief filed by the National Legal Program on Health Problems of the Poor (NLP), referring the Court to this brief for discussion of the discriminatory impact of abortion laws on the poor and non-white. The AAUW listed the religious groups that had sponsored the brief of the American Ethical Union (AEU) as support for its position that most religious groups recognized the right of a woman to decide whether to bear children (AAUW, 21).

65. PP cited the AMA's and ACOG 's policies (11, 21-4), as did the NLP in *Doe* (35) and ACOG in *Doe* (52). PP also cited the ABA's Uniform State Law (10). AAUW cited the standards articulated by a number of amici, among them the APHA and ACOG (20-3).

66. Respondent in *Roe*, 54.

67. NRLC, 20.

68. NRLC, 24-5, 46; Certain, 33;

69. ACOG in *Doe*, 5; NWL, 33; CCLA, 5; AAUW, 6-7. The brief filed by the AAUW is representative of these briefs. Here, amici stated that "Despite the numerous issues involved in these cases, this brief will address itself to only one, so as to avoid repetition of the arguments presented by Petitioners and the other briefs of amici curiae" (6-7).

70. ACOG in *Roe*, 44-45; ACOG in *Doe*, 18-20.

71. ACOG in *Roe*, 18-23; ACOG in *Doe*, 7-15

72. (Certain Physicians, 54-5; Sassone, 33-5).

73. 448 U.S. 297, 325 fn 27. The other two versions of the Hyde Amendment allowed for funding in cases of rape or incest, or where the woman's health was endangered. Justice Stewart, writing for the majority, focused on the most restrictive form of the rider, that is, the version that barred abortion funding in all cases except where the woman's life was in danger.

74. The district court found that Congress had violated the equal protection guarantee by treating medically necessary abortions differently than it treated other medically necessary services (448 U.S. 305). In addition, the district court found that the Hyde Amendment violated the free exercise provision by interfering with the decision to have an abortion, which was in part a product of one's religious beliefs (448 U.S. 306).

75. 448 U.S. 297. The Court also considered the statutory question of whether states were required to fund medically necessary abortions where the federal government provided no such funding. Justice Stewart contended that no such funding obligation existed, since Medicaid was intended to be a "cooperative endeavor" between the federal and state governments and there was nothing in the legislative history to suggest that states would have to assume these costs (448 U.S. 308-310).

76. 448 U.S. 324-6.

77. 448 U.S. 315-8.

78. 448 U.S. 328-9.

79. There are only a few references to the abortion debate throughout more than sixty pages of majority, concurring, and dissenting opinions. Justice Stewart asserts only that "abortion is inherently different from other medical provisions," in that it involves the termination of a life (448 U.S. 325). Justice Brennan writes to voice his "continuing disagreement with the Court's mischaracterization of the fundamental right recognized in *Roe v. Wade*" (448 U.S. 329). And Justice Marshall, who takes the broadest view of this case in the context of the other abortion cases, reminds that Court that the fears that he had expressed in a 1977 case, *Maher v. Doe*, have become reality, as antichoice activists had succeeded in lobbying for more abortion restrictions (448 U.S. 337).

80. The case receiving the most attention from the Justices was *Maher v. Doe*, where the Court had rejected an attempt to expand Medicaid coverage of abortions that were not medically necessary. Justice Stewart contended that *Harris* was governed by *Maher* (448 U.S. 314). Justices Stevens and Marshall, however, took pains to distinguish *Harris* from *Maher*, contending that the Hyde Amendment denied funding for therapeutic, or medically necessary, abortions (448 U.S. 345, 349).

81. 448 U.S. 330, 332.

82. Justice Blackmun criticized the majority for its "condescension" that indigent women "may go elsewhere for [their] abortions" (448 U.S. 348). Similarly, Justice Stevens contended that after Hyde, poor women could "choose" between two serious harms: either "serious health damage to themselves or abortion" (448 U.S. 350).

83. Respondents' brief, 137-9.

84. NOW brief, 28-9.

85. Attorney General of the State of New York brief, 8-10.

86. 448 U.S. 344.

87. Council, 16.

88. Respondents' brief, 125.

89. 448 U.S. 338, 332.
90. Legal Aid, 2.
91. NOW, 8.
92. 448 U.S. 331.
93. Council, 16-17, 25; NOW, 5; State of New York, 10-12.
94. In its brief, NOW cited the brief of Legal Aid as support for its position that the Hyde Amendment would result in increased sterilization abuse (NOW, p. 21 fn 16). Legal Aid's brief was focused on the coerced sterilization of poor and minority women in the pre-*Roe* era. The organization contended that the Hyde Amendment would create the conditions for sterilization abuse: women would be coerced into agreeing to sterilization in return for an abortion (Legal Aid, 28). In addition, the brief of the Legal Defense Fund for Unborn Children noted that petitions for filing amicus briefs on behalf of the unborn had been denied repeatedly by the Court from 1976 to 1980 (LDF, 9 fn1).
95. Respondent brief, 61-2.
96. See brief of the Catholic Conference and Petitioner brief, 28-38.
97. The Coalition for Human Justice argued that the Hyde Amendment did not necessarily have a negative impact on poor women's health. It contended that abortion had benefited only "abortion vendors" (p. 11), resulted in sterilization abuse (p. 8), and worsened the "oppression of the under classes" (p. 11). In contrast, the Bergen-Passaic Health Systems Agency argued that the Hyde Amendment would have serious negative consequences for women's health and would leave many indigent women without medical services (p. 7).
98. In 1978, the *Akron* City Council enacted an ordinance entitled "Regulation of Abortion." There was evidence presented at the district court level that the drafters' intent in creating this ordinance was to "enact a national model anti-abortion ordinance" (Respondent's brief, 4). The Court was asked to consider five of the provisions of this ordinance, along with the preface, which stated that from conception "the unborn child is . . . a human life" (462 U.S. 416, 421 (1983). The provisions at issue in this case required that:
    1. post–first trimester abortions be performed in a hospital;
    2. parents be notified that their minor daughters are to undergo an abortion and before abortions be performed on girls less than 16 years old, there be a parental consent or court order in place;
    3. the attending physician at an abortion inform the woman about the development of the fetus, and the date of possible viability, and read a statement prepared by the Council which warned of the physical and emotional complications from abortion, noted the availability of agencies that would provide assistance and information about birth control, adoption and childbirth;
    4. women wait at least 24 hours after signing the consent form; and
    5. fetal remains be disposed of in a humane and sanitary manner (462 U.S. 422-4).
The City of *Akron* made violation of any of these provisions a misdemeanor, punishable by a fine. This ordinance was challenged by the *Akron* Center for Reproductive Health, which was joined by two other clinics, WomenCare and the *Akron* Women's Clinic. Together, these clinics performed nearly all of the abortions in the City of Akron (5,280 out of 5,574).
99. Justice Powell cited to the brief of Americans United for Life, which was filed in another case filed with the Court during October Term 1982. He noted this brief to illustrate the conflict among courts as to whether second trimester abortions had to be performed in hospitals (462 U.S. 426 note 9).

100. 462 U.S. 465 note 10.

101. 462 U.S. 419.

102. 462 U.S. 416.

103. Respondent brief, 22-23, 25, 27-29; APHA, 31,34; California Women Lawyers, 7; Certain Law Professors, 12, 17, 22-24; National Abortion Federation, 7, 10, 16-17; NOW, 5-7, 37; Planned Parenthood, 27-28.

104. 462 U.S. 420; Certain Law Professors, 20, 41.

105. Justice O'Connor noted that "the Solicitor General argues that we should adopt the unduly burdensome standard and in so doing, should accord 'heavy deference to legislative judgment' in determining what constitutes 'an undue burden'" (462 U.S. 465).

106. U.S. brief, 2, 6, 10.

107. U.S. brief, 2.

108. U.S. brief, 6.

109. 462 U.S. 465.

110. U.S. brief, 3, 9-10.

111. Other briefs also discussed this standard (See Petitioner brief, 16, 18; Respondent-Intervenor, 35; Americans United for Life, 2, 3, 6, 11, 20; United Families Federation, 3; NOW 16-7); however, Justice O'Connor's direct citation to the amicus brief of the U.S. suggests the great extent to which she was influenced by this brief.

112. 462 U.S. 427 (citing *Doe v. Bolton*).

113. 462 U.S. 431, 434.

114. See Brennan Papers, file box 615, letters from Justices Brennan and Blackmun to Justice Powell, 3/8/83; Conference Memorandum from Justice Powell. The initial passage, encompassed in footnote 39, read "This Court's consistent recognition of the critical role of the physician in the abortion procedure has been based on the model of the competent, conscientious, and ethical physician. We are aware that, as in all professions, the degree of adherence by physicians to ideal medical and ethical standards may vary. Experience in the decade following *Roe* suggests that at some clinics abortions may be performed after only limited attention to the patient's individual needs and with virtually no involvement by the physician than performance of the abortion itself." Justices Blackmun and Brennan urged Justice Powell to strike this portion of the note, and Justice Brennan warned that "although it may well be true that some abortion clinics do not meet the standards of medical ethics, I would like to avoid making a general statement to that effect, unsupported by a specific record. It gives aid and comfort to those who would justify burdensome regulation on the basis of purportedly widespread ethical violations without investigating whether such violations are in fact occurring" (3/8/83 letter).

115. Respondent-Intervenor, 13,16-9; Feminists for Life, 6, 16-7; Womenkind, 22-6; UFF, 26.

116. 462 U.S. 429 fn11.

117. ACOG brief, 3.

118. ACOG brief, 24.

119. ACOG brief, 11-13.

120. APHA brief, 36.

121. Certain Law Professors brief, 25. It bears noting that the amicus brief of Americans for Life also recognized the central role of the physician in the abortion decision (p. 10), as did the brief of the Respondent-Intervenor (pp. 37, 40).

122. 462 U.S. 438.

123. APHA brief, 2.

124. CARASA brief, 3, 17, 23.

125. NAF brief, 20, 30.

126. NOW brief, 21. It bears noting that this argument was also made by the Respondent (p. 7-8, 12).

127. 462 U.S. 459, 461.

128. 462 U.S. 471; U.S. brief, 5; Respondent-Intervenor brief, 39.

129. 462 U.S. 455, 458.

130. 462 U.S. 456.

131. ACOG brief, 20, 26. This point was also made by NOW (p. 23 n7), CARASA (p. 23-4), and Lawyers for Life (p. 5-6).

132. Echoing the argument of the United States in its amicus brief, Justice O'Connor also contended that the state legislatures should have the discretion to decide whether or not to adopt abortion regulations based on changes in technology. Justice O'Connor contended, as did the United States, that legislatures were better able to evaluate this evidence than were courts, which lacked scientific expertise (462 U.S. 458; United States brief, 11-12).

133. In fact, the only direct cite that Justice Powell makes to an amicus brief in *Akron* is to the brief filed in another abortion case being considered by the Court, *Planned Parenthood Association of Kansas City, Missouri, Inc. v. Ashcroft*, by Americans United for Life. This brief lists the 23 states with hospitalization requirements, and Justice Powell uses this list as a way of placing the provision in context (462 U.S. 426 citing AUL brief, p. 4 footnote 1).

134. 462 U.S. 437.

135. 462 U.S. 436-7.

136. Respondent brief, 10.

137. APHA brief, 25-6, 28; NAF brief, 33.

138. ACOG brief, 18-19, 23.This point about the relative safety of clinics and hospitals was also made by amici California Women Lawyers (pp. 20-1) and Women Lawyers (35, 38).

139. 462 U.S. 434-5.

140. ACOG brief, 25.

141. ACOG brief, 4, 27, 29.

142. APHA brief, 6-7. In fact, Justice Powell employs this data, and notes that only nine second trimester abortions were performed in 1977 in the City of *Akron* (462 U.S. 435).

143. California Women Lawyers brief, 22; Certain Law Professors brief, 16; NAACP brief, 3; NOW brief, 11-12, 31, 35-6; Planned Parenthood, 59-60—in this brief, Planned Parenthood refers the Court to the amicus brief that it has already filed in *Planned Parenthood of Kansas City, Missouri v. Ashcroft*.

144. Respondent brief, 9, 11, 41.

145. Respondent brief, 41.

146. NOW brief, 43-5.

147. 426 U.S. 444.

148. 426 U.S. 445.

149. Brennan Papers, file 615, Letter from Justice Blackmun to Justice Powell, 3/8/83.

150. Respondent brief, 18; ACOG brief, 5; NAF, 23; Planned Parenthood brief, 26.

151. ACOG brief, 3, 5; Planned Parenthood brief, 19, 26.

152. This group also terms this list a "parade of medical horribles" (CRO brief, 39).

153. 426 U.S. 472 fn16.

154. Respondent brief, 23, 37.

155. CRO brief, 16-25,32-3, 51.
156. Planned Parenthood brief, 28-33.
157. ACOG brief, 10 fn19.
158. 426 U.S. 427, 441. The ordinance noted only that minors can "by-pass" parents by using an Ohio statute governing juvenile proceedings, but Justice Powell held that this juvenile delinquency statute did not provide clear alternatives for these young women (441 fn31).
159. Respondent brief, 47-8.
160. ACOG brief, 4, 15-6.
161. NAF brief, 27-8. This point is also made by California Women Lawyers (p. 20), and Certain Law Professors (p. 4, 55, 60, 63).
162. 462 U.S. 445-6.
163. ACOG brief, 6-8; APA brief, 20; Planned Parenthood brief, 17, 38-42; NAF brief, 18; California Women Lawyers brief, 26; NOW, 26-7. This point was also briefly discussed in the Petitioner's brief (p. 33-35).
164. 462 U.S. 448 fn38; NAF discusses its Counseling Standards at length in its brief (p. 24-26).
165. 462 U.S. 449 fn40. Justice Powell also employs the APA's argument that there were alternatives to requiring physician counseling and that the city could have set minimum standards for counselors (APA brief, 22).
166. APA brief, 7-14. The APA also discussed the APHA guidelines and contended that these guidelines ensured that the requirements of informed consent would be met (p. 18 n26). Justice O'Connor was also influenced by ACOG's discussion of the impact of the informed consent provision. She took note of ACOG's recommendation that special counseling be provided for abortion patients, but appears to have accepted the view of the Respondent-Intervenor that no such counseling was taking place in the *Akron* clinics prior to passage of the ordinance (462 U.S. 473; Respondent-Intervenor brief, 7-11).
167. 462 U.S. 450.
168. 462 U.S. 451; American College of Pathologists brief, 7.
169. Among the arguments that the Court did not accept were those that permitted parental consent out of concern about the family unit (United Families Foundation, 14-7) or permitted the informed consent provision because it ensured that the woman have complete information about fetal development (Feminists for Life, 10-3; UFF, 22) or was based on a model of "patient autonomy" (Womankind, Inc., 2-7). The Court also did not accept the arguments of the United Families Foundation that scientific data showed that abortion had serious risks (p. 2, 23-4). In addition, the Court did not accept the view that the informed consent provision should be struck down because it was unnecessary, since existing tort law and medical malpractice law ensured that physicians would inform patients of the risks of the abortion procedure (Planned Parenthood, 12-4, 44). The Court also rejected arguments that abortion should be treated like other medical procedures (CRO, 44) and did not address the specific burdens that the *Akron* provisions placed on women (PP, 49-51; NOW, 17-9). Finally, the Court did not entertain discussions about the inherent rights of fetuses (CLRCR, 1-3; AUL, 15).
170. These groups filed briefs that were very similar: two or more of the briefs talked about abuses in abortion clinics that had been reported in a series published in the Chicago Sun-Times in 1978 (Feminists, 16-1 ; Womankind, 22-26); described these clinics as "self-interested," (Feminists, 6; United, 26) and suggested that these clinics had a financial stake in tricking women into having abortions; provided an identical list of informed consent statutes in the states

(Feminists, 5; Womankind, 11); or said that there was a parallel between the waiting period in the *Akron* ordinance and state laws that required that women who have just given birth wait 72 hours before signing the papers to place their child for adoption (Feminists, 26; United, 27).

171. APA brief, 5.

172. APHA brief, 1, 21 n5.

173. NAF brief, 23 fn2. It bears noting, however, that one petitioner amicus also limited its discussion to one substantive area (Womankind, 7—informed consent provision).

174. APHA brief, 1, 29 n6.

175. APHA brief, ii.

176. NAF brief, 34-5.

177. California Women Lawyers brief, 3-16.

178. Certain Religious Organizations brief, 6-12.

179. Certain Law Professors brief, 45, 54.

180. The NAACP's entire brief was devoted to responding to the argument made by the U.S. The NAACP warned that if the Court heeded the U.S.'s urging to accord heavy deference to the legislature, this would "seriously threaten the enjoyment of civil, political, and personal liberties" (NAACP brief, 4).

181. The Respondent's brief was also critical of the argument made by the United States (p. 29-31).

182. 462 U.S. 458.

183. 492 U.S. 490.

184. 476 U.S. 747.

185. For an excellent discussion of interest group participation in *Webster*, see Sue Behuniak, "Friendly Fire," *Judicature*.

186. 112 S.Ct. 2791, 2803.

187. 112 S.Ct. 2854, 2849-50.

188. 112 S.Ct. 2809.

189. 112 S.Ct. 2807, 2810.

190. 112 S.Ct. 2846. Justice Blackmun also echoed the argument made by the Petitioners, as well as by the City of New York, that the abortion debate implicates gender equality (112 S.Ct. 2846; Petitioner brief, 21; City of New York, 3, 5).

191. Petitioner brief, 15; ACOG , 5.

192. Respondent brief, 109.

193. Amici in *Casey* sharply disagreed about the motives of the states in passing anti-abortion laws in the mid to late 19th century. The brief of 250 American Historians contended that these laws were based on a number of concerns, including moral and theological considerations, concern for women's health, and the medical profession's attempt to regulate and "professionalize" the practice of medicine (1). In contrast, Certain American State Legislatures argued that these laws were based solely on the states' desire to protect unborn human life (11-28).

194. 112 S.Ct. 2805.

195. 250 Historians, 5-26. In their reply brief, the Petitioners suggested that the Court look at state practices in 1791, when the Bill of Rights was ratified, and not in 1868 (Petitioners' Reply, p. 8 fn15).

196. 250 Historians, 1, 28.

197. 112 S.Ct. 2859.

198. 112 S.Ct. 2874.

199. Respondent brief, 33.

200. U.S., 7, 10-11.

201. America21, 2, 14-16; American Academy of Medical Ethics, 3, 19-25; Catholics United for Life, 9-10; Certain American State Legislators, 2, 6-7; Hyde, 8 fn8; Legal Defense for Unborn Children, 11-12, 25-26; and University Faculty for Life, 4.

202. Certain American State Legislators, 7.

203. American Academy of Medical Ethics, 3, 21-25.

204. Petitioners' reply brief, p. 8 fn 15.

205. Respondents' brief, p. 33.

206. 212 S.Ct. 2808. The only "fact" that the plurality said had changed is that advances in medical technology have made abortions safer later in pregnancy and have made fetuses viable earlier in pregnancy. The plurality contended that these facts did not affect *Roe*'s central holding, but went to the question of time limits (2811).

207. 212 S.Ct. 2810-2; Petitioner's brief, 22; ACOG, 13, Alan Guttmacher, 16-17; Don Edwards, 2, 13, 17; New York, 7-8.

208. 212 S.Ct. 2809.

209. 212 S.Ct. 2809.

210. Petitioner brief, 20; Petitioner at Oral Argument, 4-5.

211. Don Edwards, 3-4, 13; New York, 3; 178 Organizations, 10.

212. Petitioner brief, 15, 33, 62; New York, 6, 10-12.

213. The plurality asserted that "there would be a terrible price for overruling *Roe*" and that such an action "would seriously weaken the Court's capacity to exercise the judicial power and to function as the Supreme Court of a Nation dedicated to the rule of law" (212 S.Ct. 2814). Moreover, the plurality warned that the Court's decisions "must be ground truly in principle, not in compromises with social and political pressures" (2814). Justice Blackmun also argued that overturning *Roe* would "seriously weaken the Court's capacity to exercise judicial power" (2845), and Justice Stevens contended that "the societal costs of overruling *Roe* would be enormous" (2838).

214. Petitioner brief, 20; Don Edwards, 25, 27-28; 178 Organizations, 16-17, 18; NAACP, 3; New York, 15-23, 25. The Justices appear to have rejected the argument of the Respondent that these costs would not be great, since *Roe* had not been a source of stability in the law (Respondent brief, 112).

215. 212 S.Ct. 2875.

216. Respondent brief, 105; United States, 1-2, 8; Hyde, 2, 9, 11; National Right to Life, 1; Knights of Columbus, 2-3, 4.

217. 212 S.Ct. 2855, 2858.

218. United States, 5-6, 9; Catholic Conference, 5; National Right to Life, 7.

219. ACOG, 10.

220. AAME, 27-8.

221. 428 U.S. 74.

222. 212 S.Ct. 2828; Petitioner brief, 5-7, 16. The Justices of the plurality also relied extensively on the record of the federal district court in discussing the prevalence of family violence (212 S.Ct. 2826-7).

223. 212 S.Ct. 2828.

224. 212 S.Ct. 2829.

225. The Petitioner argued that fears of "physical, sexual, and psychological abuse, [as well as] abuse of other members of the family" would dissuade women from exercising their abortion right (Petitioner brief, 5-6). The Pennsylvania Coalition provided detailed information about the "serious physical and psychological injury suffered by victims of domestic battering" (Pennsylvania Co-

alition, 1, 3, 5, 7, 11, 19). The APA discussed the reasons that women might choose not to tell their husbands about their decision to abort a pregnancy, among these, the fact that the husband is not the father, that the woman has been raped, and that the husband has been emotionally and/or psychologically abusing the woman (APA, 6-16). ACOG also noted that the exceptions did not "cover the range of coercive actions" that a husband might take against his wife and that the statute did not address a compelling state interest (ACOG , 17-20).

226. 212 S.Ct. 2831. The plurality noted that the notification provision was "repugnant to present understandings of marriage" and reminded that "women don't lose their constitutional rights when they marry" (2831).

227. 212 S.Ct. 2845.

228. Petitioner brief, 16, 48; Petitioner reply brief, 16 fn28; APA, 15; 250 American Historians, 29; Rutherford Institute, 13. It bears noting that the Rutherford Institute had a much different "take" on the stereotypes than did the Petitioner or amicus 250 American Historians: it argued that certain "types" of women would not tell their husband of their intention to access abortion. For example, the Institute argued that "[a] highly dominant, independent wife who is not in touch with her emotions and who has an incapacitated husband may not tell him about an abortion" (13).

229. 212 S.Ct. 2870-1.

230. Respondent brief, 80-1; Feminists for Life, 3-6, 10, 13-4; National Legal Foundation, 20; Rutherford Institute, 2, 23; Utah, 20-28. The Chief Justice appears to have ignored the arguments of the Petitioners and the Pennsylvania Coalition that the state's interests were insufficient to justify the provision (Petitioner brief, 40-44; Pennsylvania Coalition, 24).

231. 212 S.Ct. 2870 fn2; Respondent brief, 21-2; Utah, 29.

232. 212 S.Ct. 2843; 2851 fn7; 2853. These Justices rejected the argument of the Respondent that the informed consent statement was similar to other consumer disclosures (Respondent brief, 30).

233. 462 U.S. 476.

234. Petitioners' brief, 37; Petitioners' reply brief, 1 fn3, 4, 5, 6 fn12, 6-7, 7 fn14, 8, 8 fn 15, 10(twice),19 fn36, Petitioners' oral argument trans., 8.

235. Petitioners' reply brief, 7 fn13.

236. Petitioners' reply brief, 9.

237. Petitioners' reply brief, 1 fn3.

238. Petitioners' reply brief, 13, 13 fn22, 23, 30.

239. Petitioners' reply brief, 16 fn 28.

240. Petitioners' reply brief, 10.

241. Petitioners' brief, 61 fn96.

242. Petitioners' brief, 28 fn47; Petitioners' reply brief, 7 fn14.

243. Petitioners' brief, 22 fn33.

244. Petitioners' brief, 28 fn48.

245. Petitioners' brief, 32 fn60.

246. Petitioners' brief, 39.

247. Respondents' brief, 108.

248. Respondents' brief, 58 fn24.

249. Don Edwards, 22.

250. AAME, 6 and throughout brief.

251. Certain Legislators, 7.

252. U.S., 19; AAPOG, 1 and throughout brief; Hyde, 15.

253. Hyde, 5, 13, 15; NRLCC, 3.

254. NRLCC, 3; U.S., 14, 19; UFL 15.

255. U.S., 19; UFL, 9 fn14.
256. LII, 9, 19; NRLCC, 7.
257. U.S., 19.
258. U.S., 22 fn 20; Utah, 17.
259. Certain State Legislators, 7; U.S.,10 fn6; UFL, 4 fn4.
260. Hyde, 8 fn8; U.S. 10 fn6.
261. Hyde, 23; SCLE, 18.
262. LII, 7 fn3.

4

Amici Curiae and Assistance in Dying

The United States Supreme Court has adjudicated three cases centered on the question of whether one has the constitutional right to hasten one's own death. In 1990, the Justices heard *Cruzan v. Director, Missouri Department of Health,* a case that considered whether a state regulation requiring that there be clear and convincing evidence of an incompetent's wishes before nutrition and hydration could be withdrawn violated the due process clause of the Fourteenth Amendment. In 1997, the Justices heard *Washington et al. v. Glucksberg et al.* and *Vacco v. Quill,* cases that called upon the Court to determine whether state laws prohibiting assistance in dying, specifically physician assistance in dying, violated the due process clause. There was extensive amicus curiae participation in both cases. In *Cruzan,* forty-five amici filed briefs and in *Glucksberg* and *Vacco,* there were sixty amici briefs.

The Justices perceived these three cases as turning on complicated and difficult questions about when life ceases and about the right of an individual to use medical technology to control his or her final days. The amici played a valuable role in these cases by providing a wealth of data about the sociological, physiological, and psychological processes of death and dying. Perhaps more than in any other cases under review in this study, the amici disagreed about not only the constitutional issues but also the extralegal questions. Specifically, amici were in stark disagreement about the scientific and medical data surrounding death and dying and about the historical foundation of the debate about assistance in dying. As in the abortion cases and the cases governing family relationships, the Justices ultimately accepted the views and data presented by some amici and rejected those of others. Moreover, as in the other cases under consideration, the nature of this reliance was indirect; while the Justices relied heavily on the amici, they employed very few direct citations to these briefs.

CRUZAN V. DIRECTOR, MISSOURI DEPARTMENT OF HEALTH

In its 1990 decision in *Cruzan v. Director, Missouri Department of Health*,[1] the U.S. Supreme Court upheld the decision of the Missouri Supreme Court to deny the request of the states's parents to terminate nutrition and hydration for their incompetent adult daughter. Specifically, the Court upheld a state requirement that there be clear and convincing evidence that Nancy Cruzan, who was in a persistent vegetative state following an automobile accident, would have wanted to have nutrition and hydration discontinued. The Court rejected the argument of Ms. Cruzan's parents that this evidentiary requirement ran afoul of their daughter's due process liberty right. Forty-seven amicus curiae briefs were filed with the Supreme Court in this litigation. These briefs addressed a wide range of subjects. The influence of amici is apparent in all five written opinions; however, some Justices drew more heavily on these briefs. Moreover, as in the abortion cases, not all amici were heard equally—it appears that the Justices paid closer attention to some interested parties than to others. Both legal and extralegal questions are presented in this litigation, and the influence of the amici is apparent in both areas. The principal legal question raised in *Cruzan*, whether there was a liberty interest in the termination of artificial nutrition and hydration that could be exercised by an incompetent's parents, called upon the Justices to revisit privacy and due process liberty principles. The remaining questions addressed a wide range of concerns, including the relationship of life to death, the definition of persistent vegetative state and the termination of medical treatment, and the impact of the Court's holding on the wider polity. In considering these extralegal questions, the influence of the amici was profound.

Direct Cites to Amici Briefs

As in the contraceptive and abortion cases, few direct cites to amici briefs appear in this case. In a decision that took up more than 96 pages, there were only seven direct cites, all but one of which were to the amicus brief of either the AMA or the American Association of Neurology. Most of these direct cites were to scientific or medical discussions of death and dying, and the Justices cited to the AMA almost exclusively in their opinions. For example, both Chief Justice Rehnquist and Justice

Brennan cited the AMA brief in their discussions of the prognosis for persons in a persistent vegetative state.[2] Justice Stevens also cited the AMA's brief in his discussion of the incidence of death in hospitals and nursing homes.[3] In his discussion of Ms. Cruzan's medical condition, Justice Brennan relied on the Guardian Ad Litem's brief, as well as the Position Statement included in the brief of the American Academy of Neurology, as support for the position that food and hydration is a form of medical treatment.[4] Justices Brennan and Stevens also relied upon the briefs of the AMA and the AAN in their discussion of the impact of this case on medical treatment decisions.[5]

Indirect Use of Amici Briefs

In addition to relying directly on the friends, the Justices extensively employed amici arguments and data without citing to these briefs. Amici influence is apparent in the Justices' handling of the central issues that arose in this litigation.

Due Process Liberty Interest in the Termination of Treatment
The Justices were in sharp disagreement about the nature of the right to terminate treatment, and in their arguments, there are strong hints of amici influence. In particular, the brief filed by the United States appears to have had a profound impact on the way the Justices saw this liberty right. Nancy Cruzan's parents contended their daughter had a fundamental right to discontinue treatment and that the state's refusal to honor their request to terminate this treatment violated her liberty and privacy rights. All of the Justices focused on the liberty right, and the brief filed by the U.S. likely had a profound impact on the way the Justices saw this liberty right. For example, Chief Justice Rehnquist noted that Nancy Cruzan's right was better characterized as a Fourteenth Amendment liberty interest than as a privacy right. This characterization parallels the U.S. argument that the right to refuse treatment was grounded in the due process clause, not in any "generalized right to privacy."[6] Similarly, the Chief Justice appears to have been influenced by the government's argument that the clear and convincing evidence standard was necessary where treatment was being terminated for a person who was incompetent, since "the powerful check of self-preservation" was gone for such an individual.[7] Like the U.S., Chief Justice Rehnquist contended that this standard protected the personal element of choice and served as a procedural safeguard against potential abuses.[8]

The impact of the United States on the Chief Justice's opinion is also apparent in his analysis of the equal protection clause. Both the Cruzans and the Guardian Ad Litem contended that the clear and convincing evidence standard violated not only the due process clause, but also the equal protection clause;[9] however, the Chief Justice, who was the only Justice to address this claim, asserted that competent and incompetent patients were not similarly situated, since the incompetent patient could not exercise her own right to refuse treatment.[10] Like the United States, the Chief Justice drew a distinction between the decision-making abilities of competent and incompetent individuals and concluded that incompetents could not make an informed judgment and that, because of this, their rights could be limited.[11]

The Chief Justice was not the only Justice who appears to have been influenced by amici in addressing the liberty interest at issue in *Cruzan*. Justice Brennan contended that the right of an incompetent to refuse treatment was a "fundamental right" derived from those liberties that are "deeply rooted in our Nation's history and tradition."[12] In characterizing this as a fundamental right, Justice Brennan likely drew on the briefs not only of the states and Guardian Ad Litem,[13] but also of the American Medical Association, the Society for the Right to Die, and Concern for Dying.[14] Without citing amicus AMA, he drew directly on a quote in its amicus brief, finding that "Anglo-American law is based on the premise of thorough-going self-determination."[15]

Moreover, in this conclusion that the fundamental right to be free from unwanted medical treatment could never be outweighed by state interests,[16] Justice Brennan appears to have been guided by arguments in the briefs of the Guardian Ad Litem, the National Hospice Organization, and the American College of Physicians.[17] In addition, Justice Brennan voiced many of the same doubts raised by the states and its amici about whether Missouri's interest in life was unqualified.[18] Significantly, he employed amici examples of instances in which this interest in life was not absolute, among these, the American Academy of Neurology's example of Missouri's refusal to provide adequate medical insurance to all of its citizenry,[19] and the Guardian Ad Litem's example of the state's law governing Living Wills.[20] He also agreed with amicus Society for the Right to Die that the evidentiary standard was so burdensome that it precluded the exercise of the fundamental right to refuse treatment.[21] Furthermore, Justice Brennan accepted the view of the American Medical Association that courts should consider informal statements made before incompetency in assessing whether a person would have wished to terminate treatment.[22]

Like Justice Brennan, Justice Stevens asserted that there was a fundamental right to refuse medical treatment, and he, too, appears to have been influenced by amici arguments that choices about death were "at the core of liberty" and were "so rooted in the traditions and conscience of our people as to be fundamental."[23] In contending that privacy and bodily integrity were bound together, Justice Stevens cited many of the same cases cited by amici American Academy of Neurology and AIDS Civil Rights Project as support.[24] He also noted the significance of the spiritual life in guiding choices about bodily integrity, and in so doing, echoed many of the concerns of the American College of Physicians, American Medical Association, and American Hospital Association.[25] Similarly, in characterizing Missouri's interest in life as an interest in mere "biological persistence,"[26] Justice Stevens seems to have drawn on the language in the amici briefs of the Society for the Right to Die and the Wisconsin Bioethicists.[27]

Even the arguments of Justice Scalia, who contended that liberty did not encompass a right to terminate treatment, paralleled those of amici, specifically, the United States. Like the U.S., Justice Scalia argued that such a right was not in the Constitution and would have to be constructed by the judiciary.[28] In making its argument, the U.S. noted that in its earlier decision in *City of East Cleveland v. Moore*, the Court had established that it was "most vulnerable and nearest to illegitimacy when it deals with judge-made law having little or no cognizable roots in the language or design of the Constitution."[29] This concern about judicially created rights also appeared briefly in the briefs of the National Right to Life Committee and the Rutherford Institute.[30]

Thus, even in the area of legal doctrine, where one might assume that the party briefs would have overwhelming influence, amici played an important role. The role of the United States and of certain medical organizations, like the American Academy of Neurology, the American College of Physicians, the American Hospital Association, the American Medical Association, and the Society of Critical Care Medicine, and patient advocacy groups, like the Society for the Right to Die, Concern for Dying, the National Hospice Organization, the AIDS Civil Rights Project, and Wisconsin Bioethicists, is especially notable. Moreover, the Justices' reliance on these groups was even more profound in their discussion of the medical and scientific data surrounding death and dying.

Death and Dying

Justice Brennan and Stevens were very concerned in their opinions about how to define life and death, and the influence of amici on their discussion of this issue is significant. Without attribution to amicus AIDS Civil Rights Project, Justice Brennan appears to have drawn directly on a passage found in its brief that discussed the impact of medical technology on death and dying.[31] He also employed statistics provided by the Society for the Right to Die that estimated that more than 80 percent of all deaths in the United States take place in a hospital or nursing home.[32] Justice Brennan used a quote from this brief stating that "[t]he timing of death—once a matter of fate—is now a matter of public choice," without attribution to either the amicus or the original source.[33]

Like Justice Brennan, Justice Stevens also drew heavily on the amici briefs in his discussion of death and dying. Justice Stevens contended that life should be defined to encompass not only an individual's physiological condition or function, but also his or her "history, practical manifestation of the human spirit and activity matrix."[34] This definition of life drew upon the Cruzans' brief, which heavily relied on the 1983 Report of the President's Commission and on the amici briefs, which expanded this argument.[35] While the 1983 Report had noted that "personality, memory, purposive action, social interaction, sentience, thought and even emotional states" (fn 47 original) helped to define a life, this definition of life and death was expanded upon by several amici like the United Methodist Church, who asserted that life and death were "integrative of spiritual, emotional and physical aspects of being,"[36] and the American College of Physicians, who counseled that patients in a persistent vegetative state were incapable of possessing any of the "qualities of distinctively human life."[37] Similarly, both amici Frederick R. Abrams and Barbara Burgoon asserted that life "suggests more than breathing" and implies an ability to related to one's surroundings.[38] Like amici United Methodist Church, SSM Health Care System, and National Hospice Organization, Justice Stevens reminded that death was part of the cycle of life and was a natural part of living and that the manner of dying affects how a life is remembered.[39]

Medical Science and the Persistent Vegetative State

The Justices were perhaps most affected by the amici briefs in discussing Ms. Cruzan's medical condition. At trial, it had been adduced that Ms. Cruzan was in a persistent vegetative state, and the Justices relied on the briefs filed by certain members of the medical community in discussing this condition. It bears noting that the state's brief highlights the expertise of these friends and notes that the briefs "represent the carefully considered positions of most of the doctors, nurses, and hospitals in this country," advising the Court to "defer to the medical judgment of the medical professionals" represented in these briefs.[40] The Justices appear to have heeded the state's advice. Both the Chief Justice and Justice Brennan unabashedly cited the AMA's brief in discussing what is known about the prognosis of someone in a persistent vegetative state (PVS), and Justice Stevens cited the AMA's brief in discussing the incidence of death in hospitals and nursing homes.[41] Justice Brennan also cited the brief of the Guardian Ad Litem to provide detail about Nancy Cruzan's medical condition.[42]

Of the Justices, Justice Brennan made the most use of direct citation, but his *indirect* use of amici briefs is much more striking. For example, in arguing that PVS patients are devoid of thought, emotion, and sensation, Justice Brennan drew on the brief of the American Academy of Neurology and the American Medical Association.[43] Justice Brennan also relied on amici in discussing the use of medical tests to diagnose pvs.[44] In addition to relying on amici briefs for general information about PVS patients, Justice Brennan used these briefs to conclude that artificial feeding and hydration is a form of medical treatment, and not simply "ordinary care." Justice Brennan employed the Position Paper of the American Academy of Neurology, included in the appendix of the group's brief, as support for this position[45] and appears to have relied on the amici briefs of the American Medical Association, Barbara Burgoon, the Society for the Right to Die, and Concern for Dying.[46]

The amici briefs were divided on how PVS could be defined and about whether nutrition and hydration constituted medical treatment, and the Justices clearly accepted the views of certain amici on these two issues. Most notably, they accepted the data presented by the American Medical Association, the American Academy of Neurology, and the American College of Physicians and rejected the views of other groups, among them, Doctors for Life, the American Academy of Physicians and Surgeons, the U.S. Catholic Conference, the Catholic Guild, the United States, and the Milwaukee District Attorney.[47] This selective use of amici data and arguments paralleled the patterns apparent in the abortion cases and in the two physician-assisted suicide cases discussed later in this chapter.

Decision-Making at the End of Life

At issue in this case was whether a state could employ a heightened evidentiary standard, the clear and convincing evidence standard, to determine whether statements made prior to incompetency could be used to indicate the treatment preferences of an incompetent person. The amici provided extensive information to the Court about the variation among states in evidentiary standards for medical decision-making. Respondent State of Missouri briefly noted that this variation existed and was consistent with principles of federalism, but amici United States and the AMA provided an extensive discussion of this range of options. The U.S. noted that there was no consensus about whether the courts should play a role in treatment decisions and that allowing states a wide berth in crafting decision-making procedures was consistent with "values of federalism and judicial restraint."[48] The Justices drew heavily on the amici's arguments and data in this area. For example, the influence of the U.S. brief can be discerned both in Chief Justice Rehnquist's majority opinion, which catalogued the state variation, and in Justice O'Connor's argument that the variation suggested that there was no national consensus about how to protect the individual's liberty interest in refusing treatment.[49] Justice Scalia put the most positive spin on the amici's argument, contending that state legislatures should be free to craft procedures for ensuring that treatment decisions are effectuated, warning that courts had no business deciding this issue.[50]

Justices Brennan and Stevens also implicitly made note of amici arguments about state variation, contending that only certain procedures would pass muster under the liberty right. Justice Brennan asserted that state procedural safeguards had to aim at ensuring that the treatment decision be in tune with that which the individual would have chosen. Justice Brennan accepted the view of the Cruzans and many of their amici, among these, the AIDS Civil Rights Project, American Academy of Neurology, American College of Physicians, American Hospital Association, AMA, Concern for Dying, Society for Critical Care Medicine, United Methodist Church, and the Society for the Right to Die, that the substituted judgment procedure was most preferable.[51] It bears noting that the Chief Justice had rejected substituted judgment by family members, implicitly accepting the view of the Milwaukee D.A.'s office that the prevalence of intrafamily violence and, in particular, elder abuse suggested that family relations were far less sanguine than the states and their amici suggested.[52]

The influence of amici was perhaps even more apparent in Justice Stevens' dissent, which appears to have relied exclusively on the amici briefs in endorsing the best interest test for medical decision-making, contending that the "[b]est interests of individuals, especially when buttressed by the interests of related third parties, must prevail over any general state policy."[53] The Guardian Ad Litem initially proposed this test, and amici American College of Physicians, American Medical Association, and Association of Retarded Citizens of the United States provided an expansive discussion of the benefits of it.[54]

The dissenting opinions of both Justice Brennan and Justice Stevens relied on amici arguments about the future impact of the majority holding on individual rights and medical practice. Justice Stevens directly cited the brief of the American Medical Association for support for his position that this issue would continue to be significant, and he noted that advances in medical technology were making treatment decisions more difficult.[55] Justice Brennan was concerned about the repercussions of the Court's decision on medical ethics. Again employing a quote without attributing it to the amicus brief of the AIDS Civil Rights Project, Justice Brennan cautioned that the "Missouri court's rule transforms human beings into passive subjects of medical technology."[56] Harsh warnings about the encroachment of technology on individual rights were echoed in the briefs of the Guardian Ad Litem[57] and in the amici briefs of not only the AIDS Civil Rights Project but also of Concern for Dying and the Society of Critical Care Medicine.[58]

Justice Brennan was also concerned about the impact of this case on medical practice. He, like a number of amici, contended that the Court's holding had the potential to undermine the will of doctors and families to employ medical technology.[59] Justice Brennan, along with amici AIDS Civil Rights Project, American Academy of Neurology, American Medical Association, Burgoon, and Concern for Dying, contended that the Court's decision rendered the initial decision to use "heroic" measures irrevocable, since families would have difficulty terminating this treatment. This irrevocability would discourage families and doctors from using this technology in the first instance. This point was alluded to by the states, but elaborated upon by amici.[60]

Finally, Justice Brennan ended his opinion as he began it: with a quotation that appears to have been drawn from an amicus brief, again without attribution. Warning that even the good intentions of the State of Missouri could result in a deprivation of liberty, Justice Brennan quoted Justice Holmes' dissenting opinion in *Olmstead v. U.S.*, stating that "[t]he greatest dangers to liberty lurk in insidious encroachment by men of zeal, well meaning but without understanding."[61] In using this quotation, Justice Brennan appears to have directly drawn on the brief of the American College of Physicians without attribution.[62]

Party Coordination and Cooperation

The parties engaged in very different patterns of coordination and cooperation in this case. The Cruzans cited extensively to their own amici in their initial brief, often raising points briefly and leaving elaboration to their friends. In a large number of instances, the Cruzans expressly made note of the arguments contained in their amici briefs and cited to both the briefs and the supplemental materials, like organizational policies and guidelines, contained in appendixes to these briefs. Specifically, the Cruzans attempted to focus the Court's attention on its medical amici, informing the Justices that these briefs "represent[ed] the carefully considered positions of medical professionals."[63] In this initial brief, the Cruzans made no mention of any opposing amici. In its reply brief, however, they employed a completely different strategy. The reply brief, filed with the Court after the respondent and its amici have filed their briefs, is intended to provide an opportunity for the respondent to address the arguments raised by its opponents. In this case, the Cruzans devoted almost all of their reply brief to a discussion of the brief of opposing amicus U.S. It directly cited to the U.S. six times, in an attempt to counter the arguments and data presented by this influential amicus. It is likely that the Cruzans realized the potential importance of this brief to the Justices, and they used their reply brief to address the arguments presented solely by the U.S. Much of the reply brief is devoted to a discussion of how the U.S. brief was actually compatible with the Cruzans' position, identifying a number of points of agreement between the briefs. For example, the Cruzans noted that they agreed with the U.S. that the clear and convincing evidence standard could deprive incompetent persons of a meaningful choice in making treatment decision. They also agreed with the U.S. that the right to make such a decision is protected as a due process liberty right.[64] The Cruzans pointedly disagreed, however, with the Solicitor General's argument that the clear and convincing standard is necessary to protect patients from abuse.[65]

In contrast to the Cruzans' initial and reply briefs, which attempted to make positive use of the amici briefs, even where the brief was written in support of its foe, Missouri's references to amici were almost all negative. Much of Missouri's brief aimed at undermining the arguments or data of opposing amici. In sum, there are ten direct cites either to the amici in general or to some specific friend, and nearly all are negative references. For example, in a number of instances, the State of Missouri contended that the "states and the amici" had interpreted the statute incorrectly. Moreover, Missouri repeatedly criticized certain amici, specifically, the AMA, for what it saw as misplaced reliance on "patient autonomy."[66] The state was also highly critical of the briefs of the American College of Physicians, the National Hospice Organization, and the Society for the Right to Die and argued that no third party could make the decision to terminate treatment for an incompetent person.

Just as the Cruzans' specifically targeted opposing amicus United States, which they must have seen as potentially damaging to its case, Missouri focused on those amici that it saw as most dangerous, most significantly, the AMA. While the Cruzans attempted to undercut the potential clout of the U.S. arguments by incorporating them, however, Missouri sought to undermine the AMA's brief by directly criticizing it. It appears that neither strategy was really successful: both the U.S. and the AMA were highly effective and saw the Justices employing many of their arguments and data into their decisions.

Conclusions Drawn from *Cruzan*

Amici played an important role in the Court's handling of the *Cruzan* case. Perhaps because this case raised an issue of first impression, much of the Justices' energies were devoted to addressing extralegal, as opposed to legal questions. Even in examining the constitutional provisions, however, the influence of amici is apparent. The Justices, the parties, and the amici sharply disagreed about whether the right to terminate treatment is a fundamental right, such that states must present compelling reasons for any limitations. A wide variety of groups contributed to this discussion, and the Justices appear to have adopted the arguments and information provided by a number of these groups.

Chief Justice Rehnquist and Justice Scalia vigorously contended that this right was not fundamental, and both repeatedly employed arguments that appeared only in the amicus brief of the United States as support for this position. In contrast, Justices Brennan and Stevens contended that the right to terminate treatment was a fundamental right, entitled to the greatest degree of protection. In making this argument, these Justices repeatedly employed the arguments presented in the amici briefs of the American Medical Association and the Society for the Right to Die. Other amici were also heard by these Justices, although perhaps not so loudly, among these, Concern for Dying, the National Hospice Organization, the American College of Physicians, the American Academy of Neurology, the AIDS Civil Rights Project, the American Hospital Association, the Society of Critical Care Medicine, and the Wisconsin Bioethicists.

In discussing the extralegal questions, amici influence is even more pronounced. The only direct quotes to amici briefs are in the Justices' discussions of how medical science helps us to understand Ms. Cruzan's condition. Justices Brennan and Stevens repeatedly cited the AMA brief, and Chief Justice Rehnquist also cited this brief, albeit to a lesser degree. Justice Brennan drew heavily on the briefs of several other amici and cited liberally from the briefs of the American Academy of Neurology and the Guardian Ad Litem.

Furthermore, in their discussions of life and death and how we define these states, the Justices drew on the amici briefs. Both Justices Brennan and Stevens adopted the arguments of several amici, perhaps most notably, the Society for the Right to Die, the United Methodist Church, and the National Hospice Organization, whose arguments they used repeatedly. Similarly, the Justice relied heavily on the amici briefs in discussing how treatment decisions should be made in advance of incompetence, and the impact of amici AMA is clear here. Justices Brennan and Stevens relied on alternative frameworks for decision-making, and both frameworks were presented almost entirely by amici American College of Physicians and the Association for Retarded Citizens of the United States. Finally, the Justices drew heavily on the amici briefs in discussing the impact of the *Cruzan* decision on the experience of death and dying in the United States. The impact of the District Attorney of Milwaukee is apparent in the Chief Justice's opinion, and the American Association of Neurology, Concern for Dying, the American Medical Association, the AIDS Civil Rights Project, Burgoon, and the Society for Critical Care Medicine appear to have had a significant impact on the decisions of Justices Brennan and Stevens.

It bears noting that nearly all of the amici briefs filed on behalf of the states were addressed by the Justices to a greater or lesser degree, while the arguments of most of Missouri's amici went unaddressed, even by the state. In many instances, amici presented conflicting information or arguments and the Justices simply chose which amici to favor. For example, the Justices readily embraced the arguments of the AMA in discussing the science of the persistent vegetative state, but rejected the arguments of Doctors for Life, the Catholic Lawyers Guild, and the American Academy of Physicians and Surgeons, which presented different understandings of medical science. Similarly, the Justices accepted the views of life and death encompassed in the briefs of amici United Methodist Church, American College of Physicians, Abrams, Burgoon, SSM Health Care System, and National Hospice Organization, but rejected the views of Agudath Israel, Doctors for Life, Families for Life, the International Anti-Euthanasia Task Force, National Nurses for Life, the New Jersey Right to Life Committee, and the Value of Life Committee.

Amici participation in the *Cruzan* case suggests strongly that the Justices directly cite the amici briefs relatively infrequently. Here, the only direct cites occurred in the discussion of medical science, and the Justices directly credited only the AMA's brief. In addition, mainstream groups with a significant lobbying presence in the other branches, most notably the AMA, Solicitor General, and American Academy of Neurology were most likely to be heard. In fact, the AMA is perhaps the biggest winner in this litigation. Its brief was employed not only in the discussion of the scientific and medical questions at issue in this litigation, but in the constitutional questions as well. In addition, this case suggests that even though there are few direct cites, the Justices rely to a significant extent on amici input.

WASHINGTON ET AL. V. GLUCKSBERG ET AL. AND DENNIS C. VACCO, ATTORNEY GENERAL OF NEW YORK, ET AL., V. THOMAS E. QUILL ET AL.

In 1997, the U.S. Supreme Court was called upon to consider an issue that some considered a corollary to that raised in the *Cruzan* litigation— the question of whether a terminally ill, competent person, who was not dependent upon life support, could avail herself of assistance in dying. By 1997, the larger societal debate about assisted dying had shifted from the withdrawal or withholding of nutrition and hydration to the more controversial issue of whether an individual had the right to hasten his or her death with the assistance of another person. At issue in *Glucksberg* and *Vacco* was whether state criminal laws that prohibited physicians from providing assistance in dying violated Fourteenth Amendment due process and equal protection clauses.[67]

In *Compassion in Dying v. Washington*,[68] the en banc Ninth Circuit concluded that the Washington state law violated the due process clause, holding that there is a "liberty interest in controlling the time and manner of one's death . . . in short, a constitutionally recognized 'right to die.'"[69] Drawing heavily on *Cruzan* and on the U.S. Supreme Court's 1992 decision in *Planned Parenthood of Southeastern Pennsylvania v. Casey*, the en banc court concluded that the right to avoid a painful, hopeless death constituted "one of the most, if not the most, 'intimate and personal choices a person may make in a lifetime,'" that this choice is "central to personal dignity and autonomy" and that the state law constituted an undue burden on the exercise of this right.[70] While the Ninth Circuit focused on the due process clause, the Second Circuit that heard *Quill v. Vacco* concentrated on the equal protection clause. In its hearing of *Quill*, the Second Circuit concluded that the New York law barring physician assistance in dying violated the equal protection clause because it treated two classes of similarly situated individuals differently, and that this dissimilar treatment was not rationally related to any legitimate state interest.[71] The appeals court held that terminally ill individuals in the final stages of a terminal illness, yet not in need of life-sustaining treatment like artificial nutrition or hydration, were similarly situated to those individuals requiring such treatment, but that those dependent on treatment could hasten their deaths, while those not dependent on this treatment could not.[72]

In unanimous decisions that overturned both circuit court holdings, the Justices held that the Washington and New York state laws violated neither the due process nor the equal protection clause. Seven opinions were written in this case: Chief Justice Rehnquist penned the Court's opinions in both cases; Justices Stevens, O'Connor, and Breyer each wrote a single concurrence covering the issues presented in the two cases; and Justice Souter wrote an extensive opinion in *Glucksberg* and a very brief opinion in *Quill*. The opinions hint at major disagreements among the Justices about both legal and factual issues, most notably, the nature of the right in question here and the medical, scientific, and historical data relevant to death and dying in the United States.

Sixty amicus curiae briefs were filed in this case. Nearly all were filed by private interest groups interested in this issue, and while many briefs discussed the legal dimensions of these cases, namely, whether these laws conflicted with the due process and equal protection clauses, the amici expended far more energy informing the Court of the policy implications of the cases. Amici devoted considerable space in their briefs to discussions of terminal illness and death, competence, suicide and mental illness, palliative care, the medical distinctions between withdrawal/withholding of life support and hastening death, the impact of these laws or the circuit court holdings on the medical profession, quality of life, and cost containment, public opinion, and the role of the judiciary in the federal system. In a number of instances, amici disagreed with each other about the conclusions to be drawn from their "evidence," and as in both *Cruzan* and the abortion debate, amici on either side provided conflicting data. Since the amici were far less involved in discussions about the legal dimensions of these cases, we would expect that there would be less resemblance between their briefs and the Court's decisions. In some instances, this is true; however, as in *Cruzan*, there is a striking correspondence between the Justices' handling of the legal issues in these cases and the briefs of certain amici.

Direct Cites to Amici Briefs

With the exception of Justice O'Connor's decision, which noted simply the position of "the parties and their amici" about palliative medications that hasten death, all of the Justices referred directly to specific amici briefs. For example, in his majority opinion, Chief Justice Rehnquist had six direct cites to amici briefs. He used the amici briefs of the State of California et al. and the United States as support for his position that a variety of state interests were implicated in this litigation.[73] The Chief Justice also directly referenced the briefs of the United States, Not Dead Yet, and Bioethicists for States to show that there is "no principled basis for confining this right" and referred to the AMA's brief as support for his contention that there is sufficient basis for distinguishing between the withdrawal or withholding of life support and physician-assisted dying.[74] In addition, Chief Justice Rehnquist made ample use of the New York State Task Force *Report on Death and Dying* (NYS Report), citing it a total of twelve times.[75] Justice Stevens also directly cited to a variety of amici, employing five direct cites. In addition to quoting the NYS Report several times, he cited to the brief of the Washington State Psychological Association as support for his argument that mental health workers can make determinations as to the mental capacity of dying patients.[76] Justice Stevens also directly cited the amicus brief of the Coalition of Hospice Professionals to argue that palliative care does not always eliminate all pain associated with a terminal illness and noted that the AMA endorses terminal sedation.[77] Finally, Justice Stevens employed the amici briefs of the Bioethicists Supporting the Petitioners and Dworkin et al. to argue that the individual has a right to choose an ending to her life story that is consonant with her values and desires.[78] Strangely, despite the fact that he ruled against them, Justice Stevens made much more positive use of the amici briefs of proponents of aid in dying than he did of its opponents." Justice Breyer also relied directly on amici briefs, citing to them four times. He relied on the NYS Report and on the briefs of the National Hospice Organization and AMA as support for the position that medication relieves pain for most terminally ill patients, but he also noted that, as amici AMA and Concern for Dying detailed, palliative care was often not available to those who needed it.[79]

While his brethren cited largely to the amici briefs filed by medical and scientific organizations, all five of Justice Souter's cites were to the briefs filed by legislative members. He cited to the brief of the Members of the Washington and New York Legislatures (Members), noting that neither Washington nor New York punish attempted suicide,[80] and cited to the brief of the State Legislators for the position that states should be allowed to experiment with laws regulating physician-assisted suicide than do courts.[81] He also noted the list of proposed statutes included in the State Legislators' brief and contended that state legislatures have "superior opportunities for fact finding" about assisted suicide to that of courts.[82] Finally, Justice Souter employed the brief of the State Legislators to argue that the regulatory proposals advanced by the doctors are similar to those used in the Netherlands and, like these regulations, they may not be effective.[83]

The Justices directly cited the amici briefs twenty times. This extensive use of direct cites by the Chief Justice and Associate Justices suggests the respect they paid to governmental entities and to medical and scientific organizations. Chief Justice Rehnquist relied to a significant extent on the briefs of California and the United States. Similarly, Justice Souter employed the briefs of the State Legislators and Members. Justice Stevens relied heavily on the briefs of the Washington State Psychological Association and Coalition of Hospice Professionals, as well as the AMA, Bioethicists for Respondents, and Ronald Dworkin et al. Justice Breyer also relied on the brief of the AMA, Choice in Dying and National Hospice Organization. Like the Chief Justice, Justices Stevens and Breyer explicitly relied on the NYS Report. This extensive direct citation of amici briefs is fascinating and sets these cases apart from the others in this study. The nature of decision-making in the *Washington* and *Quill* cases is consistent with the other cases, however, because of the Justices' heavy *indirect* reliance on these briefs.

Indirect Use of Amici Briefs

Despite the fact that the New York and Washington laws were challenged under both the due process and the equal protection clauses, most of the discussion among the Justices, the parties, and the amici focused on the due process clause, with relatively little discussion of equal protection. While some amici filed a brief in each case, most amici filed one brief for both cases, and these briefs devoted considerable energy to discussing how these laws implicated due process jurisprudence, particularly, the law governing abortion and assistance in dying. The Justices relied heavily on the amici to characterize the right at issue in these cases. Only Chief Justice Rehnquist employed the party's view of this right, agreeing with the state of Washington that this case was about the right to commit suicide.[84] For the rest of the Court, the amici played an important role in helping to characterize the issue. For example, Justice Breyer's claim that the right at issue could be reformulated as a "right to die with dignity" was advanced only by amici ACLU and Gay Men's Health Crisis (GMHC) et al., who both contended that human beings have a right to "dignity in dying" which could not be abridged by the state.[85] Justices O'Connor and Souter occupied more centrist positions than either the Chief Justice, who saw this as right to commit suicide, or Justice Breyer, who characterized it as the right to die with dignity. Both O'Connor and Souter seem to have agreed with amici Bioethics Professors in Support of States and Americans for Death with Dignity that the right at issue could be constructed more narrowly, as the right of a mentally competent individual experiencing significant pain and suffering to control his or her death.[86]

The Due Process Standard for Evaluating Laws

The crux of the *Glucksberg* litigation was the question of whether hastening one's imminent death is a fundamental right deserving of heightened constitutional protection. Much of the debate about fundamental rights centers on determining whether the practice in question is deeply rooted in our nation's history and traditions. All of the Justices referred to the history of assisted suicide bans as a way of determining whether a fundamental right was at issue here, and this analysis was central to Chief Justice Rehnquist's opinion. The influence of amici is obvious here, as many friends provided the Justices with often conflicting views of how American society has viewed physician assisted suicide throughout history. As in the abortion cases, the amici disagreed about the starting point for historical analysis, and amici placed varying degrees of importance on different eras. This divergence is apparent not only in the amici briefs, but in the Justices' opinions, with Chief Justice Rehnquist and Justice Souter strongly disagreeing about which historical era should be focused upon and reaching sharply different conclusions about the lessons to be learned from this history.

For the Chief Justice, the starting point in the historical analysis was the Anglo-American common law tradition. He discussed the English common law's recognition of suicide as a felony offense under thirteenth-century writer Henry de Bracton, and then discussed Coke's restatement of the law in 1644. He noted that Blackstone incorporated this view of suicide as a felonious act in his treatises in the eighteenth century and focused on the colonial period, noting that the colonies imposed severe penalties upon those who committed suicide and upon their families.[87] He noted that while colonial governments stopped punishing persons committing suicide, they continued to punish those who assisted the suicide, and that beginning in 1828, states and territories imposed criminal sanctions against those who aided others in killing themselves.[88] He noted that this ban has been part of the criminal code throughout territorial and state history and that the Washington legislature and its voters had reconsidered and decided to retain this ban at various points throughout the last two decades.[89] The Chief Justice contended that in all the states and in nearly every Western democracy, assisted suicide had been prohibited for hundreds and even thousands of years.[90]

Like the Chief Justice, Justice Souter examined this Anglo-American tradition, but he reached different conclusions about the place of history in the assisted suicide debate. He noted the argument of the physicians and patients that the laws governing both suicide and assisted suicide had been repudiated by their nonenforcement, but he refused to conclude that this repudiation created a constitutional right to die.[91] Instead, he contended that this repudiation "opens the door" to the recognition of a liberty interest in bodily integrity and autonomy in medical decision-making.[92] Justice Souter's largely ahistoric argument was echoed in the briefs of not only the doctors in *Glucksberg* and *Quill*,[93] but in the briefs of a number of amici, among them Bioethicists in Support of Respondents, Julian W. Whitaker, M.D., and the ACLU,[94] who provided extensive elaboration of this point. Bioethicists in Support of Respondents argued that since medical technology offered little in the way of effective treatment before this century, it was impossible to apply the assisted suicide statutes, which were born in the 1800s, to physician assisted death.[95] Julian W. Whitaker, M.D., argued that throughout Anglo-American history, liberty had been read broadly,[96] and the ACLU contended that assisted suicide had the "sanction of history" and was implicit in our notions of liberty.[97]

Many amici examined the history surrounding the assisted suicide debate, largely in response to the Ninth Circuit's discussion of ancient attitudes towards assisted suicide. Like the Justices, the amici offered differing analyses of this background, with some friends examining the record going as far back as ancient Greece and others focusing on the last two hundred years. It bears noting that while some amici strongly disagreed about the lessons to be learned from history, the Justices did not recognize these disagreements in their opinions.

Moreover, the only amici who appear to have been loudly heard by the Justices were those who employed a somewhat shortsighted approach, focusing on the Anglo-American tradition and not delving any more deeply into the historical record. There are striking parallels between the Chief Justice's analysis and that provided by a number of amici, among them, the American Center for Law and Justice, American Association of Homes and Services for the Aging, AMA, State of California et al., Catholic Health Association, Catholic Medical Association, Institute for Public Affairs of the Union of Orthodox Jewish Congregations et al., Legal Center for Defense of Life, Inc., National Legal Center for the Medically Dependent and Disabled, Inc., National Spinal Cord Injury Association, Rutherford Institute, U.S. Catholic Conference, and Wayne County.[98]

While the Chief Justice Rehnquist and Justice Souter provided a discussion of the history of suicide bans, Justice Stevens looked at history more broadly and contended that the Justices should not be bound in their interpretation of substantive due process to the limits of the common law protection against battery.[99] While he contended that there was no support in either tradition or history for an "open-ended constitutional right to suicide," he suggested that a narrower right might be discovered.[100] His conception of how history should be read is consistent with a number of amici, among these, the U.S., which contended that *Casey* established that the "outer limits of substantive due process" were not settled.[101] Moreover, Justice Stevens hinted at the arguments of amici National Women's Health Network et al., State Legislators, and Center for Reproductive Law and Policy, who urged the Court to reject a "historically frozen concept of constitutionally protected liberty."[102]

In addition to disagreeing about the role of history in the debate about assisted suicide, the Justices also disagreed about how to frame the legal issue in this case. While the Chief Justice relied heavily on an examination of the history and traditions of this practice, Justice Souter explicitly rejected this formulaic approach. In his concurring opinion in *Glucksberg*, Justice Souter reframed the legal issue, asserting that the question is not whether the right to hasten death is expressly governed by our nation's history and traditions, but whether the state laws "set up one of those arbitrary impositions or purposeless restraints at odds with due process."[103] In examining the obstacles created by these laws, Justice Souter explicitly relied on Justice Harlan's dissenting opinion in *Poe v. Ullman*. Interestingly, there is only passing reference to this case by the *Quill* doctors; it is the amici who focus on its importance to these cases.[104]

Justice Souter rejected what he characterized as the Chief Justice's reliance on past practices in defining due process and embraced a more fluid conception of this clause.[105] Like National Women's Health Network et al., Justice Souter argued that Justice Harlan's *Poe* dissent established that substantive due process could not be "reduced to any formula nor determined by reference to any code."[106] The amici briefs of Senator Hatch, 36 Religious Organizations, and the ACLU also noted that for Justice Harlan, liberty was a "living thing." Like these amici, Justice Souter argued that liberty was located on a rational continuum and was reflected in the "balance that our nation has struck between individual rights and the needs of an ordered society," and he cited to the *Poe* dissent for the principle that this balance may change over time.[107]

Moreover, Justice Souter argued forcefully that the Court has been engaged in substantive review throughout the history of the nation and that assisted suicide bans did not violate substantive due process because the states had clear justification for adopting them.[108] Much of his concurrence in *Glucksberg* focused on the foundations for substantive due process and closely paralleled the amici briefs of Representative Hatch and Wayne County. Both Justice Souter's opinion and these briefs examined the Court's substantive due process cases, beginning in the eighteenth century, with Souter beginning with *Fletcher v. Peck,* and both Souter and the amici continuing on to *Dred Scott v. Sanford,* the Slaughterhouse Cases, *Meyer v. Nebraska,* and *Lochner v. New York.*[109]

Liberty Interest of a Terminally Ill, Competent Adult in Hastening Death
While the doctors in *Glucksberg* argued that the right to hasten one's death was fundamental, the doctors in *Quill* avoided this issue and took a different tack, mostly arguing that the right raised important liberty interests. While none of the Justices agreed that these interests were at play in this litigation, Justices Stevens, O'Connor, and Breyer suggested that they might be in future litigation. The most significant obstacle for all of the Justices seemed to have been that there were no terminally ill individuals suffering from intolerable pain who had brought this litigation. The terminally ill adults who brought the Washington case had died by the time this case reached the U.S. Supreme Court, and the Justices did not seem convinced that the most important liberty interests could be raised by the remaining doctors, all of whom were physicians. The debate about the nature of the due process liberty interest centered on two issues: first, how death and dying and, in particular, the experience of pain and suffering shaped the due process liberty right; and second, how the Supreme Court's decisions in *Cruzan* and *Casey* helped to define this right. The amici's influence is clearly apparent in discussions of both these questions, and the amici marshaled a wealth of legal arguments and scientific and medical data in support of their positions.

The Liberty Interest and Pain and Suffering. All of the Justices except Chief Justice Rehnquist concluded that the right to hasten one's death might be exercised by a terminally ill, mentally competent person suffering intolerable, irremediable pain and seeking to control the circumstances of his or her death. Justice O'Connor recognized that such a person would have "a constitutionally cognizable interest in controlling the circumstances of his or her imminent death."[110] Similarly, Justice Stevens stated that the now-deceased plaintiffs had a liberty interest in avoiding unbearable pain and the indignity of living one's final days "incapacitated and in agony" and that the Court had articulated such an interest in *Casey* and *Cruzan*.[111] Justice Breyer was even more willing to recognize a liberty interest in avoiding unbearable pain and retaining personal control over "the manner of death, professional medical assistance, and the avoidance of unnecessary and severe physical suffering."[112] He argued that this interest would likely become compelling if terminally ill individuals were not permitted sufficient palliative care. For Justice Breyer, the avoidance of serious, unwanted pain would be an essential part of any successful challenge to these state laws,[113] but both he and Justice O'Connor agreed that since neither Washington nor New York had barred the use of palliative care, this interest was not at play in this litigation.[114]

The issue of pain and suffering was probably the linchpin of the Justices' due process analysis, and the parties and their amici provided compelling medical and scientific information about this issue. Significantly, it was the amici who forcefully argued that terminally ill persons have a liberty interest in avoiding pain and suffering and that this interest might form the basis for a right to hasten death. Perhaps most compellingly, in its *Glucksberg* brief, amicus United States focused on this interest in avoiding pain and argued that competent, terminally ill adults have a "cognizable liberty interest in avoiding the kind of suffering experienced by the plaintiffs in this case." The United States contended that this interest encompassed not only "an interest in avoiding severe physical pain, but also the despair and distress that comes from physical deterioration and the inability to control basic bodily or mental functions in the terminal stage of an illness."[115] In an argument about palliative care that paralleled those of Justices O'Connor and Souter, the United States argued that the liberty interest was implicated when the state forced an individual to endure such pain and suffering by barring access to medication that would alleviate it.[116] Other amici echoed this argument, specifically, the Council for Secular Humanism et al., which argued that there is a "fundamental liberty interest in not being compelled to live in irremediably painful and degrading conditions" and that the absolute ban accomplished by these laws "results in the state's appropriation of lives."[117]

Many other amici provided extensive information about the nature of pain and the usefulness of palliative care at the end of life, and Justices O'Connor, Stevens, and Souter likely employed this data. While the states and doctors only briefly discussed pain and suffering,[118] this was a central concern for a number of amici. For example, the American Geriatrics Society, the AMA, the American Medical Student Association, Concern for Dying, Coalition of Hospice Professionals, and National Association of Prolife Nurses et al. provided extensive support for their conclusion that palliative care has dramatically improved over the last two decades, and that for many terminally ill patients, pain can be controlled throughout the dying process.[119] Several of these amici admitted, however, that there is a group of patients for whom this care does not provide relief.[120] Other amici noted that palliative care itself had a cost to patients and that it sometimes impaired "basic bodily functions" and brought about extended periods of sedation, and possibly greater physical pain.[121] Many amici also wrote to inform the Court that even effective palliative care was unavailable to large sectors of the population.[122]

The impact of the amici on helping to inform the Justices about pain and suffering and palliative care is apparent. Significantly, Justice Breyer directly cited to the briefs of the National Hospice Organization, the American Medical Association, and Concern for Dying, noting that "[m]edical technology, we are repeatedly told [by amici], makes the administration of pain-relieving drugs sufficient, except for whom the ineffectiveness of pain control medicines can mean, not pain, but the need for sedation which can end in a coma."[123] Similarly, Justice Stevens cited to the brief of the Coalition of Hospice Professionals as support for his conclusion that palliative care is not available to all who need it and that those in pain are much more likely request physician assisted aid in dying.[124] Justice O'Connor also employed this amici data and upheld the statutes in large part because Washington and New York did not bar access to palliative medication, even where this treatment hastened death. These direct and indirect cites, and the centrality of the issue of pain and suffering to the concurring justices' opinions, strongly suggest that these amici briefs played a role in this important aspect of the decision-making process.

The amici also provided the Justices with information about the experience of dying in the United States. In this area, however, it is more difficult to discern amici influence because there are few comments about death in the Justices' opinions. In her concurrence, Justice O'Connor noted only that "[d]eath will be different for each of us."[125] Chief Justice Rehnquist noted only that Americans are much more likely to die in institutions from chronic diseases than they have ever been.[126] One of the most striking facets of this discussion is how the states and doctors deferred to the expertise of the amici and the way the debate about dying occurred largely between amici, with each countering the other's arguments.[127] While the Justices may have been aware of this disagreement, they did not address it in their opinions.

The Court's Precedent in Cruzan *and* Casey. The *Cruzan* and *Casey* decisions were central to the Justices' discussions of the due process liberty clause, and the party and amici briefs provided the Justices with varying interpretations of how these decisions applied to the cases under discussion. Because of the apparent connection between the factual circumstances surrounding *Glucksberg*, *Vacco*, and *Cruzan*, the parties and their amici repeatedly invoked the Court's decision in *Cruzan*. For example, the *Glucksberg* doctors simply argued that in *Cruzan*, the Court had "recognized the profoundly personal and protected nature of the decision to die" through the withdrawal of life support and that this protection extended to the right at issue in these cases.[128] Amici expanded this argument, urging the Court to accept this interpretation of *Cruzan*. Among these amici was the United States, which forcefully argued that *Cruzan* compelled recognition of a liberty interest in these cases since the patients were facing severe pain and suffering.[129] The State Legislators urged the Court to go even further than *Cruzan*, contending that the patient-plaintiffs in *Glucksberg* and *Vacco* had a stronger interest than did Cruzan because they had explicitly stated that they wanted to hasten their deaths, while Nancy Cruzan had made more vague statements about her desires in hypothetical situations.[130]

The impact of the United States and State Legislators on Justice Stevens cannot be understated. Justice Stevens interpreted *Cruzan* as resting on the fundamental right to make "this deeply personal decision" to terminate treatment,[131] and he cited to his dissent in this case, noting that one has an interest in both dignity and "in determining the character of the memories that will survive long after [his]/her death."[132] The issue of pain was a critical one for both Justice Stevens and these amici. Justice Stevens combined the U.S.'s discussion of *Cruzan* with the State Legislators' assertion that the plaintiffs in these cases were entitled to more protection than had been Nancy Cruzan, and he concluded that the patients in this case had an even more compelling interest than had Nancy Cruzan because they had been suffering severe and constant pain. Justice Stevens also based his decision on *Casey v. Planned Parenthood of Southeastern Pennsylvania*, arguing that this holding established the principle that the avoidance of unwanted pain is "at the heart of [the] liberty . . . to define one's own concept of existence, of meaning, or the universe, and of the mystery of human life."[133]

The only other Justice to address either *Cruzan* or *Casey*, Chief Justice Rehnquist, had a much narrower view of these precedents. For example, he accepted the argument presented by the states and several amici that *Cruzan* was based upon the common law right to refuse treatment.[134] He also rejected the Ninth Circuit's extensive reliance on *Casey*, instead adopting the view of the states and amici that the decision did not establish sweeping protections of all "important, intimate and personal choices."[135]

The Equal Protection Standard for Evaluating the Laws

While the Ninth Circuit evaluated the assisted suicide ban under the due process clause of the Fourteenth Amendment, the Second Circuit employed the equal protection clause to strike them down.[136] Much of the Justices' attention in these cases was devoted to the due process clause, and the only consideration of equal protection was in the assessments of the New York law made by the Chief Justice and Justice Stevens. Moreover, the Justices' evaluation of equal protection focused narrowly on the issues of intent and double effect, in stark contrast to the Court's extensive discussion of due process.

Intent to Cause Death. Both the Chief Justice and Justice Stevens rejected the Second Circuit's holding that New York's assisted suicide ban violated equal protection by treating two groups of similarly situated individuals, those seeking physician assistance in dying and those seeking to terminate life sustaining treatment, differently. In discussing the equal protection challenge, the issue of intent was central to both Justices. For example, the Chief Justice noted that "the law has long used an actor's intent or purpose to distinguish among two acts that may have the same result,"[137] and Justice Stevens noted that "the differences . . . in causation and intent . . . support the Court's rejection of the doctors's facial challenge."[138]

Significantly, this issue of intent, so central to the Justices' disposition of the equal protection claim, was presented almost entirely by the amici. The only reference to intent by the parties occurs in the doctors' brief in *Glucksberg*, where they note simply that the intent of the two groups was the same, in that they both sought to bring about death.[139] While the doctors' amici embraced this view of intent, the states' amici sharply disagreed with it, and all of the debate about this issue took place in the amici briefs. For example, the doctors' amici argued that there were no material or morally relevant differences between the two groups.[140] The states' amici vehemently disagreed, contending that while those seeking death-hastening drugs certainly intended to die, patients seeking to terminate treatment might not have this intent.[141]

Double Effect. The debate about double effect was also waged in the amici briefs, and in this debate, the Chief Justice and Justice Stevens took opposing sides. According to the principle of double effect, a medication taken to ease severe pain by sedation may in fact bring about death by depressing respiration. Many amici argued that a physician's use of a medication with a double effect was closer to euthanasia than was a patient's ingestion of death-hastening medications and that the existence of double effect blurred the distinction between physician-assisted suicide and the termination of treatment.[142] Justice Stevens embraced this argument, agreeing with amici that the practice of terminal sedation did in fact blur the lines between the termination of life support and physician-assisted suicide and that physicians using both forms of "treatment" might have the same intent, that is, to ease patient suffering and to bring about death.[143] This discussion of terminal sedation was an important element of the amici briefs of the ACLU and State Legislators, as well as the AMA, and Justice Stevens joined the *Vacco* doctors and the ACLU in directly citing to the AMA's brief, which noted the contradictory character of the practice of terminal sedation.[144]

In contrast, the Chief Justice appears to have been influenced by the arguments made by opposing amici about the principle of double effect, and he argued forcefully that differences in physician intent distinguished double effect from assisted suicide. Like amici American Geriatrics Society, Bioethicists for States, and the U.S. Catholic Conference, Chief Justice Rehnquist contended that the physician's intent in prescribing medication was to palliate suffering and not to bring about death, and this was true even where this medication had the secondary effect of hastening death.[145]

Distinction Recognized at Common Law and by Professional Organizations. The Chief Justice was also influenced by amici arguments about the common law basis of the right to terminate treatment and the view of professional organizations about this right. Specifically, many amici attempted to appeal to the Chief Justice by reiterating his view in *Cruzan* that the right to terminate treatment was grounded in the common law. In *Quill* and *Vacco*, these amici provided an extensive catalogue of state cases to distinguish this practice from physician-assisted suicide.[146] For example, the American Association of Homes and Services for the Aging, American Geriatrics Society, American Hospital Association, AMA, Bioethicists for States, California et al., Catholic Medical Association, Clarendon Foundation, Medical Society of New Jersey, U.S., and U.S. Catholic Conference all concluded that the right to bodily integrity extended to the termination of medical treatment but not to physician-assisted suicide.[147] The Chief Justice, who appears to have employed this analysis of the common law, in *Vacco* provided a detailed summary of state court holdings governing the termination of treatment.[148]

The Chief Justice also appears to have been influenced by amici who presented extensive information about how legal and medical organizations view the distinction between physician-assisted suicide and the termination of treatment. Once again, this issue was discussed almost entirely by amici, and the friends who did discuss it were all medical and legal associations who noted that they joined other professional organizations in the view that these two practices were distinct.[149] While the Chief Justice recognized that there was some disagreement among medical professionals about how to view these two practices,[150] he accepted the view of those organizations who filed in this litigation.[151]

State Interests at Issue

As in the abortion cases, in *Vasco v. Quill* the Justices devoted significant attention to a discussion of the states' interests in adopting the controversial laws. Washington and New York argued that the bans against physician-assisted suicide were necessary to advance the state's interests in the preservation of life, the prevention of abuse and error, the preservation of the integrity of the medical profession, and the protection of innocent third parties.[152] In weighing these interests, the Justices were presented with extensive medical, scientific, and social science data by the amici. It is then perhaps not surprising that amici played a prominent role in this discussion.

State Interest in Protecting Life. There was significant disagreement among the Justices about the strength of the states' articulated interest in protecting life, and this disagreement paralleled discussions among amici. For example, the Chief Justice's perception that there is an unqualified and absolute interest in life, apparent in his conclusion that this interest was "symbolic and inspirational as well as practical,"[153] was apparent in the states' briefs and elaborated upon in the amici briefs. The states in both cases argued that the assisted suicide ban reflected the high value the state placed on the protection of life,[154] and amici expanded upon this point. Perhaps most notably, the United States argued that states have "an interest of the highest order" in prohibiting physician assistance in dying.[155] In addition, thirteen other friends argued forcefully that a state could choose to protect all life based on its inherent sanctity and the inalienability of the right to life.[156]

Justice Stevens rejected this view that the state always had an absolute, unqualified interest in life, particularly for terminally ill, competent individuals. He noted that "state interests do not have the same force in all cases"[157] and that this interest does not "always outweigh the interests of a person who because of pain, incapacity or sedation finds her life intolerable."[158] Moreover, he argued that the use of capital punishment suggested that states did not have an unqualified interest in life and that they did place less value on some lives than on others.[159] Justice Stevens' assessment of this state interest echoed the arguments not only of the doctors, but of seven of their amici.[160] In particular, his discussion of capital punishment closely paralleled that of amicus Bioethicists, who contended that capital punishment is evidence that states have qualified their interest in life.[161]

The use of "quality of life" arguments in the opinions of both Chief Justice Rehnquist and Justice Stevens also underscore the influence of amici in these cases, because these were arguments made only by amici. For example, the Chief Justice contended that the assisted suicide ban "reflect[ed] and reinforce[d] the policy that the lives of the terminally ill, disabled, and elderly much be no less valued than the lives of the young and healthy."[162] This argument about the quality of life is made by many amici, and a large number of them warned that the lower courts' decisions devalued the lives of the elderly and infirm by forcing states to treat the terminally ill differently than others.[163] Only one amici offered a different view of the quality of life issue: the GMHC argued that assistance in dying is consistent with the goals of self-determination, independence, and autonomy and that quality of life considerations had no bearing on this case.[164] Justice Stevens appears to have agreed with this lone amicus: he contended that allowing an individual to make a decision to hasten death might enable that person to "choose a final chapter that accords with her life story, rather than one that demeans her values and poisons memories of her."[165]

State Interest in Preventing Error and Abuse. In assessing the assisted suicide bans, the Justices focused on the states' articulated interest in preventing abuse and mistake. All of the Justices wrote extensively about this interest, and relying heavily on the arguments and information presented in the party and amici briefs. Once again, the amici's central goal seems to have been to provide elaboration for points that were only very briefly raised in the party briefs. The coordination of party and amici briefs, so apparent in many other areas of this litigation, was significant here as well. Specifically, amici participation had profound importance in helping the Justices understand four aspects relating to the state's interest in safeguarding against abuse and neglect: first, the risk of error; second, the possibility of abuse; third, the danger to the integrity of the medical profession; and fourth, the risk of assisted suicide being employed more broadly.

1. Risk of Error. In his opinion for the Court, Chief Justice Rehnquist focused on the state's interest in protecting vulnerable groups, defined

as the disabled, poor, and elderly, from abuse, mistake, and neglect.[166] For the Chief Justice, states were to be given substantial latitude in protecting these vulnerable groups from "prejudice, negative and inaccurate stereotypes, and societal indifference."[167] Much of his discussion of the state's interest focused not on the risk of error attendant in the decision to hasten one's death, but in the danger of abuse or coercion in the decision-making process. Moreover, while no other opinion defined this state interest so broadly, all of the concurring Justices were concerned about the risk of error. Justice O'Connor's concurrence focused on this risk, holding that a concern about errors relating to competency, terminal illness, and voluntariness justified the state's decision to ban assistance in dying.[168] Justice Souter argued that the assisted suicide ban protected terminally ill individuals from "involuntary suicide and euthanasia" and noted that there was a significant risk of error and coercion in end of life decisions.[169] He left open the possibility that states might not be permitted to ban physician-assisted suicide for those who made a "knowing and responsible" decision to hasten their death.[170]

The parties and amici wrote extensively about the risk of error in end of life decisions, in particular, in the diagnosis of terminal illness, the assessment of pain, and the determination of competency. These three issues, terminality, pain, and competency, were critical in this litigation, since doctors and patients seeking to strike down the bans were arguing that physician-assisted suicide would be strictly limited and available only to those who were terminally ill, suffering unbearable pain, and capable of making decisions. The amici fiercely disagreed about how to define terminal illness and how to assess pain and competency, and their role in helping the Justices to understand these issues was significant in a number of ways. First, the states that brought these cases cited extensively to their "friends" briefs and urged the Justices to accept these amici as experts. For example, in discussing the definition of terminality and the measurement of pain, New York State incorporated and cited much of what was in the briefs of the American Geriatrics Society and the National Hospice Organization.[171] Second, both the doctors and the states briefly raised points in their briefs that were then "fleshed out," often quite substantially, by amici. For example, the two sides vehemently disagreed about whether an illness could reliably be deemed terminal, but the debate about terminality was waged in the amici briefs. The states' amici, among them the American Medical Association, Choice in Dying, Clarendon Foundation, National Catholic Office for Persons with Disabilities et al., Project on Death in America, United States, and U.S. Catholic Conference, all argued that mistakes are often made in both the diagnosis and prognosis of illness.[172]

The doctors' amici sharply disagreed with this assessment of terminality, contending that it is not difficult to assess terminal illness and that the risk of misdiagnosis is not sufficient to justify a blanket prohibition on physician assistance in dying. For example, both the ACLU and Americans for Death with Dignity provided an extensive discussion of how the right could be limited to those with terminal illness, and several other amici argued that the risk of misdiagnosis was no greater in these cases than it was where patients sought to discontinue treatment.[173] Amici Americans for Death and Dying and Coalition of Hospice Professionals also argued that physician-assisted death occurs even though it is prohibited and that striking down the laws would likely compel state legislatures to regulate the practice. With more regulation, these amici argued, the risk of error would be much reduced.[174]

2. Risk of Abuse. The Justices were quite concerned about the risk of abuse that might attend a decision to hasten one's own death and, in particular, that the decision would be made involuntarily or by someone without mental capacity. The Chief Justice and Justices O'Connor, Stevens, and Souter all were concerned about the risks of coercion, abuse, and undue influence, as well as the prevalence of untreated pain and depression among those with terminal illnesses. All held that states could ban assisted suicide to limit the risk of abuse for patients who lacked capacity or were unable to make a voluntary decision.[175]

There is both direct and indirect evidence of amici influence on the Justices' assessments of the risk of abuse. In his discussion of the state's interest in this area, Justice Stevens directly cited to the amicus brief of the Washington State Psychological Association as support for his argument that some individuals could make a "rational and voluntary decision to seek assistance in dying."[176] Furthermore, the indirect evidence of amici influence is even more compelling than the direct evidence. Once again, amici raised very few new issues, devoting most of their energies elaborating on points raised very briefly in the party briefs. For example, in both cases, the parties briefly discussed pain and depression in their briefs, but many amici, most notably the AMA and the American Suicide Foundation, devoted large portions of their briefs to these issues.[177] These amici provided extensive information to the Justices about the prevalence of depression among terminally ill individuals, and most referred the Justices to the New York State *Report on Death and Dying* for additional information.[178]

In addition to discussing depression, many amici wrote to provide the Justices with information about how untreated and untreatable pain could render one unable to make a knowing and voluntary decision to choose death.[179] Interestingly, medical organizations, like the AMA and the American Suicide Foundation, noted that the physician's role in assessing capacity might be quite limited, since depression and pain were often very difficult to diagnose and treat among terminally ill individuals.[180] This point about the difficulty of assessing capacity was very important, since the Ninth Circuit seems to have assumed that physicians and mental health workers could readily make this determination and that such a determination was critical to the granting of a right to hasten death. The Justices seem to have been influenced by the amicis' arguments and marshalling of data about depression and pain, and all of the concurrences established that even if there were a right to hasten one's death, it could only be invoked by terminally ill individuals who were free from depression and pain.

As in the discussion of pain, depression, and mental capacity, the argument about coercion, undue influence, and abuse was made almost entirely by amici. While the states noted simply that financial pressures might increase the risk of coercion by families, physicians, and managed care organizations concerned about financial pressures,[181] amici provided ample support for this position. For example, American Association of Homes and Services for the Aging, Catholic Health Association, Evangelical Lutheran Church, Law Professors, and the United States were all concerned about the possibility that physicians might subtly pressure patients to choose death.[182] Similarly, amici AMA, Milwaukee District Attorney, National Association of Prolife Nurses et al., and U.S. discussed the potential for elder abuse in families and the strong possibility that some families would pressure seriously ill patients to hasten their deaths.[183] Finally, amici American Life League, American Geriatrics Society, AMA, International Anti-Euthanasia Task Force, National Association of Prolife Nurses et al., Not Dead Yet et al., and Project on Death in America all provided data in support of the argument that cost considerations, including pressures from managed care companies, would compel patients to choose death.[184] The doctors and their amici attempted to counter these arguments, contending that the conclusions drawn from the data were flawed and that the risk of abuse was greater given the current prohibitions.[185] However, it seems that these counterarguments and data did not allay the fears of the Justices, who clearly accepted the views of the states' amici in this area and rejected those of the doctors' amici.

3. Integrity of the Medical Profession. Several justices accepted the argument, raised solely by amici, that assisted suicide bans protected the integrity of the medical profession. Chief Justice Rehnquist concluded that these laws protected the "integrity and ethics of the medical profession," noting that the American Medical Association and many other medical groups believed that physician assisted dying was "fundamentally incompatible with [the] physician's role as healer."[186] The

amici briefs of medical organizations appear to have been the source of much of the Chief Justice's discussion of this issue. For example, the AMA's briefs in both cases focused on the effects of physician-assisted suicide on the integrity of the profession and presented the organization's Opinions of the Council on Ethical and Judicial Affairs, which was directly cited by the Chief Justice.[187] The brief submitted by the National Association of Prolife Nurses et al. was also focused on how these laws protected the integrity of the medical profession, and almost the entire brief was devoted to a discussion of how striking down these laws will "erode the personal and professional ethics of nurses."[188] Many other amici also discussed how allowing physicians to aid in dying would harm the medical profession, among these, the American Association of Homes and Services for the Aging, Christian Legal Society, Catholic Medical Association, Evangelical Lutheran Church, Family Research Council, Legal Center for Defense of Life, Inc., Legal Center for Defense of Life, Inc., Medical Society of New Jersey, Richard Thompson, D.A., and the U.S.[189]

Justices Stevens and Souter were also concerned about the role of the medical profession in this debate; however, they employed the data and arguments of opposing amici who contended that it was the assisted suicide bans themselves that threatened the integrity of the medical profession. For example, Justice Stevens noted that doctors' obligations to their dying patients are not as clear as the state would suggest and that, for some patients, it would be "a physician's refusal to dispense medication to ease their suffering and make their death tolerable and dignified that would be inconsistent with [their] healing role."[190] Similarly, Justice Souter argued that the doctor has an obligation to treat the person, not the disease, and that "serving the whole person is the source of high value traditionally placed on the medical relationship."[191] Justice Souter also noted that the doctor's obligation to serve the individual as a person and not just a disease is apparent not only in these cases, but in instances where doctors are called upon to perform abortions.[192]

Again, this argument that the physician may have an ethical obligation to provide aid in dying was presented exclusively by the amici.[193] The ACLU, Americans for Death with Dignity et al., American Medical Student Association, Bioethicists in Support of Respondents, the Coalition of Hospice Professionals, and State Legislators all argued that allowing physicians to aid in dying would improve the doctor-patient relationship and enhance the public's view of the medical profession.[194] Several amici also noted that the Hippocratic Oath should not control in these cases, since the meaning of the oath has changed over time to permit abortion, surgery, and accepting fees for teaching medicine.[195] Furthermore, State Legislators contended, as Justice Souter had, that the argument that physician assistance in dying harmed the medical profession had "no greater purchase than in the abortion debate."[196]

Justice Stevens also noted that a significant number of physicians supported assistance in dying and cited to a poll of Washington physicians as support for his position that doctors are already hastening the deaths of certain patients. This poll figured prominently in the brief of the Washington State Psychological Association, which argued that surveys of psychiatrists in Washington and Oregon revealed support for the view that individuals could make "rational decisions to control the time and manner of death."[197] Several amici noted that medical professionals are already providing aid in dying,[198] and others contended that many physicians support hastening death for some patients.[199]

4. The "Slippery Slope." The parties and many of their amici also argued about whether the right to physician assistance in dying could be limited and about whether states could limit this right through regulation. While the states discussed this issue at length, the doctors made only a passing reference, arguing simply that there would be no slippery slope to "assisted suicide on demand."[200] Only Chief Justice Rehnquist and Justice Souter addressed this state interest, and both held that the state's concern about being able to limit such a right could justify its prohibition. The contribution of amici to this discussion is apparent: they provided arguments and data that were distinct from those provided by the parties, and they were relied upon by the Justices. For example, Chief Justice Rehnquist argued that the state's fears that assisted suicide would not be limited to the terminally ill were reasonable and that what was being presented "as a limited right to physician assisted suicide is likely, in effect, to be a much broader license"; as support for this position, he directly cited the briefs of the U.S., Not Dead Yet, and the Bioethicists for States.[201] Similarly, Justice Souter contended that the state had made a plausible case that the right to assistance in dying was not readily containable. He contended that the requirements imposed by the lower courts, that is, that a person be terminally ill, competent, and in great pain, were flexible and not easy to contain.[202] Moreover, he was concerned about the financial incentives imposed by managed care and the effects these incentives might have in encouraging physicians and patients to choose death.[203] In making this argument, Justice Souter was likely relying on the information presented by the AMA, American Hospital Association, and American Geriatrics Society, who all warned that physicians would have difficulty in containing the class of people eligible for aid in dying[204] and that financial incentives would militate in favor of death.[205] As in so many other areas, the Justices chose among competing amici: while the Chief Justice and Justice Souter accepted the views of amici who

feared the "slippery slope," they rejected the arguments of many others who attempted to allay fears about what would happen if assisted suicide bans were struck down.[206]

A large number of amici also used the Netherlands, where physician aid in dying is permitted in certain circumstances, to advance their argument. The parties confined their discussion of the Dutch experience to footnote references; however, the amici presented extensive evidence that seems to have been pondered by both the Chief Justice and Justice Souter. For example, many amici argued that Holland's experience demonstrated the pitfalls of allowing doctors to assist in dying,[207] while other amici contended that the incidence of abuse in the Netherlands was quite low and that the right was strictly limited.[208] In his discussion, Chief Justice Rehnquist clearly accepted the views of those who held out the Netherlands as an example of all that could go wrong with assisted dying, noting that there has been concern in the Netherlands about whether physician aid in dying is rendered to those who are truly competent and about whether involuntary euthanasia occurs.[209] Justice Souter also appears to have read the conflicting analyses of the Dutch experience presented by amici, and he concluded that it was impossible to determine what was really happening in the Netherlands.[210] He also cited to the proposals offered by State Legislators, noting the similarity between these guidelines and those in place in the Netherlands and concluding that it was impossible to evaluate either set of guidelines.[211]

The Role of the Court and Public Opinion

Both the Chief Justice and Justice Souter discussed the Court's role in the debate about assisted dying, and both argued that the judicial branch should defer to legislative action in this area. The Chief Justice noted that state legislatures were already debating this issue and that courts should decline from issuing a holding that would preempt this activity.[212] Similarly, Justice Souter noted that debate about physician-assisted death should be centered in the legislatures and not the courts, because of legislatures' "superior opportunities to obtain the facts necessary for judgment."[213] He noted that legislatures had better fact-finding abilities and the "power to experiment," and he cited the amicus brief of the State Legislators as support for his argument that states were crafting various approaches to this issue.[214]

In addition to the State Legislators, other amici appear to have been heard by Chief Justice Rehnquist and Justice Souter. Both the states and their amici urged the Court to stay out of this debate, lest it preempt state initiatives in this area.[215] Notably, several amici noted that the state legislatures could serve as laboratories for change,[216] and a number of amici pointed to state legislative activities and laws passed in the last decade as evidence that the states were taking a leading role in this debate.[217] Similarly, like Justice Souter, amicus American Center for Law and Justice contended that the calculus of costs and benefits attendant to the practice of physician-assisted dying should be left to the legislatures,[218] and Clarendon Foundation noted that legislatures had greater information-gathering abilities and the ability to easily modify laws if "things turn[ed] out differently than expected."[219]

One amici appears to have had a profound impact on the Justices' discussions about the impact of public opinion on the debate about assisted dying. In her concurrence, Justice O'Connor argued that the democratic process protected the rights of those affected by terminal illness and that the existence of legislative activity in the area of death and dying could be taken as evidence of the responsivity of states to the needs of their citizens.[220] Similarly, the Chief Justice briefly noted that since most Americans die in institutions from chronic diseases, they have an interest in this issue and have placed pressure on the state governments to craft responses to their needs.[221] This argument about political mobilization was made only by the United States. In its *Glucksberg* brief, the U.S. argued that "since terminal illness potentially affects all Americans—all races, genders, income groups—there is every reason to believe that state legislatures will address the urgent issues involved in this cases in a fair and impartial way."[222] While amicus ACLU attempted to rebut this argument, by contending that the political process had never acted to safeguard the needs of the terminally ill, the Justices were unconvinced by this argument.[223]

Party Coordination and Cooperation

The parties and their amici were clearly addressing each other in their briefs. The states and the doctors extensively employed the briefs of their "friends," and amici used these briefs to wage battles with their foes. As in the abortion cases, the amici used this forum to strengthen the arguments of their allies and to undermine those of their opponents.

Party Use of Amici Briefs

The states and doctors made ample use of the arguments and data incorporated in the briefs of amici filing in support of them. The states' brief in *Quill* employed the briefs of allies AMA, American College of Physicians, and American Geriatrics Society, and its reply brief cited the briefs of the American Geriatrics Society, National Hospice Organization, Project on Death in America, AMA, International Anti-Euthanasia Task Force, Senator Hatch et al., and the American Suicide Foundation, as well as the writings of amicus attorney Lawrence Tribe.[224] While the states in *Glucksberg* did not cite to any amici briefs in their initial brief on the merits, they made ample use of amici arguments and data in their reply brief, citing the amici briefs of the U.S., American Suicide Foundation, American Geriatrics Society, State Legislators, State of California et al., National Spinal Cord Injury Association (NSC), National Legal Center for the Medically Dependent and Disabled, Inc., ACLU, Julian W. Whitaker, M.D., Washington State Psychological Association, Gary Lee, Gay Men's Health Crisis et al., Washington State Psychological Association, National Women's Health Network et al., Council for Secular Humanism et al., and Milwaukee District Attorney.[225]

While the states' discussions relied heavily on the briefs of amici filing on their behalf, the doctors expended significant energy on a discussion of the briefs of opposing amici, perhaps in an attempt to discredit their arguments and data. For example, in its brief, the *Quill* doctors cited repeatedly (and negatively) to the briefs of the AMA, American Geriatrics Society, Bioethicists for States, National Hospice Organization, U.S., and U.S. Catholic Conference, as well as to "some amici,"[226] all of which supported their opponents. In particular, the *Quill* doctors focused on attempting to refute the arguments of the AMA and American Geriatrics Society and cited each of these seven and three times, respectively.[227] Similarly, the *Glucksberg* doctors repeatedly cited to the briefs of opposing amici AMA, Bioethicists for States, Catholic Health Association, Evangelical Lutheran Church, MC, State Legislators, U.S., and "states' amici."[228] In particular, the *Glucksberg* doctors cited the U.S. brief six times.[229] Furthermore, the *Glucksberg* doctors used their own amici defensively—they used these briefs principally to rebut the arguments of opposing amici, citing to the briefs of the American College of Legal Medicine, Bioethicists in Support of Respondents, Coalition of Hospice Professionals, Gay Men's Health Crisis et al., 36 Religious Organizations, and Surviving Family Members in an attempt to discredit their opponents.[230]

Amicus Use of Amici Briefs

As in the use of amici briefs by the parties, a pattern can be discerned in the way that the amici themselves used these briefs. Amici filing briefs in support of the states cited only to the amici briefs filed in support of their position. Nine amici briefs cited to the briefs of other amici, and all of these "honored" amici were friends filing in support of the states.[231] These briefs were used only to support the arguments and data presented by the amici. There was a great deal of cooperation and coordination of amici positions for this group. In contrast, the doctors' amici relied very little on the briefs of their friends and, with only a few exceptions, used the amici of opposing counsel as "straw men" to knock down. Only the Council for Secular Humanism et al. and

American Medical Student Association used their own "friends'" briefs to support their positions[232]; the other sixteen amici negatively cited to amici on the opposing side.[233] Moreover, these amici concentrated on only a few "straw men," firing at the AMA, the U.S., the American Geriatrics Society, and Bioethicists for Petitioners (the states) when they identified the amicus. Of the sixteen amici, four aimed at the AMA brief and seven attempted to rebut some argument or data in the U.S. brief.[234] Most of these briefs cited to the AMA or U.S. numerous times. The remaining amici rebutted the positions of the opposing amici more generally.

The amici made good use of each other's briefs, and to a great extent, there appears to have been a coalescing of opinions among the amici on the issues presented in these cases. Perhaps in more than in any other cases discussed in this book, the amici in these two cases were adroit at summarizing and using the arguments and data presented by other "friends." While the states' and doctors' strategies were different, with the states' amici elevating the briefs of their colleagues and the doctors' amici denigrating the briefs of their opponents, both groups seem to have recognized the importance of putting a "spin" on these briefs for the Justices. There were a huge number of briefs filed in these two cases, and the amici briefs themselves may have helped the Justices to sort through the vast array of information presented in these briefs. In these cases, one can see clearly that the amici and the parties recognized that the briefs of certain amici, like the AMA and the U.S., carried more weight than others, and the amici concentrated on either emphasizing or undermining the arguments presented in these briefs. In addition, the amici and parties correctly recognized the importance of certain documents, most significantly, the *NYS Report on Death and Dying*, that were outside the litigation. The parties and their amici, especially those seeking to uphold the laws banning physician-assisted dying, repeatedly brought into the litigation the findings and conclusions of this report. This litigation suggests a great deal of coordination and cooperation among amici and a recognition of the importance of helping the Court to analyze the substance of *other* amici briefs, particularly those of one's opponents.

Conclusions Drawn from Glucksberg and Quill

Amici curiae played an important role in the debate about physician assistance in dying heard by the U.S. Supreme Court in *Washington et al. v. Glucksberg et al.* and *Vacco et al. v. Quill et al.* The presence of amici arguments and information may be discerned not only in direct citations to the amici briefs made by the Justices, but also in indirect use of amici briefs. Moreover, the Justices' use of amici arguments and scientific and technical data was extensive, with all of the Justices relying on the briefs to help resolve both the legal and the extralegal issues raised in this litigation.

All of the Justices directly cited the amici briefs as support for arguments made about both the legal issues and the scientific and medical questions that arose in these two cases. In addition, the Justices appear to have made extensive use of the amici briefs *without* direct citation. In numerous instances the Justices employed arguments or data provided solely in the amici briefs. These arguments and data related to a range of legal and extralegal issues in this litigation. For example, the Justices employed amici arguments to examine due process questions at play and to understand the nation's history and traditions with regard to assisted suicide. Moreover, the Justices employed the amici briefs to discuss whether the pain and suffering of those suffering from terminal illness affects due process liberty rights, and they made use of the amicis' discussions about *Cruzan* and *Casey*, which all the Justices saw as important to the two cases at issue. The Justices also used the amici briefs to understand whether the state laws violated the equal protection clause and to examine whether the states' articulated interests justified the assisted suicide bans. Finally, the Justices utilized the amici briefs to consider the role of the Supreme Court in the debate about assisted dying and the impact of public opinion on this issue.

In a significant number of instances, the Justices employed amici briefs to discuss an issue raised only by amici. It was the amici who provided the discussion of the common law history of assisted suicide bans relied upon by the Chief Justice. Similarly, the Chief Justice appears to have relied upon the argument of amici that the Court should not create any new substantive due process protections. Justice Stevens appears to have accepted the argument of amici that this history does not definitively establish the scope of due process rights. Furthermore, it was amici who alone raised the *Poe v. Ullman* case that was relied upon by Justice Souter in his concurrence. In cataloguing the state court holdings that distinguished between cases involving the withholding or termination of treatment, the Chief Justice likely drew upon amici briefs, which provided the only discussion of these cases. Furthermore, the Chief Justice's concerns about the effect of striking down the bans on the integrity of the medical profession were voiced only by amici, many of whom argued that it was the physician's obligation to provide aid in dying, an obligation hinted at by Justices Stevens and Souter. Finally, amicus U.S. was the only party to argue that the democratic process can be relied upon to ensure that individual rights will not be trampled upon, an argument embraced by the Chief Justice and Justice O'Connor.

In addition to instances in which amici alone raised issues that were then addressed by the Justices, in many circumstances amici elaborated on points raised only in passing by the parties, which were then addressed at length by the Justices. The states and their amici worked in tandem to convince the Chief Justice that the right at issue should be characterized as a right to commit suicide. Similarly, the doctors only briefly addressed the history of non-enforcement of assisted suicide, but this point, which was embraced by Justice Souter, was elaborated upon by a number of "friends." Perhaps even more significant, the states and the doctors only very briefly addressed the impact that pain and suffering have on one's due process rights, but this issue, which Justices O'Connor, Stevens, and Breyer focused on, was discussed in detail by a large number of medical and legal organizations. In addition, the parties provided only a cursory discussion of the *Casey* and *Cruzan* decisions, and it appears to have been the extensive examination of these cases by amici that was employed by the Chief Justice and Justice Stevens.

In discussing the equal protection claims, the parties also only briefly raised some issues that were then expanded upon by the amici. The states' discussion of the factual differences between those seeking to terminate life support and those seeking physician assistance in dying was cursory. In contrast, the Chief Justice's expansive discussion of these differences appears to have derived from the amici briefs. Similarly, the contrary view of Justice Stevens, that there were no real differences between the two groups in terms of intent, was hinted at in the doctors' briefs, but expanded upon in the opposing amici briefs. Similarly, the states briefly contended that state legislatures and professional organizations recognized distinctions between these two groups, a point much elaborated upon by various friends.

Furthermore, in examining the interests articulated by the states, the states' argument that the interest in life is unqualified was expanded upon by amici, and this discussion was accepted by the Chief Justice. Similarly, Justice Stevens's contention that the state's interest in life is not always absolute and that states are not devaluing lives by allowing individuals to hasten their deaths was only superficially raised by the states, but was elaborated upon by amici. Moreover, the Justices' weighing of the states' interest in preventing error and abuse was likely inspired by amici briefs, which greatly expanded upon the states' briefs.

Moreover, the expansive discussion of the risks of abuse, incompetence, and lack of voluntariness, present in a large number of amici briefs, likely affected the Chief Justice and Justices O'Connor, Souter, and Stevens to a far greater degree than the superficial discussions provided by the parties. In addition, the states' interest in avoiding the slippery slope was raised only in passing by the states and doctors, who noted simply that states could or could not limit physician-assisted suicide. Concern about the impact of these cases upon future assisted dying cases was central to the opinions of the Chief Justice and Justice Souter and, again, was present in expanded form in the briefs of the amici, not the parties. Similarly, amici provided an extensive discussions of the Netherlands, which was alluded to in the opinions of the Chief Justice and Justice Souter, but only touched upon by the parties. The amici also provided an extensive discussion of the proper role of the Court in the debate over assisted dying, an issue only briefly mentioned by the parties.

It bears noting that there was significant disagreement among the amici about a number of issues and that in their analyses, the Justices were called upon to choose sides in these debates. For example, there was fierce disagreement among the amici about how to characterize the right at issue, as well as disagreement about the correct starting point for historical analysis and the degree of importance to attach to the historical underpinnings of assisted suicide bans. In addition, amici disagreed about whether there were differences in intent and in the cause of death for those who sought to terminate treatment and those who wanted access to lethal prescriptions. Similarly, the amici argued fiercely about whether the state interest in life was unqualified and about whether states were rating the quality of life by allowing some to hasten their own deaths. There was strong disagreement about how to define terminality and about whether assisted suicide could be limited to those who were adult, competent, terminally ill, and suffering great pain. Amici also disagreed about whether prohibitions against assisted suicide increased the risk of abuse or guarded against abuse.

There is strong evidence of party and amici cooperation and coordination in these cases. The parties made extensive use of the amici briefs in their arguments, with the *Quill* states citing to the briefs of nine amici, the *Glucksberg* states citing to the briefs of sixteen amici, the *Quill* doctors citing to the briefs of eight amici, and the *Glucksberg* doctors citing to thirteen amici. Moreover, there is a pattern in this coordination and cooperation: the states cited to the briefs of both friends and foes in their efforts to convince the Court to uphold the assisted suicide bans, but the doctors cited only to their foes, specifically seeking to undermine the briefs of the AMA and the American Geriatrics Society, which were each cited seven times in the *Glucksberg* brief.

There is also a pattern in the use of amici briefs by other amici. The states' amici used only those briefs of amici who were on their side in this litigation. Nine amici briefs cited to other amici briefs. States' amici also made extensive use of the Task Force Report, citing it in twenty-five briefs. In contrast, the doctors cited the briefs of their foes in all but two out of sixteen briefs. These amici used the briefs of the AMA, U.S.,

American Geriatrics Society, and Bioethics Professors in Support of States as "straw men" and sought to weaken the arguments and data presented in these amici briefs. The doctors' amici cited the Task Force Report far fewer times, providing only three references to it.

This study of amici participation suggests strongly that in these two 1997 cases, the amici were adroit at summarizing and using the arguments and data presented by other friends and foes. The states' amici tended to elevate the briefs of their colleagues, while the doctors' amici tended to denigrate opposing amici. Perhaps because of the sheer number of amici briefs filed in these two cases, the amici recognized the importance of putting a spin on the briefs. In particular, the amici seem to have recognized that certain amici would have more influence; in particular, the briefs of the AMA, the American Geriatrics Society, and U.S. seem to have attracted significant attention among both the parties and the amici.

CONCLUDING REMARKS ABOUT ASSISTED DYING CASES

Amici influence is apparent in all three assisted dying cases heard by the U.S. Supreme Court in the 1990s. In *Cruzan*, the amici made significant contributions to the debate about the termination of life support, and in *Glucksberg* and *Quill*, the amici seem to have influenced the Court's handling of challenges to state bans on assisted suicide. The influence of amici in these three cases is apparent in the direct cites made by the Justices to the amici briefs and in the Justices' indirect reliance on the arguments and data provided in these briefs. Moreover, taken together, these cases suggest that the Court has become more willing to use amici briefs over the course of the last decade.

There is some direct citation of amici briefs in the *Cruzan* decision: the Chief Justice cited the AMA brief once, Justice Stevens cited this brief twice, and Justice Brennan cited the AMA brief once, the American Association of Homes and Services for the Aging brief twice and the Guardian Ad Litem brief once. This direct citation is even more apparent in the two cases involving physician assistance in dying. In *Glucksberg* and *Quill*, the Chief Justice cited amici briefs five times, as did Justice Stevens. Justice Breyer cited amici four times, Justice Souter cited amici three times, and Justice O'Connor alluded to "the parties and their amici" once. While the *Cruzan* cites were mostly to the AMA brief, the *Glucksberg* and *Quill* cites were not only to medical organizations, like the AMA, Coalition of Hospice Professionals, and Washington State Psychological Association, but to patient advocacy groups like Choice in Dying and Not Dead Yet et al., governmental entities like the

United States, State Legislators, Members, and State of California et al., and groups of ethicists like Bioethicists in Support of Respondents and Ronald Dworkin et al.

In the *Cruzan* case, Justice Brennan used direct quotes from the amici briefs of the American College of Physicians, the AIDS Civil Rights Project, the AMA, and the Society for the Right to Die, but he did not attribute these quotes to the briefs. In contrast, no passages were drawn from amici briefs without attribution in *Glucksberg* and *Quill*. It bears noting, however, that in these later cases, the Justices appear to have been much more willing to employ amici arguments and data and may have relied even more heavily on these briefs than they did in *Cruzan*.

The use of direct cites in *Glucksberg* and *Quill* was slightly different for the Chief Justice than it was for Justices Stevens, Souter, and Breyer. While Chief Justice Rehnquist used the direct cites as endorsements for his positions on largely legal issues, the other Justices employed these cites to draw conclusions about extralegal questions. For example, Chief Justice Rehnquist cited the U.S. and State of California et al. as support for his position that a variety of state interests were at play in this litigation. In contrast, Justice Stevens used the Coalition of Hospice Professionals brief to conclude that pain cannot always be eliminated for those suffering from a terminal illness, and he employed the briefs of the Bioethicists in Support of Respondents and Ronald Dworkin et al. to argue that one's death should be in accord with one's life story. Similarly, Justice Breyer employed the briefs of the AMA and Choice in Dying to conclude that palliative care is not always available for terminally ill individuals, and Justice Souter used the brief of the State Legislators to contend that states should be allowed to experiment with legislation and regulations governing aid in dying.

In addition to using direct cites to amici briefs, the Justices in all three cases relied indirectly on the arguments and data in the briefs. In *Cruzan*, the indirect reliance on amici was most apparent in Justice Brennan's dissent. In a decision that was twenty-nine pages long, he employed thirteen briefs and relied on an amicus argument or information in forty-seven instances. In contrast, Justice Stevens' decision, which was twenty-seven pages long, used eleven briefs and relied on amicus data fourteen times; and the Chief Justice's majority decision, twenty-two pages long, relied on six amici in nine instances. Justices Scalia and O'Connor relied on amici to a lesser extent: Justice Scalia's eight-page concurrence employed the data from four amici in five instances, and Justice O'Connor's five-page concurrence used one amicus' brief one time.

The *Cruzan* decisions were relatively long: altogether, the majority, concurring, and dissenting opinions took up ninety-one pages. Interestingly, the *Glucksberg* and *Quill* opinions were much shorter. The seven opinions in these cases spanned only forty-eight pages. Despite the relative brevity of these two decisions, indirect reliance on amici briefs was more extensive than it had been in *Cruzan*. In twenty pages of text in these two cases, the Chief Justice's opinions corresponded with amici briefs one hundred fifty-six times. In his nineteen pages, Justice Souter's opinions coalesced with amici briefs eighty-eight times. Justice Stevens' six-page opinion used information found in amici briefs seventy-four times. Justice O'Connor's one-page opinion correlated with data found in amici briefs forty-eight times, and Justice Breyer's two-page opinion employed amici information thirty-seven times. Moreover, the Justices' opinions corresponded with a variety of amici. Justice Souter's opinion corresponded with the briefs of forty-one amici; the Chief Justice's opinion was in sync with forty amici; Justice Stevens's opinion corresponded with thirty-seven amici; and Justices O'Connor and Breyer were in sync with twenty-eight amici each.

In all three cases, the Justices used amici briefs to consider an issue or employ information contained only in an amicus brief. For example, in *Cruzan*, the amici alone raised a number of issues that the Justices considered; among these were the nature of the liberty and equal protection rights at issue, the state's interest in life, the definition and nature of death and dying, the experience of those in a persistent vegetative state, state variation in decision-making for incompetents, and the impact of this case on medical treatment. Similarly, in *Glucksberg* and *Quill*, the amici were the only ones providing the Court with information about the common law history of assisted suicide bans, the impact of the *Poe v. Ullman* case on these cases, the parallels between abortion and assisted dying, precedent distinguishing the termination of medical treatment from the provision of lethal medication, the impact of these cases on the integrity of the medical profession, the obligation of physicians to provide aid in dying, and the role of the democratic process in resolving this debate.

The close correspondence between the Justices' decisions and the arguments and information in the amici briefs suggests that the amici had a significant role in all three cases, especially the 1997 cases. Moreover, there is evidence of partisanship in some of the Justices' opinions. For example, the only briefs that Justices Stevens and Brennan directly cited to in *Cruzan* were those that supported the Cruzans, with whom the Justices sided. Similarly, in the physician aid in dying cases, Chief Justice Rehnquist cited only those amici who supported the winning side, that is, U.S., State of California et al., the AMA, and Not Dead Yet et al. Similarly, with the sole exception of the AMA, Justice Stevens cited only doctors' amici. It bears noting, however, that Justices on both side of the debate in the three cases cited the AMA, maybe because it was seen as more neutral than the other "friends."

While there is evidence of partisanship in direct citation, there is no real pattern in the indirect use of amici briefs. While the briefs of the amici who wrote in opposition of a right to terminate treatment went largely unaddressed in *Cruzan*, in *Glucksberg* and *Quill* the Justices relied on the arguments and information provided in amici briefs from both sides of the debate. It is important to note, however, that certain amici seem to have more influence in all three cases, and there is correspondence between the briefs of these amici and all of the Justices. For example, in *Cruzan*, the Justices relied to a significant degree on the briefs of the AMA, AAN, AIDS, Choice in Dying , Guardian Ad Litem, Society for the Right to Die, and U.S.[235] Similarly, in *Glucksberg* and *Quill*, the Justices indirectly relied on the briefs of the AMA, United States, California et al., American Association of Homes and Services for the Aging, American Geriatrics Society, and State Legislators.[236] The parties and their amici also recognized that certain amici, most notably, the U.S. and the AMA, were most influential; and in *Glucksberg* and *Quill*, they referred to these briefs, in an attempt either to buttress their own arguments or to undermine the arguments of these two amici.

It also bears noting that there appears to have been significant coordination and cooperation in all three cases, although this coordination is even more apparent in the 1997 cases than in *Cruzan*. This coordination is apparent in a number of areas. First, the amici in all three cases disagreed about a number of issues, which suggests that they were reading the briefs of other friends as well as those of the parties. For example, in *Cruzan*, the amici disagreed about critical issues relating to Nancy Cruzan's medical condition, the character of food and hydration, and the definition of death and dying. Similarly, in the *Glucksberg* and *Quill* cases, the amici disagreed about a range of questions relating to both legal and medical or scientific questions. Second, amici and party coordination and cooperation is apparent in the amici's elaboration of points raised in the party briefs. In these two cases, the parties and their amici appear to have devised a divide and conquer strategy: the parties raised a point very briefly in either their brief on the merits or their reply brief, and the amici picked up this point and provided much more extensive discussion. Third, coordination is apparent in the citation by both parties and amici to the briefs of other amici. This pattern is apparent in *Glucksberg* and *Quill*, but not in *Cruzan*.

Finally, in *Glucksberg* and *Quill*, far fewer amici arguments went unnoticed by the Justices than in *Cruzan*. In *Cruzan*, the amici wrote about the sanctity of life, the risk that a Court holding allowing the termination of treatment would threaten the most vulnerable in society and lead to lethal injections for members of these groups and undermine suicide and homicide laws, the parallels between abortion and the termination of treatment or euthanasia, and the lessons to be learned from the Nazi era. In *Glucksberg* and *Quill*, very few amici arguments were unheard by the Justices. In fact, the only arguments that were completely ignored related to the Nazi era, the history of assisted suicide prohibitions in the ancient and medieval periods and in the Roman Catholic Church, and the relationship between assisted suicide bans and the establishment clause and the right to intimate association. Interestingly, the unnoticed *Cruzan* arguments about the effects of these laws on the most vulnerable in society, the parallels between abortion and assisted dying, and the states' interest in preserving the sanctity of life were all eventually addressed in *Glucksberg* and *Quill*.

In sum, even though the *Glucksberg* and *Quill* opinions were much shorter than the *Cruzan* opinions, there was even more direct and indirect evidence of amici influence in the two cases. This coalescing of arguments and data in the Justices' opinions and the amici briefs may have a number of explanations. We know that there was increasing overlap between what was in the party and amici briefs in these cases. The amici were often "seconding," "thirding," and "fourthing" the information provided in each other's briefs. It may be that the parties and amici were becoming more adroit at guessing what was of interest to the Justices and focusing on these issues. It is also possible that the Justices were just more willing to rely on amici briefs in *Quill* and *Glucksberg* than they were in *Cruzan*. This willingness is apparent in the number of direct cites as well as in the conscious use of information provided only in amici briefs. It is possible that the Justices saw these two cases as raising more complicated issues than those raised in the *Cruzan* litigation, and the Justices may have needed to rely on amici discussions about the nature of death and dying, the prevalence of depression and the effects of palliative care, and the impact of these cases on the medical treatment of those with terminal illnesses. This need for medical and scientific information is highlighted by the Justices' unabashed use of the *NYS Report*, which was issued by the New York State Legislature and provided detailed information about the experience of death and dying in the United States. The Justices' lack of information and expertise may have highlighted the role of the amici in these three cases, allowing virtually all of the amici to enter into the debate.

NOTES

1. *Cruzan v. Director, Missouri Department of Health et al.* 497 U.S. 261, 110 S.Ct. 2841 (1990).
2. 497 U.S. 266, 309-10 note 8.
3. 497 U.S. 339.
4. 497 U.S. 311-2, 308.

5. 497 U.S. 314, 339.

6. For example, in his majority opinion, Chief Justice Rehnquist noted that "[t]his issue [was] more properly analyzed in terms of the fourteenth amendment liberty interest" (497 U.S. 279 fn 7). It is possible that the amicus brief of the United States influenced the Chief Justice. In this brief, the U.S. notes that "the source of any due process right to refuse unwanted medical treatment or procedures should be drawn from history and traditions, not [from] a generalized right to privacy" (United States, 6).

7. United States, 24. Similarly, one of the Chief Justice's key concerns was that for incompetents, the liberty interest would be exercised not by the individual, but by someone else acting on her behalf. He argued that this possibility justified a heightened evidentiary standard to ensure that the individual's treatment preferences were protected. This was a major concern of both the Free Speech Advocates and the SSM Health Care System, which both focused on the questionable exercise of Ms. Cruzan's liberty right by someone other than her (Free Speech Advocates, p. 10-11; SSM Health Care Systems, p. 4).

8. 497 U.S. 262, 280.

9. Petitioner's brief, 21-2; Guardian Ad Litem, 5-8.

10. 497 U.S. 279-80.

11. United States, 19-20.

12. 497 U.S. 304.

13. Petitioner's brief, 11-5; Guardian Ad Litem, 4-5.

14. American Medical Association, p. 17; Society for the Right to Die, p. 4; Concern in Dying, 6.

15. 497 U.S. 305, cited from *Natanson v. Kline* 186 Kans. 393, 406-7 (1960), cited in AMA, 25.

16. 497 U.S. 313.

17. Guardian Ad Litem, p. 25; National Hospice Organization, p. 15; and the American College of Physicians, pp. 9, 24.

18. Petitioners, 8-9, 15.

19. 497 U.S. 314; American Academy of Neurology, p. 21.

20. 497 U.S. 314; American Academy of Neurology, p. 21; Guardian Ad Litem, 29.

21. 497 U.S. 303; Society for the Right to Die, 25-6. The Petitioner Brief also notes that the practical effect of this standard is to bar the exercise of the liberty right. The Petitioner asserts that this burden is so heavy that "virtually no incompetent person would ever be able to meet it" (33).

22. 497 U.S. 324-5; American Medical Association, 32, 41-42.

23. 497 U.S. 343; American Medical Association, 17; Society for the Right to Die, 4; Society of Critical Care Medicine et al., 22.

24. 497 U.S. 342-3; American Academy of Neurology, 16-17; AIDS Civil Rights Project, 5.

25. 497 U.S. 342; American College of Physicians, p. 8; National Hospice Organization, p. 9; American Medical Association, p. 25.

26. 497 U.S. 345.

27. 497 U.S. 344-5; SRD, 16; Wisconsin, 7.

28. 497 U.S. 300; U.S. 10-1.

29. United States, p. 10.

30. Rutherford Institute, 18-19; National Right to Life Committee, 6.

31. Like the ACRP, Justice Brennan warned that "[m]edical technology has effectively created a twilight zone of suspended animation where death commences while life, in some form, continues. Some patients, however, want no

part of a life sustained only by medical technology. Instead, they prefer a plan of medical treatment that allows nature to take its course and permits them to die with dignity" (Cited from *Rasmussen v. Fleming* 154 Ariz. 207, 211 (1987) in 497 U.S. 301; AIDS Civil Rights Project, 21-1).

32. 497 U.S. 302, 329; Society for the Right to Die, p. 2.

33. 497 U.S. 302; Society for the Right to Die, p. 2.

34. 497 U.S. 346.

35. Petitioner's brief, 14.

36. United Methodist Church, p. 5.

37. American College of Physicians, 27.

38. Frederick R. Abrams et al., 5; Barbara Burgoon and Ruth Fields, 16.

39. 497 U.S. 343-4; NHO, 2, 4, UMC, 8; SSM, 17.

40. Petitioner brief, 14.

41. 497 U.S. 261, 287 (Chief Justice); 497 U.S. 261, 310 (Justice Brennan); 497 U.S. 261, 357 (Justice Stevens).

42. 497 U.S. 261, 339.

43. 497 U.S. 310; American Academy of Neurology stated that pvs patients are "unable to express emotion, sensation or pain" (p. 3); the American Medical Association stated that individuals in a pvs do "not feel pain or sense anyone or anything" (p. 8).

44. 497 U.S. 309-10, note 8; American Medical Association, p. 10; American College of Physicians, p. 6-7.

45. 497 U.S. 308.

46. American Medical Association, 15; Barbara Burgoon, 11; Society for the Right to Die, 18-19; Concern in Dying, 10-12.

47. These groups argued that the persistent vegetative state is not readily definable, and that food and nutrition might not be medical treatment (Doctors for Life (p. 2, 7-8), American Academy of Physicians and Surgeons (pp. 1-2, 17, 22), U.S. Catholic Conference (p. 27), the Catholic Guild (pp. 8, 11-12), the United States (p. 7), and the District Attorney of Milwaukee (p. 17).

48. United States, p. 25, 29.

49. 497 U.S. 292.

50. 497 U.S. 293.

51. 497 U.S. 328; Petitioner brief, 22, 26; Barbara Burgoon, 4, 6; Frederick R. Abrams, 10-1; the AIDS Civil Rights Project, 3; the American Academy of Neurology, 15, 25; the American College of Physicians; the American Hospital Association, 9-10, 16-7; the AMA, 3a; Concern in Dying,17; the Guardian Ad Litem, 3, 17; the Society of Critical Care Medicine, 16-8; the United Methodist Church, 10; and the Society for the Right to Die, 28, 30.

52. 497 U.S. 286; D.A., p. 28.

53. 497 U.S. 350.

54. Amici briefs of the American College of Physicians, 23-24; American Medical Association 1a; Association of Retarded Citizens of the United States, 23; and Guardian Ad Litem 21.

55. 497 U.S. 339. District Attorney, p. 26. Concern about caregiver stress and the impact that such stress would have on family members contemplating discontinuance of treatment was also a part of the briefs of the Association of Retarded Citizens of the United States and the Right to Life League of Southern California (ARC, 13; RLLSC, 32-35).

56. 497 U.S. 325; AIDS Civil Rights Project, 18 (noting that Nancy Cruzan "remains a passive subject of medical technology that offers no hope for cognitive human life").

57. Guardian Ad Litem, 4.

58. Concern in Dying, 25 ("medical treatment has come to symbolize a prototypically modern form of torture"); Society of Critical Care Medicine, 30.

59. 497 U.S. 314.

60. Petitioner, 9; AIDS Civil Rights Project, 15; American Academy of Neurology, 11; American Medical Association, 48; Burgoon, 15; Concern in Dying, 23; Petitioner brief, 32.

61. 497 U.S. 330.

62. American College of Physicians, p. 21.

63. Petitioner's brief, note 11, p. 27–28.

64. Petitioner's reply brief, p. 5 fn 6.

65. Petitioner's reply brief, p. 2 citing United States p. 8.

66. Respondents brief, p. 11–16, specifically notes 10, 11.

67. Under the Washington law, a person is guilty of promoting a suicide attempt when "he knowingly causes or aids another person to attempt suicide." Under this law, promoting a suicide attempt is a class C felony (Washington Revised Code Section 9A.36.060). The New York law decreed that a person is guilty of manslaughter in the second degree, also a class C felony, when "he intentionally causes or aids another person to commit suicide." Aiding an (unsuccessful) suicide attempt is punishable as a class E felony (New York Penal Law Section 125.15, 120.30).

68. This case was initially brought to the federal district and appeals courts by four physicians, three terminally ill individuals, and the nonprofit organization Compassion in Dying. Compassion in Dying dropped out of the case before it reached the Supreme Court because the three terminally ill persons represented by the group had died, leaving the physicians as parties to the case.

69. 79 F.3d 790, 816.

70. 79 F.3d 814. The federal district court had recognized a right to hasten one's death in its examination of this case (850 F.Supp. 1454 (W.D.Wash. 1994)), but the Ninth Circuit initially reversed the decision, finding that there is no such right embodied in the right to privacy (49 F.3d 586 (1995)).

71. 80 F.3d 716, 729 (1996). The Second Circuit rejected a due process claim, arguing that "the Supreme Court has drawn a line, albeit a shaky one, on the expansion of fundamental rights that are without support in the text of the Constitution" (724).

72. 80 F.3d 729.

73. 117 S.Ct. 2272.

74. 117 S.Ct. 2274, 2298.

75. 117 S.Ct. 2263, 2272, 2273, 2274, 2276, 2274, 2298, 2301.

76. Cites to NYS Report: 117 S.CT. 2308, 2309. Cites to WSPA 2308.

77. 117 S.Ct. 2308, 2310.

78. 117 S.Ct. 2308.

79. 117 S.Ct. 2311-2.

80. 117 S.Ct. 2286.

81. 117 S.Ct. 2293.

82. 117 S.Ct. 2293.

83. 117 S.Ct. 2291.

84. 117 S.Ct. 2269.

85. American College of Legal Medicine (ACLM), 4; GMHC, 24.

86. AD, 3; BP-pet, 9.; 117 S.Ct. 2353.

87. 117 S.CT. 2264-5. Much of the Chief Justice's discussion of the early colonial period draws on Justice Antonin Scalia's opinion in *Cruzan*.

88. 117 S.CT. 2261, 2265.

89. 117 S.CT. 2266. For example, in 1975, the legislature revised its criminal code and included this practice, and in 1991, Washington voters rejected a ballot initiative that would have permitted some types of physician-assisted suicide (2266).

90. According to Chief Justice Rehnquist, "[o]pposition to and condemnation of suicide and assisting suicide are consistent and enduring themes of our philosophical, legal and cultural heritages" (117 S.CT. 2263).

91. 117 S.CT. 2286.

92. 117 S.CT. 2287.

93. Respondents' brief in *Glucksberg*, 17-8; Respondents' brief in *Quill*, 27.

94. The Petitioner in *Glucksberg* and Members contended that this non-enforcement did not constitute a repudiation of the statutes, since suicide and assisted suicide continue to be viewed as crimes in Washington and New York (Petitioner, 23; Members, 15).

95. B/P, 12.

96. JW, 10-11, 16, 19.

97. ACLU, 1.

98. ACLJ, 8; AA, 6; AMA in *Glucksberg*, 22, 28; California in *Glucksberg*, 13, 15-6; CHA, 10; CMA, 4-5, 10-1; IPA, 6; LC, 20-3; NLC in *Glucksberg* 10; NSCI in *Glucksberg*, 14; RI in *Glucksberg*, 5; USCC in *Glucksberg* 14; WC, 28-9.

99. 117 S.CT. 2307.

100. 117 S.CT. 2305, 2307.

101. 117 S.CT. 2307; United States in *Glucksberg*, 11.

102. NW, 3, 9, 11, 13. The SL referred to this approach as "narrow historicism" (9, 11), and CRLP contended that the Court should never be "confined to historic notions of equality . . . [or] due process (21).

103. 117 S.CT. 2275.

104. 117 S.CT. 2312; While Justice Breyer also noted the *Poe* opinion in his concurrence, it is only a passing reference (117 S.Ct. 2312).

105. 117 S.CT. 2284.

106. 117 S.Ct. 2281; NW, 10-1.

107. Hatch, 20, 21; 36, 3; NW, 7; 36, 2; ACLU, 3.

108. One of the most interesting aspects of these opinions is the extent to which the Justices accept that due process encompasses not only procedural but substantive dimensions. Since the repudiation of *Lochner v. New York* in the late 1930s, the Court had taken pains to disassociate itself from substantive due process, attempting to frame rights in other terms. It can be argued that the right to privacy was created to shield the Court from criticism that it was employing substantive due process. In these cases, however, the Justices expressly use substantive due process. The Chief Justice is clearly cagier about employing this "right." For example, the Chief Justice criticized Justice Souter for his reliance on the Harlan dissent in *Poe*, arguing that the Court has "never abandoned our fundamental rights-based method," and that *Poe*, while often cited in later cases, like *Casey v. Southeastern Pennsylvania Planned Parenthood*, did not set the parameters for substantive due process (117 S.Ct. 2268, n17).

109. 117 S.CT. 2278.

110. 117 S.CT. 2303.

111. 117 S.CT. 2307.

112. 117 S.CT. 2311.

113. 117 S.CT. 2311.

114. 117 S.CT. 2303, 2311.

115. United States in *Glucksberg*, 8.

116. United States in *Glucksberg*, 13.

117. CSH, 4. Similarly, the Center for Reproductive Law and Policy contended that a state could not override the right of a terminal ill patient to avoid unbearable pain in his/her last days (24); and Surviving Family Members and Julian W. Whitaker, M.D., urged the Court to consider that the laws compel some to suffer horrific and unrelenting pain in their final days (SFM, 9; JW, 2-3).

118. Interestingly, even though this would seem to be a critical issue for the doctors, they noted simply that medical technology did not ease the pain and suffering of the patient-plaintiffs or of many others, and that doctors often employed "terminal sedation" to aid these patients (respondents' brief in *Glucksberg*, 20-1). In terminal sedation, a person is medicated to the point at which he or she is no longer conscious, and then is not fed or given hydration. These patients die of starvation or dehydration. Similarly, the *Quill* respondents note simply that palliative care forces some patients to choose between pain control and mental acuity (respondents' brief in *Quill*, 8-9). The doctors in both cases argued that pain and suffering encompassed not only physical pain, but emotional anguish and a loss of dignity (Respondents' brief in *Glucksberg*, 21; Respondents' brief in *Quill*, 4).

119. AGS, 9; AMA in *Glucksberg*, 6-7; AMSA, 2; CID, 17; CHP, 4; NAPN, 11-3.

120. United States in *Glucksberg*, n1, 15-6; AMSA, 2; SFM, 8 n9; JW, 3.

121. AMSA, 10; CHP, 10-1.

122. These amici drew heavily on the findings of the 1994 New York State Task Force Report on Life and the Law, which concluded that palliative care was often not available to minorities, the elderly, and women. For example, the AMA argued in both cases that such care was "grossly inadequate (AMA in *Quill* and *Glucksberg* citing to NYSTF, 7). Choice in Dying contended that possibly one half of all terminally ill people died in pain (CID, 15). The American Geriatrics Society, International Anti-Euthanasia Task Force and Choice in Dying all claimed that a lack of insurance coverage and a lack of education among health care providers and the general public were the principal obstacles to adequate palliation (AGS, 8a-10a; CID, 19-20; IAET, 26). Moreover, the AMA, the National Hospice Organization, and the U.S. Catholic Conference voiced their strong opinion that a decision by the Court striking down the laws would reverse the trend toward improving palliative care (AMA in *Quill*, 22; AMA in *Glucksberg*, 18, 29; National Hospice Organization, 17-8; USCC in *Quill*, 27).

123. 117 S.CT. 2311-2.

124. 117 S.CT. 2308.

125. 117 S.Ct. 2303.

126. 117 S.CT. 2265.

127. For example, the doctors and their amici contended that barring assistance in dying consigned many to a horrific and inhuman death and that allowing assistance would ensure dignity and bodily integrity (Quill, 14, 31; LP, 25; AMSA, 16 n15; 10, 1-4, 5-6, 12-3, 16, 22; AD, 21-3. The Petitioner's amici attempted to counter this bleak picture. For example, AA argues that even Alzheimer's Disease patients have "day to day ebbs and flows" in lucidity (AA, 14); the AGS contends that severe pain can be relieved for nearly all persons (AGS, 3). The AGS also note that most die "quietly, in their sleep . . . [and with the support of] hospice and palliative care programs (AGS, 7). Several employed the *NYS Report* as support for their position that most terminally ill individuals seeking assistance in dying are suffering from depression and that depression is a treatable condition.

128. Respondents' brief in *Glucksberg*, 23-4.

129. The Court held that the interest was implicated "at the point at which avoiding severe pain or suffering and ending life coalesce" (8). This point was also made by Ronald Dworkin and the Center for Reproductive Law and Policy, which argued that *Cruzan* mandated a finding that a liberty interest was a stake in this case (RD, 10; CRLP, 15-6).

130. SL, 8.

131. 117 S.Ct. 2307.

132. 117 S.Ct. 2306.

133. 117 S.Ct. 2307.

134. AA, 9; AHA, 5-6; CA in Glucksberg, 8-9, 23; CHA, 12-3; ELC, 11; Members, 2-3. Other amici arguments about the significance of the *Cruzan* decision to the present cases do not appear to have been adopted by the Justices. For example, the *Quill* doctors and several amici urged the Court to employ what they saw as the balancing test adopted in *Cruzan*: they contended that the absolute ban should be weighed against the states' interests (Respondents' brief in *Quill*, 33; CRLP, 23; SL, 6-7). Other amici invoked Justice Scalia's argument in *Cruzan* that states may have a compelling interest in human life and do not have to make decisions about whether to employ quality of life assessments in protecting this life (California in *Quill*, 16; CMA, 16; MSNJ in *Quill*, 15; NRLC in *Glucksberg*, 19; NSCI in *Glucksberg*, 15; RI in *Glucksberg*, 5). Still others argued that the *Cruzan* decision had no relevance in this debate or that *Cruzan* should be overturned (The Petitioner in *Quill* (11) and WC (22) argued that *Cruzan* was inapposite, and ALL in *Quill* contended that *Cruzan* should be overturned because it allowed the "intentional killing of innocent, non-aggressor persons" in contravention of the Fourteenth Amendment due process clause (8, 19). Moreover, as has been noted, most of the Justices agreed that the individual might have a liberty interest in controlling the circumstances of his or her death, and all referred to "decisional autonomy." This theme runs through many of the briefs, including those of the states and their amici, who urged the Court not to embrace the concept of "autonomous self-determination," and contended that there is no right to "absolute liberty" (Petitioner' brief in *Quill*,10-1, 19; California in *Glucksberg*, 17; ED, 8; NSCI, 10; WC, 33-4; CMA, 10; AMA, 3-4). The Chief Justice appeared to have agreed with this conclusion; however, the other Justices writing opinions may have agreed with the many other amici that detailed how these laws interfered with these liberty interests. In its brief, the GMHC focused on the right to personal autonomy, arguing that the state laws "effectively force a person to continue living against his or her will [and] destroy the autonomy that has been central to the struggles of people with disabilities" (GMHC, 6). Similarly, ADD, CHP, CRLP, CSH, and NW urged the Court to consider how these laws crippled the ability of a terminally ill person to make decisions about how to spend his/her last days of life (ADD, 2-3; CHP, 5; CRLP, 19; CSH, 2-3, 15; NW, 8). For example, the CRLP contends that these laws make terminally ill individuals "captives of machinery," and limit them to only two choices—to either remain on treatment regimens or to refuse treatment (CRLP, 20). A similar argument is made by JW, who contends that the laws make the terminally ill "prisoners of medical procedures" (JW, 5).The *Glucksberg* and *Quill* respondents both argue that the decision of a terminally ill individual to end one's life should be guided by one's individual conscience and that one's religious or spiritual beliefs often influence one's choice (Respondents in *Glucksberg*, 19; Respondents in *Quill*, 1). This argument is echoed by several amici, perhaps most notably 36, which contends that the decision whether to hasten death "will be resolved differently for different individuals, based on [their] own philosophical, ethical

and religious beliefs" (36, 15). 36, along with RD and B/R, claim that the Washington and New York laws run afoul of the First Amendment establishment and free exercise clauses because they promote one religious view over other views (36, 6-9, 15, 16-7; RD, 3; B/R, 10).

135. 117 S.Ct. 2271.

136. Most amici filed in both cases, and their briefs contained detailed discussions of both clauses. Some of the Justices also wrote only one opinion, writing more generally about the alleged violations of the clauses, and other Justices, notably the Chief Justice, wrote two opinions and divided up the due process and equal protection arguments to correspond with each case. Justice Souter also filed two opinions, but his opinion in the *Vacco* case was very brief and contained no additional arguments or information.

137. 117 S.Ct. 2299.

138. 117 S.Ct. 2310.

139. Respondents' brief in *Glucksberg*, 46. The doctors and their amici contended that the state's disparate treatment of the two groups could not be justified by intent, since both groups had the same intent, that is, the intent to bring about their own deaths (Respondents' brief in *Vacco*, 10, 45). The Doctors criticized New York State for inquiring into intent only in cases where parties sought to hasten their deaths through the ingestion of medication, but not where they sought to hasten their deaths through the termination of life support (Respondents' brief in *Vacco*, 12). The doctors also argued that the line between these two groups was further blurred by the fact that intentional and nonconsensual termination of life support could be prosecuted as murder under state law (Respondents' brief in *Vacco*, 11).

140. ACLM, 26; ACLU, 25-6; AD, 7; AGS, 14; AMSA, 4-5; BP/P, 14; B/R, 13, CID, 2, 7; RD,11-2; SFM, 27; SL, 7.

141. ACLJ, 25; AHA, 14; Bioethicists for Petitioner , 13, CHA, 17-8, 25; CMA, 18-21, Members, 27-8; NRLC in *Vacco*, 21; USCC in *Vacco*, 19-21. Some of these amici argued that there were real differences in the two populations: those who sought to terminate treatment were usually close to death and already receiving medical assistance, while those seeking PAS might not be receiving adequate medical attention, and in particular, might have treatable mental illness (AGS, 12-13; ASF in *Glucksberg*, 13).

142. CID, 11-2; AMSA, 16. The *Vacco* doctors only very briefly made this point, contending that the treatment of patients with medications that had a double effect was closer to euthanasia than was physician-assisted suicide (Respondents's brief in *Vacco*, 15).

143. 117 S.Ct. 2310.

144. 117 S.Ct. 2301; Respondents' briefs in *Vacco*, 16-7, 49; ACLU, 26; SL, 28-9.

145. 117 S.CT. 2301; Petitioner' Reply Brief in *Vacco*, 11; AGS, "Position Statement on PAS and Voluntary Active Euthanasia," 2a; Bioethicists for Petitioner , 18; USCC in *Vacco*, 21.

146. Once again, the parties paid little attention to this issue. The states in *Vacco* noted only that the right to decline or withdraw treatment "derives from the common law right of bodily integrity" (Petitioner' brief in *Vacco*, 18), and that it is "erroneous, as a matter of history, law, medicine and logic, to treat these practices as the same" (32).

147. AA, 22-3; AGS, 3, 14-5; AMA in *Glucksberg*, 18-20; AMA in *Vacco*, 19-20; Bioethicists for Petitioner , 2-3, 5, 7-11, 17; California et al. in *Vacco*, 11, California et al. in *Glucksberg*, 13-6; CMA, 5-6; Clarendon in *Vacco*, 15-6; MSNJ, 10, 16-7; United States in *Glucksberg*, 9; U.S. in *Vacco*, 15; USCC, 4, 13.

148. 117 S.Ct. 2299.

149. AA, 24; AGS, 11; AMA in *Glucksberg*, 20-1; CLS, 18, 20-1; MSNJ, 6-9.

150. The states in both cases argued simply that there was disagreement among medical and legal professionals about how to view these practices (Petitioner' brief in *Glucksberg*, 10-2; Petitioner' brief in *Vacco*, 7).

151. 117 S.Ct. 2298.

152. Had the Justices accepted that the statutes interfered with the doctors' due process rights, by either placing an undue burden on the right to hasten dying or finding that there was a fundamental right to hasten dying, they would have engaged in a weighing of the state interest. Similarly, if the Court had found that the states treated similarly situated groups differently and in so doing violated the equal protection clause, the Justices would also have examined the state's interest in adopting the assisted suicide ban, by looking at whether the ban was rationally related to the state's articulated goals.

153. 117 S.Ct. 2272.

154. Petitioner' reply brief in *Glucksberg*, 19; Petitioner' brief in *Quill*, 20.

155. United States in *Glucksberg*, 18.

156. AA, 11; AI, 1-2; ACLJ, 2; California et al. in *Glucksberg*, 27; California et al. in *Quill*, 5, 20-1, 23; CHA, 19-21; CMA, 13, 15, 17; ELC, 20, 24; LCDL in *Quill*, 3; NCOP, 6, 25; NLC in *Glucksberg*, 7-9; NRLC in *Glucksberg*, 1, 24-5; NSCI, 3, 9; RI in *Glucksberg*, 1; WC, 26-7).

157. 117 S.Ct. 2307.

158. 117 S.Ct. 2307-8.

159. 117 S.Ct. 2304.

160. Petitioner' brief in *Quill*, 20; CRLP, 26; CSH, 12; NW, 24; SL, 8, 17-8; ACLU, 18; AD, 9-10; GM, 14.

161. B/R, 10.The briefs of the Catholic Medical Association and the Milwaukee D.A. also discussed capital punishment, but both friends used this discussion as evidence of the state's strong interest in life (CMA, 7; D/A, 19).

162. 117 S.Ct. 2273.

163. AA, 2-3; AGS, 2; AI, 21-2; California in *Glucksberg*, 27-9; ELC, 25-9; FRC, 4-5; Members, 1; NCOP, 2, 9, 17-8, 21, 23-4; NLC in *Glucksberg*, 5-9, 12, 16, 25; NSCI, 17, 20-2, 25-6; NDY in *Quill*, 4-6, 11, 28-30.

164. GM, 2, 16.

165. 117 S.Ct. 2308.

166. 117 S.Ct. 2273.

167. 117 S.Ct. 2273.

168. 117 S.Ct. 2303.

169. 117 S.Ct. 2290.

170. 117 S.Ct. 2290.

171. Petitioner' reply brief in *Quill*, 13.

172. For example, CID contended that there is a lack of consensus among states as to what constitutes a terminal illness: some states define terminal illness as resulting in death within six months (New Jersey), others as death within one year, and others as "imminent death" (Illinois) or death in a "short time" (Missouri) 12-3. See also, Clarendon Institute, 3; PDA 27-9; United States, 22; USCC in *Quill*, 24. Furthermore, one amicus pointed to the activities of Dr. Jack Kevorkian, arguing that he had extended his assistance to number of patients who did not have terminal illnesses (RT, 8).

173. ACLU, 23-24. AD, 16, 23, 36; AMSA, 18, 36, 23; RD, 14. This point was also briefly made by the doctors in both cases (Respondents in *Quill*, 4; Respondents in *Glucksberg*, 40).

174. AD, 16; 36, 23; CHP, 5.

175. 117 S.Ct. 2272-4 (Rehnquist); 2303 (O'Connor); 2290, 2292 (Souter); 2308 (Stevens).

176. 117 S.Ct. 2308.

177. Respondents' brief in *Glucksberg*, 32 note 20; Petitioner' reply brief in *Quill*, 15; AA, 14-6; AMA in *Glucksberg*, 9-10; AMA in *Quill*, 8; ASF in *Glucksberg*, 5-11, 27-30; Hatch, 7; Gary Lee, 11-8; NAPN, 9; NLC in *Glucksberg*, 22; PDA, 25; RT, 26-7; United States in *Glucksberg*, 9, 19-20.

178. AMA in *Glucksberg*, 9, 10; Hatch, 3-10 (eight out of fifteen quotes are from this report); Gary Lee, 10-4 (cited repeatedly); NAPN, 9; RT, 26-7; United States in *Glucksberg*, 19-20.

179. Petitioner in *Quill*, 13, 29; AMA in *Glucksberg*, 6-8, 13, ASF, 14-6; PDA, 18-9.

180. AMA in *Quill*, 13-4, 16; ASF, 14-6.

181. Petitioner' reply brief in *Vacco*, 13, 16, 29.

182. AA, 15-6, 18; CHA, 24-5; ELC, 20-4; LP, 16-7; United States in *Glucksberg*, 22.

183. AMA in *Glucksberg*, 15; DA in *Glucksberg*, 8-9; NAPN, 10; United States in *Glucksberg*, 20-2.

184. ALL in *Quill*, 15; AGS, 10; AMA in *Glucksberg*, 13; IAET, 3-18, 29 (almost this entire brief was devoted to this issue); NAPN, 10-1; NDY in *Quill*, 24, 27; PDA, 22.

185. Several amici contended that the data about suicide were inapposite in these cases, because a terminally ill person's decision to hasten death could not be viewed as suicide (B/R, 11; WSPA, 16-7, 20). Other amici contended that the bans actually increased the risk that end of life decisions would be subject to abuse, since these decisions were shrouded in secrecy and not the result of adequate communication between patient and health care professional (LP, 4, 22-3, 25-6; SL, 21; WSPA, 28-9). The doctors and their amici argued that the state could advance its interest in preventing abuse by crafting regulations that would require competency determinations and would involve health care workers at the beginning of the process (Respondents in Quill, 38; GM, 21; SL, 22; WSPA, 25-6).

186. 117 S.Ct. 2273.

187. In both cases, the AMA devoted more than seventeen pages to its discussion of the impact of physician-assisted suicide on the ethical and legal obligations of doctors (AMA in *Glucksberg, Vacco*, 1-17). In its briefs, the AMA highlights the Hippocratic oath and the AMA's examination of physician assistance in dying from 1977-1996 (5 in both briefs). It bears noting that the text of these two briefs are identical from pages 1-17.

188. NAPN, 2; see generally, 3, 5-8, 11, 15-23, 26-9.

189. AA, 18-21; CLS, 1-13; CMA, 1-2; ELC, 5-6; FRC, 1; LC, 5-6; LCDL in *Quill*, 6-9; MSNJ in *Quill*, 4-5, 9; RT, 18, 20; US in *Quill*, 11-2.

190. 117 S.CT. 2308.

191. 117 S.Ct. 2288.

192. 117 S.Ct. 2288-9.

193. The only allusion to this argument in the doctors' briefs occurs in the *Glucksberg* case, where the doctors cites to the amici briefs of the B/R and ACLM as support for its argument that striking down the laws will bring the practice of physician assistance in dying out into the open and will enhance the physician-patient relationship (Respondents' brief in *Glucksberg*, 26 note 14).

194. ACLU, 22-3; AD, 19; AMSA, 12-6; B/R, 11-2; CHP, 23-5; SL, 25-6.

195. B/R, 7-8; ACLM, 26-7.

196. SL, 25.

197. WSPA, 23.

198. CHP, 15-7.

199. B/R, 9; SL, 26; WSPA, 21.

200. Petitioner brief in *Glucksberg*, 34-5, 44-47; Petitioner reply brief in *Glucksberg*, 9, 15-8; Petitioner brief in *Quill*, 21-4), Respondents' brief in *Glucksberg*, 33-7; Respondents in *Quill*, 41 note 21.

201. 117 S.Ct. 2274, 2274 note 23.

202. 117 S.Ct. 2291.

203. 117 S.Ct. 2291.

204. AMA in *Quill*, 11-2; AMA in *Glucksberg*, 27; AHA, 9; AGS, 15-27.

205. AMA in *Quill*, 13.

206. Both the ACLM and the WSPA provided extensive discussion about how existing regulations guarded against an expansion of the right to hasten death (see ACLM, 2-3, 7-21, 28-9; appendix B-1; WSPA, 2-13, 22-4). See also the briefs of the ACLU, 21-3; AMSA, 17, 19-20, 22-29; B/R, 13-5; CHP, 17-9; CSH, 13-4; CRLP, 26; GMHC, 8, 14, 19; NW, 18; RD, 21.

207. AGS, 27; AMA in *Glucksberg*, 11; AMA in *Quill*, 10-1, 25; ASF, 18-24; IAET, 27; LCDL, 13, 21, 25-6; NSCI, 24 note 7; US in *Glucksberg*, 23-4; USCC, 22-3.

208. ACLU, 21-2 note 33; AMSA, 18 note 18; B/R, 16-8 note 3; GM, 20.

209. 117 S.Ct. 2274. The Chief Justice also notes that like the United States, other countries are embroiled in the controversy over assisted dying (2266).

210. 117 S.Ct. 2292-3.

211. 117 S.Ct. 2291-2.

212. 117 S.Ct. 2268 2275.

213. 117 S.Ct. 2293.

214. 117 S.Ct. 2293.

215. Petitioner reply brief in *Glucksberg*, 20; Petitioner brief in *Quill*, 26; Petitioner brief in *Glucksberg*, 47-9, 16; Petitioner reply brief in *Glucksberg*, 2.

216. CA et al. in *Glucksberg*, 4, 28-9; Hatch, 11; PDA, 7-13.

217. Hatch, 28; SL, Appendix A, p. 29.

218. ACLJ, 25-7; AGS, 11; AHA, 6; California et al. in *Glucksberg*, 1-2; CA et al. in *Quill*, 1, 27-9; Clarendon, 15; ELC, 9; Hatch, 10-3; LCDL, 4; PDA, 5; RT, 29-30; SL, 27; WC, 4, 13-4.

219. Clarendon, 15.

220. 117 S.Ct. 2302-3.

221. 117 S.Ct. 2265-6.

222. United States in *Glucksberg*, 10. The *Glucksberg* Petitioner argued only that this issue was being "discussed and debated throughout the nation in a variety of media" (Petitioner' brief in *Glucksberg*, 13, 14-5). Several amici debated the importance of public opinion to the debate about physician-assisted dying, with groups like CHP and the GMHC arguing that public opinion ran strongly in favor of the practice (CHP, 9; GMHC, 4-5), and the NSCI and RT contending that public opinion had to be tempered to protect the rights of the vulnerable (NSCI, 8 note 2; RT, 28).

223. ACLU, 28. The ACLU also argued that the disjunction between the letter of the law, which barred assisted suicide, and the actual functioning of the law, which operated to allow some to hasten their deaths, further undermined faith in the democratic process (28 note 39).

224. Petitioners' brief in *Quill*, 14; Petitioners' reply brief, 4 note 2, 5 note 4, 13, 15; Petitioners' brief in *Quill*, 10-1 note 5.

225. Petitioners' reply brief in *Glucksberg*, 1 note 1, 1, 4, 4 note 3-4, 8, 9 notes 8, 9; 10, 11, 11 note 11, 12-3 note 13, 14, 15, 15 note 16, 17 note 18-9, 18 note 21.

226. Respondents' briefs in *Vacco*, 3, 4, 11, 16, 17, 19, 24 note 10, 27, 32, 33-4, 36 note 14, 37, 38, 39 note 19, 40, 41, 43, 46-7, 48, 49.

227. Respondents' briefs in *Vacco*, 16, 17, 37, 38, 43, 49.

228. Respondents' briefs in *Glucksberg*, 8 note 5, 15, 18 note 10, 20-1, 20, 23, 24, 25, 26 note 14, 34, 35, 37, 39 note 26, 40, 45.

229. Respondents' briefs in *Glucksberg*, 15, 20, 24, 25, 39 note 26.

230. Respondents' briefs in *Glucksberg*, 5 note 3, 9 note 6, 14-5, 19, 21, 26 note 14, 27 note 15, 27 note 17, 29 note 18, 32 note 20, 35-6 note 24, 38, 46.

231. AHA, 2, 12-3; AGS, 3, 27; Bioethicists for Petitioners , 13, 28; CHP, 6, 26-7, 13, 10-1; FRC, 10; Hatch, 25; LCDL, 6; RT, 3-4; US, 11; USCC in *Glucksberg*, 9, 21 note 13.

232. CSH, 10 note 7; AMSA, 16 note 15.

233. AMSA, 10, 12, 14, 15 note 14, 17, 17-8 note 17, 18 note 18; ACLU,12, 13, 13 note 18, 20 note 31, 21, 21-2 note 33, 22, 26, 28 note 39; AD, 14, 15 note 6; B/R 2, 10-2, 13, 14-5; CRLP 26, 27-8; CHP, 19; CSH, 5, 5 note 3, 7 note 4, 12, 19; JW, 15, 16, 19; LP, 4, 16-7, 20, 20-1; NW, 3, 9, 10, 10 note 11, 13, 14, 16, 22; RD, 8-9, 10, 13, 16, 17, 18, 19; SFM, 24-5; SL, 3-4, 7, 9, 9 note 4, 11, 16 note 9, 21 note 12, 26 note 15, 28-9; WSPA, 15, 20 note 7, 25; 36, 13 note 16, 14 note 17, 17 note 19.

234. AMA brief cited in AMSA 12, 15 note 14, ACLU, 26, SL 3-4, 21 note 12, 26 note 15, 28-9, B/R 9; United States cited in ACLU 12, 13, 13 note 18, 20 note 31, 28 note 39; CRLP 27-8, CSH, 5, 12, LP 4, RD 8-9, 10, 13, 16, 17, 18, 19, SL 9 note 4, 21 note 12, NW 9, 13, 14, 16.

235. In *Cruzan*, Chief Justice relied on the U.S. the largest number of times (4), and Justice Brennan relied on the AMA eight times, the AAN six times, the AIDS Civil Rights Project, Concern in Dying, and the Guardian Ad Litem five times, and the Society for the Right to Die four times.

236. In *Glucksberg* and *Quill*, Chief Justice Rehnquist relied on the AMA fourteen times, the U.S. eleven times, California et al. ten times, and the AA and AGS nine times. Justice Stevens relied on the U.S. and AMA seven times and the SL six times. Justice O'Connor relied on the U.S. eight times and the AMA six times. Justice Souter relied on the AMA ten times and the U.S. nine times. Finally, Justice Breyer relied on the AMA four times, and the U.S. and NAPN three times.

5

Amici Curiae and Protected Relationships

The U.S. Supreme Court has heard two cases in the last three decades that have set the parameters for determining which relationships are entitled to heightened due process protection. In 1977, the Court decided *Moore v. City of East Cleveland* and evaluated a municipal ordinance that required that all persons living in a dwelling unit be part of a single family, but defined family in such a way that only nuclear families were granted protection and thus permitted to live together. In 1986, the Court heard *Bowers v. Hardwick* and considered a Georgia criminal sodomy statute that barred sodomy, even when engaged in by two consenting adults. Both laws were challenged under the due process clause, and the petitioners in both cases asserted that the laws violated their constitutional right to privacy. The Court struck down the city zoning ordinance in *Moore* as violative of the right to privacy, but upheld the state statute in *Bowers*, finding that there was no right to privacy at play in this case. Amicus curiae participation was quite different in these two cases: only one amicus filed in *Moore*, but thirteen filed in *Bowers*. Furthermore, the role of the amicus in *Moore* was far more muted than was the role of many of the amici filing in *Bowers*.

MOORE V. CITY OF EAST CLEVELAND

The housing code for the City of East Cleveland barred any group of persons who were not in a "family" from living together; it defined "family" as consisting of the head of a household, his or her spouse, and the unmarried children or parents of the head or spouse. The city found Inez Moore guilty of violating the ordinance, ruling that the residents of her home—her son, Dale Sr., his dependent son, Dale Jr., and her grandson, John—did not constitute a family.

Mrs. Moore alleged that the city ordinance ran afoul of her due process right to live with her family. She contended that families are entitled to heightened protection under the due process clause and that the justifications offered by the city for the ordinance were inadequate. Writing for a closely divided Court, Justice Powell struck down the zoning ordinance, finding that it violated the Moores' right to privacy and the due process right of nontraditional families to reside together. While five Justices agreed with this result, only three, Justices Brennan, Marshall, and Blackmun, signed on to Justice Powell's opinion; the fifth, Justice Stevens, penned a concurring opinion. Justice Brennan also filed a concurrence. Chief Justice Burger and Justice Stewart filed dissents in this case. There was only one amicus brief in this case, filed by the American Civil Liberties Union. Much of the debate among the Justices in this case centered on the legal arguments offered by the two sides. Unlike the other ten cases discussed in this book, there was almost no discussion of historical, sociological, scientific, or medical data. Moreover, unlike the other cases, the role of the amicus was quite limited. In fact, the ACLU brief offered very little in the way of additional information. Its role in this litigation was limited to seconding the legal arguments offered by Mrs. Moore.

Taken together, the plurality, concurring, and dissenting opinions raised a series of largely doctrinal questions: among these, whether the due process clause provides heightened protection to families and whether the state interests advanced are sufficient to outweigh the ordinance's interference with individual rights. The Justices drew heavily on the party briefs and employed not only the legal arguments, but the extralegal data provided in Moore's brief. The amicus's role in this case was muted: there were no direct cites to the ACLU's brief, and the brief provided no additional information.

The Due Process Clause and Family Relations

Moore claimed that the family had a central role in American society and that the due process clause provided heightened protection not only to nuclear families, but to extended families as well.[1] Moreover, she argued that the right to live as a family was a fundamental right and that states could interfere with this right only for a compelling reason. Moore asserted that the city had offered no such reason in this case.[2] The ACLU seconded Moore's argument without offering any additional data, noting that there was special constitutional protection afforded was to families and that this protection extended beyond nuclear families.[3] In contrast to Moore's brief, which offered not only legal arguments but also some discussion of the sociological and histor-ical foundations of family life in the United States, the city's brief relied almost exclusively on legal precedent and employed a fairly narrow reading of substantive due process in support of its position.[4]

The Justices were very selective about whose briefs they relied upon in this case: the Justices who agreed with petitioner Moore relied heavily on the arguments raised in her brief and reiterated in the ACLU brief. On the other hand, the dissenting Justices relied exclu-sively on the narrow reading of due process offered by the city. For example, Justice Powell wholly adopted Moore's reasoning, contend-ing that the strong constitutional protection of the sanctity of the family extended beyond the nuclear family and that the nation's history and traditions embraced a larger conception of family.[5] Draw-ing upon Moore's data, Justice Powell noted that the decline in the number of extended families in the United States had been of relatively recent vintage and that extended families are created "out of choice, necessity, or a sense of family responsibility."[6] His argument that extended families offered many benefits to their members was clearly articulated in Moore's brief, and he drew upon the citations in this brief to underscore his conclusions.[7] Justice Brennan's concurring opinion employed Moore's brief to an even greater extent. He em-ployed many of the same articles and books cited in her brief as support for his position that nuclear families were characteristic of white, middle-class suburbia, but that among African American fam-ilies, extended families were the norm and that East Cleveland's ordinance was evidence of "cultural myopia."[8] Over the course of three pages, he used data provided in Moore's brief at least eighteen times, employing not only her conclusions but also her citations.

Conference memoranda suggest strongly that the Justices were di-vided about how to define "family." For example, in his Memo to the Conference, the Chief Justice provided an extensive discussion of how the right to privacy was limited to "single" families, which he argued were the "most intimate familial relations" and the "basic building block [s] of society."[9] Justices Brennan and Marshall both fiercely criti-cized this formulation of the family in letters to the Chief Justice. Justice Brennan argued that the Chief Justice's "'nuclear family' concept [was] . . . completely out of touch with the reality of a vast number of relations in our society" and held out his own experience as an example.[10] Similarly, Justice Marshall contended that the Court was not bound by the narrow construction of family proposed by the Chief Justice and argued that he had "seen too many situations where a strong grandpar-ent literally held the family together . . . to agree that as a matter of constitutional law . . . the 'nuclear' family is 'the basic building block of our society.'"[11] In turn, Justice Stewart decried what he saw as the insinuations of racism and racial stereotyping in the responses of Justices Brennan and Marshall and warned that he would include his criticism in his opinion.[12]

It bears noting that the due process right was at the heart of this litigation and that the right to privacy was largely absent. While Ms. Moore argued that the privacy right extended to protecting the nurturing and rearing of children, she made this argument largely without amicus support.[13] Moreover, only Justice Stewart's concurring opinion referred to this right, holding that the right was narrow and did not apply here, since the city was not dictating whether individuals could have children or how they would be reared by their parents.[14] The reticence of Justices Powell and Brennan about founding Ms. Moore's right upon the privacy clause can be traced to discussions in the Justices' personal papers, which suggest strongly that the Justices were lukewarm about the privacy right. Chief Justice Burger argued that "constitutional privacy is limited to the most intimate familial relations" and did not extend to a mother and her grandchildren.[15] Justice Marshall was unclear about whether the right at issue was based upon association or privacy, and he sidestepped this issue in his letter to the Chief Justice.[16] Moreover, in his Memo to the Conference explaining why he had changed his mind and decided to vote to overturn the municipal ordinance, Justice Stevens clearly backed away from the privacy right, noting that a focus on Ms. Moore's property rights allowed the Court to avoid having to rely on the "open-ended concepts of liberty or privacy."[17]

The Articulated Interest for the Zoning Ordinance

The parties and the ACLU devoted considerable discussion to the reasons offered by East Cleveland for its ordinance, believing this to be an important component of this litigation. Only Justice Stevens discussed this interest, however, concluding that the city had not demonstrated why the ordinance was necessary.[18] What is interesting about this discussion is that Justice Stevens looked beyond the city's brief to examine the justifications for the ban and conducted his own research on other state cases involving "single family" zoning ordinances. In a Memo to the Conference, Justice Stevens argued that the state cases had convinced him that there was no justification for excluding "*any* related persons from living together [emphasis in original]."[19] He seems to have agreed with Moore and the ACLU that there was no reasonable relation between the means and ends, that is, between the ordinance and the city's articulated concerns about overcrowding, increased traffic, insufficient parking, or an overburdened school system. This argument seems to have influenced Justice Stevens' decision and may have been part of the reason he did not join the other Justices in what would otherwise have been a majority holding.

While only Justice Stevens examined the city's reasons for adopting the law, several other Justices did discuss the administrative remedy offered to Moore under its variance proceedings. These discussions are apparent in the Justices' opinions, as well as in the letters and conference memoranda exchanged among the Justices. East Cleveland made much of the fact that it had an "escape hatch" for persons like Mrs. Moore, arguing that since Mrs. Moore had not applied for a variance, she could not prevail in court.[20] Chief Justice Burger adopted this argument, noting that Mrs. Moore's "deliberate refusal to use the plainly adequate remedy provided by the city" foreclosed her from bringing this case to Court.[21] The Chief Justice initially thought he would write the majority opinion upholding the zoning ordinance, but the other Justices who had been in the majority before Justice Stevens switched his vote did not agree that Ms. Moore's failure to use the variance procedure was pivotal in this litigation.[22] The Chief Justice ultimately made the decision to assign the opinion to Justice Potter Stewart and to write a separate concurrence focusing on the variance issue. Obviously, when Justice Stevens changed his vote, both Justice Stewart's majority opinion and Chief Justice Burger's concurrence became dissents. Justice Brennan also discussed the "safety hatch," but he argued that its "existence . . . only heightens the irrationality" of the ordinance, an argument made forcefully by Moore.[23]

Conclusions about *Moore v. City of East Cleveland*

Thus, the amicus role in *Moore* was confined to seconding the arguments of the petitioner. The ACLU provided no new information or arguments, and the Justices relied almost entirely on the arguments of the parties. *Moore* is unusual in this study for a number of reasons, perhaps most obviously because, in this case, there was only one amicus. The decision by other potential amici to sit out this case is interesting, especially given that a number of organizations might have weighed in with discussions about the history and traditions of the American family. In *Bowers v. Hardwick*, decided nearly a decade later, many of these potential amici decided to become involved and filed briefs that provided elaborate detail about these historical and sociological foundations, along with extensive discussions of the possible policy implications of the Court's holding. All of this was notably absent in *Moore*.

Another notable aspect of the *Moore* litigation is the extent to which legal arguments dominated the debate among the Justices and the degree to which the parties were able to control this discussion. The

Justices relied almost exclusively upon the party briefs in their examination of the legal precedent surrounding the city ordinances, and the only time that a Justice looked beyond these briefs was to conduct research on a purely legal question, that is, the adjudication of other cases involving single-family ordinances in state courts. The Justices focused exclusively on the legal issues at play in the *Moore* litigation, eschewing any real discussion of larger sociological or policy issues. Moreover, the lone amicus in this case performed a very different role than did amici in other cases. Here, the ACLU "toed the party line" and did not encourage the Justices to adopt a broader approach. Amicus participation in *Moore* stands in stark contrast to participation in other cases, like *Bowers v. Hardwick,* where amici provided the Court not only with novel legal arguments, but also with extensive information about history, medicine, science, sociology, and public policy.

BOWERS V. HARDWICK

In 1986, the U.S. Supreme Court handed down its decision in *Bowers v. Hardwick* and upheld a Georgia statute barring consensual sodomy. In his majority opinion, Justice Byron White held that the statute, which criminalized anal and oral sex between consenting adults, did not violate Michael Hardwick's right to privacy, since there was no fundamental right to engage in these activities.[24] Like nearly all of the cases in this book, the Court's decision was closely divided, with a number of concurrences and dissents. Thirteen amici curiae briefs were filed in this litigation; four were filed on behalf of the petitioner, Michael Bowers, Attorney General of the State of Georgia, and nine were filed in support of respondent Michael Hardwick. These briefs focused on a range of issues, and many provided the Court with information about the historical foundations of sodomy statutes, the state's rationale in enacting the sodomy statute, and the applicability of the First, Fourth, Eighth, and Fourteenth Amendments to Hardwick's claim. Amici provided a wealth of data that bore not only on the legal questions at play but also on the larger historical, political, and social issues.

Unlike the Court's handling of *Moore,* which focused almost exclusively on the narrow due process issue, its approach to *Bowers* was multifaceted. In this case, the Justices explored both the narrow doctrinal questions and the broader extralegal issues; their opinions and intra-Court discussions are focused on five principal areas. First, the Justices worked toward determining which activities and relationships were protected under the right to privacy. Second, the Court grappled with how to determine whether a right was fundamental and deserving of heightened due process protection. Third, the Justices considered whether laws barring homosexual sodomy would be better assessed under the rational relation standard than under the compelling state interest standard. The fourth question the Justices considered was whether constitutional rights, other than the right to privacy, could be used to assess the Georgia law. Finally, the fifth question the Justices dealt with concerned the proper role of the Court in this litigation. These five questions were central not only to the Justices' opinions but to their discussions and letters to each other. By examining these opinions, memoranda, and letters, the influence of amici can be readily discerned. While there were only two direct cites to amici briefs, an analysis of amici participation in this case reveals that the influence of amici was pervasive and can be seen in the Court's discussions of the privacy right, alternative constitutional bases for engaging in consensual sodomy, and the Court's role in the larger debate about gay and lesbian rights. *Bowers* was overturned by the Court in its 2003 decision in *Lawrence et al. v. Texas*. In this case, six Justices struck down the Texas statute barring consensual sodomy that had been upheld in *Bowers*, finding that this law violated the due process liberty rights of individuals.

The Scope of the Privacy Right

In their opinions, Justices White and Blackmun were very concerned about sorting out which relationships are protected under the right to privacy. The two opinions defined the scope of this right very differently, and the amici briefs figured prominently in these opinions. In his majority opinion, Justice White contended that the line of privacy cases decided by the Supreme Court did not confer a right to privacy upon homosexual activity, and he argued that these cases established that only those activities within the protected spheres of family, marriage, and procreation would receive constitutional protection. Since Hardwick was not engaged in activities within one of the protected spheres, he was subject to state regulation of that conduct.[25] Furthermore, Justice White emphatically rejected Hardwick's argument that there was a fundamental right to engage in consensual sodomy and held that states could regulate or even bar such activity.

Attorney General Bowers was joined by a number of amici who argued that sodomy fell outside of the activities that were protected under the right to privacy was consistent with the briefs of the petitioner and various amici. In his brief, the Attorney General argued that the privacy right extended only to marital relationships, other "familial" relationships, and decisions about conception, childbearing, childrearing, and education.[26] He claimed that homosexual sodomy was "the anathema of the basic units of our society—marriage and family" and that this activity had to be kept separate from these protected relationships to preserve societal order.[27] This argument was seconded by both the Catholic League, which argued that the privacy right was "family oriented,"[28] and the Rutherford Institute, which contended that the right to privacy protected only monogamous marriage, childbearing, and the family, since these activities have "historically and traditionally been basic to our society."[29] Similarly, the Attorney General was joined by the Catholic League in arguing that there is no unlimited right to engage in sexual activities.[30] Despite the fact that the amicus Presbyterian Church, filing on behalf of Hardwick, claimed that he was not seeking "unfettered sexual autonomy,"[31] Justice White nonetheless accepted the Catholic League's contention that this case turned on whether the state was prohibited from regulating all sexual activity.

While amici Catholic League and the Rutherford Institute largely seconded the arguments of the Attorney General, amici filing on behalf of Hardwick provided arguments that were more nuanced and distinct from those of Hardwick. These alternative views of the privacy right appear to have influenced Justices Blackmun and Stevens. For example, Hardwick only briefly argued that the right to privacy extended beyond marriage, childbearing, or child rearing and protected "associational intimacy" even where it was not procreative,[32] but some amici went much further. The Bar Association of the City of New York, National Gay Rights Advocates, the American Public Health Association, the Lambda Legal Defense Fund, and the Lesbian Rights Project all argued that the right to privacy had both "decisional and spatial aspects." In particular, the Bar Association and National Gay Rights Advocates argued that there are two zones of privacy, one that protects the home and the other that protects personal decisions, and that both zones were invaded by Hardwick's arrest.[33] In his holding, Justice Blackmun largely adopted this argument, holding that the privacy right has two prongs: first, individuals have the right to make decisions about their intimate relationships; and second, individuals have the right to be secure in their homes.[34] Justice Brennan also embraced this two-pronged approach. In his Memorandum to the Conference, he argued that the case implicated both "the privacy right and the sanctity of the home."[35]

In addition to adopting amici arguments about the two-pronged nature of the right to privacy, Justice Blackmun also appears to have accepted the view of amici that all individuals, homosexual and heterosexual, have the right to make their own decisions about their activities and relationships. For example, Justice Blackmun rejected the majority's view that Hardwick's right to privacy was dependent upon whether the homosexual sodomy was within the categories of cases involving privacy doctrine. According to Justice Blackmun, these cases all turned on the understanding that individuals have a right to determine the nature of their intimate associations with others.[36] Justice Brennan's Memorandum to the Conference also reflected this belief that the privacy right protected individuals who sought to engage in consensual sodomy. He categorized the right at issue as the right to "sexual privacy" and argued that individuals could engage in sodomy regardless of their marital status or gender.[37] Both Justices Blackmun and Brennan drew heavily on the briefs of amici American Psychological Association, National Organization for Women, Bar Association, and Lambda Legal Defense Fund, who argued that the privacy right extended to marital and nonmarital heterosexual relationships,[38] and encompassed decisions about whether to engage in intimate associations[39] and, if so, with whom.[40] Justices Blackmun and Brennan also appear to have accepted the view of amici Lambda Legal Defense Fund and the Presbyterian Church that privacy is not rooted in marriage or procreation, but is instead based on the right of individuals to seek self-fulfillment.[41] Similarly, Justice Stevens' dissenting opinion asserted that these prior cases established that an individual has the right to make the "unusually important decisions that will affect his own, or his family's destiny."[42] Justice Stevens claimed that this fundamental right was at the core of the Court's privacy cases and necessitated the striking down of the Georgia statute.

In what may have been the most striking example of amici influence, Justice Blackmun adopted the view that our nation's commitment to pluralism barred statutes like the one at issue in this case. He argued that in a diverse nation like the United States, individuals may have different ways of conducting their relationships and that states should not impose on these individuals their view of the "correct" way.[43] In his call to respect pluralism, Justice Blackmun seems to have been strongly influenced by the amicus brief of the Bar Association of the City of New York, which posited that the Court's decision in *West Virginia Board of Education v. Barnette* governed the disposition of this case. The Bar Association contended that *Barnette* required that certain subjects be withdrawn "from the vicissitudes of political controversy, to place them beyond the right of majorities and officials and to establish them as principles to be applied by the courts."[44] In his conclusion, Justice Blackmun cited *Barnette*, holding that the decision establishes that individuals have the right to conduct their relationship, even if they make choices that are not popular.[45]

Furthermore, Justice Blackmun's call for tolerance was echoed in the amicus brief of the Presbyterian Church. In its brief, the Church contended that the movement toward decriminalizing sodomy, already underway in twenty-five states by 1986, evinced "a new aspiration of our people: to enforce tolerance for diversity in our society."[46] Justice

Blackmun appears to have accepted this argument in concluding that our nation has a history of "tolerance of nonconformity."[47] For Justice Blackmun, as well as the Bar Association of the City of New York and Presbyterian Church, diversity required that the Georgia statute be struck down.

Thus, in determining whom the right to privacy protects, the Justices were likely influenced not only by the briefs of the petitioner and respondent, but by the briefs of amici as well. The influence of the amici is perhaps most apparent in Justice Blackmun's holding. Justice Blackmun's view of privacy as encompassing two distinct areas, individual decision-making and the protected sphere of the home, likely drew on the briefs of the New York City Bar Association and National Gay Rights Advocates. Moreover, Justice Blackmun appears to have been influenced by amici use of various Supreme Court holdings, perhaps most significant, *Barnette*. Moreover, Justice Blackmun likely embraced the view of the New York City Bar and the Presbyterian Church that the Georgia statute violated central American tenets of pluralism and tolerance.

The Nature of Fundamental Rights

While all members of the Court agreed that the right to privacy extended to those personal rights that were fundamental, they disagreed about which rights were, in fact, fundamental. Chief Justice Burger and Justices White, Blackmun, and Stevens all applied the fundamental rights test articulated in *Palko v. Connecticut*: that is, that fundamental rights are those that are "of the very essence of a scheme of ordered liberty" and "rooted in the traditions and conscience of our people."[48] Much of Justice White's opinion and all of Chief Justice Burger's opinion aimed at determining whether the right to engage in homosexual sodomy could be deemed a fundamental right, given what both saw as "ancient proscriptions against sodomy."[49] Justices Blackmun and Stevens looked at much the same history and reached the opposite conclusion about whether the right to engage in consensual sodomy was a fundamental right. This focus on history provided the amici with a significant opportunity to provide the Justices with much-needed information.

Justice White and Chief Justice Burger contended that since sodomy was condemned as immoral for much of the last two thousand years, it could not be within the scheme of ordered liberty or fundamental rights. Both justices catalogued the proscriptions against sodomy that have existed since Ancient Greece. Justice White focused his attention on the period of time since our nation's founding, while Chief Justice Burger examined the earlier roots of antisodomy statutes. After surveying the history of these statutes in this country, Justice White concluded that the claim that the right to engage in sodomy was "deeply rooted in the Nation's history and traditions" or "implicit in the concept of ordered liberty" was "at best facetious."[50] Similarly, the Chief Justice contended that "[t]o hold that the act of homosexual sodomy is somehow protected as a fundamental right would be to cast aside millennia of moral teaching."[51] For both Justices, the lessons of history were incontrovertible: the history of the Western world was one that had uniformly condemned homosexuality.[52]

Justice White and Chief Justice Burger were likely influenced not only by the Attorney General in this case, but by various amici as well. The petitioner provided a detailed history, from the Old Testament through the present, to demonstrate that sodomy was abhorred in both the Judeo-Christian tradition and under English common law.[53] The Concerned Women Education and Legal Defense Fund and the Rutherford Institute provided a much more extensive history for antisodomy statutes, and Justice White integrated much of this history in writing his majority opinion. The Concerned Women Education and Legal Defense Fund provided a list of states with antisodomy statutes for various points in American history: at the time that the Constitution was passed; at the ratification of the Fourteenth Amendment in 1868; and in 1960, immediately prior to the first state court declaring a statute invalid.[54] This list was adopted without attribution and in its totality by Justice White, who provided an identical catalogue of states who had anti-sodomy statutes in place in 1791, 1868, and 1960.[55] The Rutherford Institute provided a rationale for using the historical method to determine the meaning of the Constitution,[56] and it warned that a failure to use this approach would shake "the very foundations of society."[57]

Justices Blackmun and Stevens rejected this view of history, contending that American legal history was not grounded in universal condemnation of homosexuality, but was instead based on a tradition of liberty and tolerance. Justice Stevens argued that the right to engage in homosexual relationships was based on the "American heritage of freedom,"[58] and Justice Blackmun focused on the fact that prohibitions against homosexuality had not been secular in nature, but religious.[59] In fact, Justice Blackmun was troubled by the religious basis of this statute, and claimed that Georgia was employing its secular power for ecclesiastical reasons.[60]

Amici appear to have played an important part in helping the Justices to understand the historical background of these statutes. While Hardwick noted simply that the existence of these laws did not, in itself, confer legitimacy upon them and reminded the Justices that twenty-six states had already decriminalized sodomy,[61] the amici went much further, providing a wealth of information about American legal history and the religious basis of these laws. In particular, Justice Blackmun was probably heavily influenced by the American Psychological Association (APA), which contended that Christianity ushered in an era of repression against homosexuality and that this statute was based solely on religious principles. The APA also suggested that the Georgia statute was "based on the disproved, religiously based concept of 'unnatural acts.'"[62]

In discussing the historical justifications for this statute, Justice Blackmun was also influenced by the briefs of the Presbyterian Church and the New York City Bar Association. Justice Blackmun contended that the Georgia statute could not be validated solely on the basis of the historical record. Blackmun implied that even if the record condemned homosexuality, this history was not sufficient to validate this statute. Employing the *exact words* of the Bar Association without directly citing its brief, Justice Blackmun claimed that "the length of time a majority has held its convictions or the passions with which it defends them" were not enough to "withdraw legislation from th[e] Court's scrutiny."[63] This ahistorical approach was embraced not only by the Bar Association, but by the Presbyterian Church, which argued that the Court should be guided by its holding in *Loving v. Virginia* and that popular views should not determine fundamental rights. Hardwick made only one oblique reference to *Loving*, noting simply that this case had struck down state antimiscegenation statutes. Justice Blackmun provided a much more extensive discussion of *Loving* and appears to have accepted the argument of the Presbyterian Church that the "parallel between [*Bowers*] and *Loving* is uncanny."[64] Justice Blackmun appears to have agreed with this amicus that popular sentiment did not define fundamental rights and that history was not the only factor to consider when determining whether a right was fundamental or implicit in ordered liberty. Interestingly, the historical basis for antisodomy laws was again the focus of the Justices' inquiry in the 2003 *Lawrence et al. v. Texas* case. In *Lawrence*, however, the majority rejected the view that these bans had been passed to specifically target gays and lesbians and instead contended that they were aimed much more generally at nonprocreative sexual activity. Thus, in *Lawrence*, the majority opinion penned by Justice Kennedy employed a much broader historical view of these statutes and embraced much of the historical analysis used by the dissenters in *Bowers*.

Thus, the Justices employed the arguments of a number of amici in assessing whether Hardwick had a fundamental right to engage in homosexual sodomy. Justice White and Chief Justice Burger relied heavily on the Attorney General's amici, who urged the Court to consider this case in light of the nation's history of antisodomy statutes. Both Justice White and Chief Justice Burger used the historical examples provided by amici, and Justice White employed the view of some amici that this historical approach was necessary to ensure societal stability and order.

Justices Blackmun and Stevens were also influenced by the arguments of amici about the nature of fundamental rights. Both agreed with amici that the lessons to be gleaned from history were not altogether clear. Justices Blackmun and Stevens contended that the guiding principles of our nation's history have been those of liberty and tolerance. These justices were also influenced by the arguments of amici who claimed that antisodomy statutes were based on impermissible religious principles and that states were not permitted to employ these principles as justification for the statutes. Finally, Blackmun accepted the contention of several amici that history is not dispositive in determining the nature of fundamental rights and that the Court may choose to ignore the historical foundations of antisodomy laws.

Evaluating the Georgia Statute under the Rational Relation Standard

Much of the Justices' opinions, as well as the briefs filed by the parties and by amici, focused on assessing whether homosexual sodomy should be protected under the right to privacy. It bears noting, however, that all of these parties, in a sense, "couched their bets" about this issue: they asked not only whether the right was fundamental, but also whether the statute could be justified if the right was found not to be fundamental. It is easier for a state to justify legislation that does not interfere with a fundamental right, because the state need show only that its statute has a rational relation to a legitimate state goal. The parties disagreed about whether public morality could provide a rational basis for the statute, and this split was apparent in both the amici briefs and the Justices' decisions.

Justice White argued fiercely that a state could base its statutes on morality. He claimed that the law "is constantly based on notions of morality" and that statutes based on such moral choices are valid under the due process clause of the Fourteenth Amendment.[65] The Georgia Attorney General contended that even in the absence of empirical proof of a cause and effect relationship, Georgia could create an antisodomy statute to guard against certain societal ills, among these, sexual promiscuity and the spread of Acquired Immune Deficiency Syndrome. While Justice White accepted the state's argument that it could base a law upon perceptions of morality, Justice Blackmun rejected this view, focusing on the fact that there was no established relationship between homosexuality and harm to the society.[66]

While Hardwick had noted simply that there was no relationship between homosexuality and the public welfare,[67] amici provided substantial elaboration of this argument. In particular, the American Jewish Congress, the American Psychological Association, the Lesbian Rights Project, and the New York City Bar Association all argued that there was no relationship between the antisodomy laws and the articulated state interest in safeguarding public health. The impact of these amici on Justice Blackmun is clear. In one of only two direct cites to amici briefs in this case, Justice Blackmun pointed to the briefs of the Attorney General and its amicus, David Robinson, on the one hand, and the amici briefs of New York, the American Psychological Association, and the American Public Health Association on the other, as evidence of the strong societal disagreement about whether homosexuality is a societal ill.[68]

In the second direct cite to an amicus brief, Justice Blackmun explicitly accepted the views of the American Psychological Association and the American Public Health Association, who both argued that the "ills" that Georgia sought to protect its citizenry against were, in fact, specious. He directly cited the APA and APHA briefs, noting that "mental health professionals did not see homosexuality as a 'disease' or disorder."[69] Justice Blackmun's conclusion that there was no consensus about whether homosexuality was "evil" was also articulated in the amici briefs of the Lambda Legal Defense Fund[70] and the Presbyterian Church,[71] which both contended that there is significant societal disagreement about sexual orthodoxy. Moreover, Blackmun's contention that religious groups did not agree about the morality or immorality of homosexuality[72] was likely buttressed by his reading of the amici briefs of the American Psychological Association and the Lesbian Rights Project, who both claimed that the statute was much more harmful than the activity it aimed at restricting.[73]

The Application of Other Constitutional Rights to Hardwick's Claims

The Justices were also concerned about the extent to which Hardwick's claims could be evaluated under constitutional principles other than the right to privacy. In particular, the Justices examined the application of the First, Fourth, and Eighth Amendments, as well as the equal protection clause of the Fourteenth Amendment. The Justices' discussions about these amendments appear in both their opinions and in the intra-Court memoranda of Justices Powell and Blackmun. Hardwick's only mention of an alternative basis for his claim was a brief discussion of how the Fourth and Fourteenth Amendments established heightened protection for privacy within the home.[74] Interestingly, most of the Court's discussion of the Fourth Amendment and all of its discussion of the Eighth and Fourteenth Amendments derived from amici briefs.

First and Fourth Amendments

There was significant disagreement among the Justices about the relevance of the Court's 1969 decision in *Stanley v. Georgia* to Hardwick's claims. Justice Blackmun argued that *Stanley*'s central holding was that one's First Amendment freedom of expression and Fourth Amendment right to be free from unreasonable search and seizure provided enhanced protection for activities in the home. In his dissent, he argued that these amendments protected Hardwick's right to engage in consensual intimate relations in his own home.[75] According to Justice Blackmun, both the site of the activity and the activity itself were protected, and the state had to meet a heavy burden to justify its regulation as it applied to Hardwick.

Justice Blackmun drew upon Hardwick's argument about the application of *Stanley* to his case, but he went beyond it, as well. While Hardwick focused on the special protection given to the home, some amici zeroed in on the activities themselves. In his brief, Hardwick argued that states had to demonstrate either a compelling government interest or legitimate governmental objective before being allowed to intrude into individuals' bedrooms,[76] but amici American Jewish Congress and National Organization for Women focused on the act of consensual sodomy, viewing it within the ambit of the *Stanley* decision. For example, the American Jewish Congress contended that *Stanley* and other Supreme Court holdings established the principle that "sexual expression and sexual intimacy depend to a large extent on where the activities take place"[77] and that strict scrutiny applied whenever the protected activities take place in the home. Similarly, NOW claimed that where consensual, private activity occurred in the home, the state's burden of justifying the regulation increased.[78]

Justice White rejected this interpretation of *Stanley*, relying largely on arguments made by the State of Georgia and seconded by amicus Catholic League. In his majority decision, Justice White wholly accepted the contention of the Attorney General and its amicus that *Stanley* did not immunize illegal activities simply because they occurred within the home.[79] Like the state, he argued that "homosexual conduct" could be analogized to adultery and incest and that the state could prohibit any of these activities.[80]

Thus, in considering the application of *Stanley* to this case, Justices White and Blackmun employed the legal arguments presented by the litigants and their friends. While Justice White accepted the state's argument that *Stanley* did not apply, however, Justice Blackmun seems to have relied heavily on the amici briefs. Like the American Jewish Congress and NOW, Justice Blackmun contended that the fact that these protected activities were engaged in at home triggered heightened constitutional protection and required that the state meet a heavy burden in justifying its law.

Eighth Amendment

In another clear example of amici influence in this case, all of the Justices mentioned the Eighth Amendment prohibition against cruel and unusual punishment in their opinions, but this provision was employed only by amici. For example, Justice White casually noted that Hardwick had not invoked a number of constitutional provision, including the Eighth Amendment and that, for this reason, the Court could not consider these provisions.[81] Justice Powell mentioned this amendment in both his Memorandum to the Conference and in his decision, contending that if Hardwick had been convicted of a single act of sodomy and sentenced to a lengthy jail term, he likely would have struck down the law as violative of the cruel and unusual punishment provision, but since there was no conviction, he viewed this provision as irrelevant.[82] Justice Blackmun provided an extensive discussion of the cruel and unusual punishment clause, contending that the state had violated this provision by punishing Hardwick solely for his sexual orientation.

The Eighth Amendment was likely "on the table" in this case only because amici Lesbian Rights Project and National Gay Rights Advocates placed it there, arguing that criminalization is an inappropriate means for discouraging homosexual activity.[83] The Lesbian Rights Project claimed that it didn't matter "how you get to be gay," but that if sexual orientation was outside of the individual's control, criminalization would be patently unfair. The Project analogized homosexuality to the Court's handling of cases involving drug addiction and alcoholism, reminding the Justices that the Court has held that incarceration of individuals solely because of their addictions is unfair. The impact of these arguments on Justice Blackmun's disposition of the Eighth Amendment claim is very clear. He agreed with these amici that the "involuntariness" of homosexuality barred criminalization, and he cited the same drug addiction cases cited by the Lesbian Rights Project as support. Like the Project, Justice Blackmun's assessment of involuntariness was based on his view that sexual orientation was not a matter of choice, or "personal election," but was "part of the very fiber of an individual's personality."[84]

Fourteenth Amendment

Similarly, the claim that the antisodomy law violated the Fourteenth Amendment's equal protection clause, an argument accepted by both Justices Blackmun and Stevens, was raised only by amici. Several amici addressed the equal protection claim, focusing on the state's repeated claim that it would prosecute only homosexual sodomy, not heterosexual sodomy.[85] NOW argued that by singling out gays and lesbians, Georgia was violating the equal protection clause, and it urged the Court to consider sexual orientation to be a "suspect class" deserving of the highest level of protection.[86] In contrast, the Rutherford Institute contended that homosexuality was not a suspect or quasi-suspect classification and that Hardwick's claim failed under equal protection analysis.[87] Justice Blackmun fully endorsed NOW's argument that the equal protection clause had been violated and hinted that sexual orientation is akin to race and should be a suspect class.[88]

Justice Stevens focused on the selective enforcement of this statute, criticizing Georgia for enforcing the antisodomy ban only against gays and lesbians and arguing that the state had to provide a neutral and legitimate reason for the selective prosecution of gays and lesbians. He rejected the state's argument that selective prosecution was justified by public morality and an abhorrence of homosexuality, challenging the state to offer another rationale.[89] In his decision, Justice Stevens seems to have drawn heavily upon the briefs of amici Lesbian Rights Project and NOW, who alone argued that the state's enforcement scheme violated equal protection. For example, the Lesbian Rights Project claimed that the statute created "built-in discrimination in law enforcement" and that "its terms beg[ged] for discrimination in enforcement, hypocrisy and arbitrariness,"[90] and NOW criticized the state's attempt "to focus on an undesirable minority group."[91]

Thus, in considering the application of the First, Fourth, Eighth, and Fourteenth Amendments to Hardwick's claims, several Justices drew heavily on legal arguments raised primarily in amici briefs. In considering the First and Fourth Amendments and the application of the *Stanley* decision, Justice Blackmun accepted the views articulated in amici briefs. Similarly, Justices Blackmun, Powell and Stevens employed arguments about the Eighth and Fourteenth amendments that were raised solely by amici.

The Role of the Court in the Debate about Anti-Sodomy Laws

While Justice White contended that this case was "not about whether state laws, or the repeal of these laws, are wise and desirable,"[92] the Justices were clearly concerned about the role of the Court in the ongoing debate about gay and lesbian rights. In discussions about the judiciary's role in this debate, echoes of arguments made solely by the amici can be clearly heard. For example, Justice White and Chief Justice Burger urged a very limited role for the Court in this debate, arguing that the Court should embrace the principle of judicial restraint and resist the temptation to interfere with the legislative authority of the State by expanding the substantive reach of the right to privacy.[93] Only the Catholic League and Rutherford Institute made this point in their briefs, warning against judicial activism and urging the Court to allow the state legislatures to make decisions about public morality.[94]

Like these amici, who urged judicial restraint, those "friends" who looked to the Court to take an active role in protecting minority rights were also heard. Justice Blackmun rejected the strict adherence to principles of judicial restraint and contended that the Court had an important role to play in cases like these that involved minority rights, and that the Court was not barred from considering state statutes simply because the statutes were long-lived or based on principles that were popular.[95] Moreover, Justice Blackmun argued that the Court had a special role in protecting individual liberties. He argued that our principles of liberty required that "a certain private sphere of individual liberty" be kept beyond the government's reach.[96] Justice Blackmun contended that majority views could jeopardize minority rights and that the Court had to ready and willing to defend these rights.[97] In framing this as an issue that pitted the majority against individual rights, Justice Blackmun appears to have been influenced by the briefs of the Lambda Legal Defense Fund and the Lesbian Rights Project, who both urged the Court to step in to protect gays, lesbians, and bisexuals from discrimination and homophobia.[98]

Coordination and Cooperation among Amici

There is some evidence of amici and party coordination in this case; however, there appears to have been less concerted action here than there has been in other cases. For example, in several instances, the parties raised a point and the point was seconded by amici. Amici seconded the Attorney General's arguments about the scope of the privacy right, the application of the rational relation test, and the applicability of the *Stanley* decision. Similarly, amici on both sides provided additional elaboration of points only briefly made by the parties. In discussing the nature of fundamental rights, the Concerned Women Legal Defense and Education Fund and Rutherford Institute provided additional information to the Court about the historical basis for antisodomy laws, as did opponents American Psychological Association, Presbyterian Church, and Bar Association. Amici American Jewish Congress, APA, Lesbian Rights Project, and Bar Association also provided substantial elaboration of Hardwick's point that there was no link between homosexuality and societal ills.

In some situations, however, the amici appear to have acted on their own and did not attempt to coordinate their activities with those of the formal litigants. Interestingly, on a number of occasions, this independence was rewarded, and the Justices adopted a position or employed some data or information provided solely by an amicus. For example, in discussing the nature of the privacy rights, Hardwick's amici went much further than he did, interpreting the right at issue as a right to engage in intimate association. The APA, NOW, the Bar Association, the Lambda Legal Defense Fund, and the Presbyterian Church all offered a much different interpretation of this right than had been presented by the litigants, and at least one Justice accepted this interpretation. Similarly, the argument of the American Jewish Congress and NOW that the *Stanley* decision extended protection not only to the home but also to activities was accepted by the Court regardless of the fact that it appeared only in amici briefs. And perhaps most tellingly, in a number of examples, the Justices considered arguments or data that appeared *solely* in amici briefs. For example, only amici raised the issue of pluralism, which was embraced by Justice Blackmun, and amici alone presented arguments and data related to the Justices' discussions about the Eighth and Fourteenth Amendments and the role of the Court in the larger debate about gay and lesbian rights. This lack of cooperation and coordination may not have harmed the friends, however, as the Justices appear to have read, considered, and adopted their arguments.

Conclusions about *Bowers v. Hardwick*

Interest groups had a significant impact on the Court's decision-making process in *Bowers v. Hardwick,* and in five separate areas, amici influenced the way the Court interpreted the right to privacy. First, the amici briefs likely had an impact on the way the Justices interpreted the scope of this right. Justice White, writing for the majority, accepted the view of the state attorney general and its amici that the privacy right was quite narrow and applied only to decisions or activities bearing on marriage, procreation, or child rearing. For Justice Blackmun, who filed a dissenting opinion, the briefs of the Bar Association, National Gay Rights Advocates, and Presbyterian Church were likely compelling and probably influenced his view that the right was much broader, encompassing not only decisional but spatial characteristics as well. For both Blackmun and the amici, concerns about the principles of tolerance and diversity were critically important.

Second, amici had a significant impact on the way the Court defined fundamental rights. Justice White appears to have been strongly influenced by the briefs of the Concerned Women and the Rutherford Institute, and in fact he adopted the list of anti-sodomy statutes provided by the CWA. Amici also had a significant impact on Justice Blackmun's view of fundamental rights. Not only did Blackmun adopt the arguments of the American Psychological Association, the Bar Association of the City of New York, and the Presbyterian Church in dealing with this question, he used the exact language of amici to describe this right.

Third, the Justices relied on amici arguments in discussing the role of the Court in cases involving the privacy doctrine. Justice White and Chief Justice Burger relied on the principles of judicial restraint articulated by the Catholic League and the Rutherford Institute, while Justice Blackmun relied on the view of the Court as protector of minority rights that was set out by the Lambda Legal Defense Fund and the Lesbian Rights Project.

Fourth, the Justices appear to have been guided by amici arguments in discussing whether the Georgia statute bore any rational relation to a legitimate state objective. Drawing heavily on amici briefs, Justice Blackmun contended that such a basis did not exist. Moreover, he directly cited the amici briefs of David Robinson, New York State, and the APA and noted that there was societal disagreement about whether homosexuality causes or contributes to social ills.

Finally, amici influence is perhaps most striking in the Justices' discussions of the First, Fourth, Eighth, and Fourteenth Amendments. These alternative bases for providing constitutional protection to consensual sodomy were articulated *only* by the amici, and were not raised by either the Attorney General or Hardwick. The amici provided an extensive discussion of *Stanley* and the First and Fourth Amendments, and they alone examined the relevance of the Eighth Amendment prohibition against cruel and unusual punishment and the Fourteenth Amendment equal protection clause. That Justices Powell, Blackmun, and Stevens seriously considered these claims in intra-Court memoranda and in their opinions strongly suggests that they read the amici briefs, considered amici arguments, and employed these arguments to reach their own decisions.

This chapter suggests that the Court was strongly influenced by interest groups filing briefs in *Bowers v. Hardwick*. For some Justices, like Justice White, amici influence was muted: Justice White appears to have drawn on those amici arguments that were also present in the state's brief. For other Justices, like Justice Blackmun, this influence was more obvious: Justice Blackmun explicitly cited amici briefs and, in some instances, used the exact words or identical case law used by amici for support. For all the Justices, the briefs appear to have been viewed as supplements to the briefs of the formal parties. Interestingly, the Justices who wrote opinions supporting Attorney General Bowers relied only on the briefs of Bowers or his amici, while those writing in support of the Hardwick relied only on his briefs and the briefs of his amici.

CONCLUDING REMARKS ABOUT CASES CONCERNING PROTECTED RELATIONSHIPS

Both *Moore v. City of East Cleveland* and *Bowers v. Hardwick* challenged the Court to clarify the test for fundamental rights and to delineate the contours of privacy analysis. The key question in both cases was of a legal nature: to what extent did the right to privacy extend to persons outside the marital relationship? In these two cases, there are hints of the Court's coming reticence about the right to privacy that became so apparent in the abortion cases of the late 1980s and early 1990s. The parties attempted to raise alternative constitutional bases in these cases; however, the privacy right remained central. Ultimately, the Court extended protection to Ms. Moore and her grandchildren, but denied it to Mr. Hardwick, and this choice likely reflected an understanding that the privacy right can be exercised only by individuals making decisions about marriage, procreation, and the rearing of children, or by traditional family groupings.

While the Court's decisions in *Moore* and *Bowers* both addressed the right to privacy, the Justices' approaches to these cases were much different. In *Moore*, the plurality, concurring, and dissenting opinions focused on more purely legal arguments. In particular, the Justices assessed whether the due process clause applied to extended families, whether there was a right of association at issue, and whether the municipality's interests in crafting this zoning ordinance outweighed the burden placed upon Ms. Moore. In considering the due process clause, the Justices limited themselves almost entirely to the case law governing the right to privacy. In *Bowers*, the Justices also examined legal questions—they pondered whether the right to privacy encompassed consensual sexual activity, whether the law would pass muster under the less rigorous rational relation test, and whether the protections against unreasonable search and seizure, cruel and unusual punishment, and unequal treatment before the law could be exercised by Mr. Hardwick. In *Bowers*, however, the Justices also considered extralegal questions, most significantly, the policy ramifications of antisodomy laws and the role of the Court in this debate. In addition, even the legal issues in *Bowers* were evaluated by considering "extralegal" information: the Justices pondered not only the case law on privacy, but the historical and sociological foundations of antisodomy laws, as well

as the policy rationales for the laws and the nation's embrace of tolerance and diversity.

The Court's willingness to look beyond the legal precedent in *Bowers*
was in part a result of amici presence in this case. Thirteen amici filed
in this litigation, and the arguments and information provided in their
briefs became a part of the Justices' intra-Court discussions and, ultimately, of their decisions. In several instances, the amici expanded upon
issues raised by the parties. For example, in attempting to determine
what the right to privacy encompasses, Justice White drew upon not
only the brief of the Attorney General, but those of amici. Similarly, in
his dissent, Justice Blackmun employed the briefs of both Hardwick and
his amici. Moreover, the amici not only expanded on the arguments of
the Bowers and Hardwick, they also raised new issues or provided
information that was not part of the record. For example, Justice White's
catalogue of state laws barring sodomy seems to have been derived
from an amicus brief, and Justice Blackmun's exposition of ecclesiastical history seems to have come from the briefs of several amici. Similarly, the discussion by Justice White, Chief Justice Burger, and Justice
Blackmun about the role of the Court in this litigation derived only from
a number of amici briefs. Furthermore, the Justices discussion of the
Eighth andFourteenth Amendments and much of their examination of
the First and Fourth Amendments derived only from the briefs of amici.

Amici in *Bowers* provided the Court with a fuller record upon which
to base their decisions, and the Justices' majority, concurring, and
dissenting opinions reflect this contribution. In contrast, the sole amicus in *Moore* provided little new information to the Court. The ACLU
brief was limited to seconding the legal arguments of petitioner Moore.
This amicus brief provided only a limited discussion of the historical
and sociological foundations of either the family or single-family zoning ordinances and provided no discussion of the policy ramifications
of the ordinance. Justice Powell's majority opinion was based almost
entirely on a recitation of the case law governing the right to privacy,
and the concurrences and dissents of all the Justices, except that of
Justice Brennan, also were focused on the legal precedent. Justice
Brennan's concurrence relied on the petitioner's brief for a discussion
of the configuration of families in American society and cited the same
articles and statistics employed in this brief. Unlike *Bowers*, and nearly
all the other cases in this book, the *Moore* Court was limited to the record
of the parties and the courts below in reaching its decision. Amicus
participation had only a negligible impact on the Justices' deliberations
or decisions. In the recent *Lawrence et al. v. Texas*, thirty organizations
filed briefs, sixteen opposing the Texas sodomy ban and fourteen supporting it. Many of these had been involved in the *Bowers* litigation
more than fifteen years before, and there was likely much more coop-

eration and coordination in *Lawrence* than there had been in the earlier case.

Together, these two cases suggest that even where the Justices are examining cases that primarily call upon them to clarify legal doctrine, amici can have an important role. In these two cases, the amici sought to shape the Justices' interpretation of the constitutional right to privacy, and the Justices seem to have relied, to a significant extent, on amici participation. As in the other cases examined in this book, some amici appear to have been more successful in seeing their arguments or data integrated into the Justices' decisions or discussions. There were no direct cites to the ACLU brief in *Moore*, and only two direct cites, both by Justice Blackmun, in *Bowers*. These two *Bowers* cites were to the briefs of David Robinson, New York State, the American Psychological Association, and the American Public Health Association. The APA and APHA were included in both cites.

There was also only limited indirect reliance on the ACLU brief in *Moore*, since this brief seconded the petitioner's brief and provided no new information. In contrast, there was significant indirect reliance on amici briefs in *Bowers*, with a number of amici providing arguments and information that was not present in either of the party briefs. Many of the thirteen amici filing briefs saw some unique aspect of their briefs appear in the Court's opinions in *Bowers*. Those who were successful were the American Psychological Association, American Public Health Association, Bar Association for the City of New York, Catholic League, Concerned Women, Lambda Legal Defense Fund, Lesbian Rights Project, National Gay Rights Advocates, National Organization for Women, Presbyterian Church, and Rutherford Institute. Even the remaining briefs of David Robinson and New York State were either directly cited by the Justices or provided a strong "second" to a party brief.

Interestingly, the Justices who upheld the Georgia law tended to employ the amici briefs filed on behalf of Georgia, while those who voted to overturn the law used the briefs filed in support of Mr. Hardwick. Unlike the abortion or assisted dying cases, there was far less coordination and cooperation among parties and amici in these two cases than in other cases. With the exception of the "seconding" of party briefs by amici, there was no evidence of a coordinated effort. There were no direct cites in the party briefs of amici arguments or data, and no citation to amici briefs by amici.

NOTES

1. Petitioner brief, 8-11.
2. Petitioner brief, 37-9.
3. ACLU brief, 6-7.
4. Respondent brief, 18.

5. 431 U.S. 494, 504.

6. 431 U.S. 504-5.

7. 431 U.S. 504-5. Justice Powell cited to the 1970 Census, as well as to two articles cited by the petitioner.

8. 431 U.S. 507-10.

9. Brennan Papers, file 453, Marshall Papers, file 194, Conference Memorandum from Chief Justice Burger, 11/22/76.

10. Brennan Papers, file 453, Marshall Papers, file 194, Letter from Justice Brennan to Chief Justice Burger, 11/23/76. Justice Brennan contended that "[o]nly a minority of American families still can afford to warehouse old people in retirement communities." He continued, "[in] urban areas a grouping such as the Moores' remains an economic necessity. East Cleveland is definitely not Fairfax County. In short, I cannot believe that the Constitution embraces purely and simply an affluent suburban concept of what is a family."

11. Brennan Papers, file 453, Marshall Papers, file 194, Letter from Justice Marshall to Chief Justice Burger, 11/23/76.

12. In a Memo to the Conference, Justice Stewart noted that "[in] view of Mr. Justice Brennan's [then] dissenting opinion, a final word is appropriate. His dissenting opinion seeks to convey the invidious message that the ordinance before us is racially discriminatory. Nothing could be further from the truth. . . ." He continued, "Mr. Justice Brennan's dissenting opinion boils down to the proposition that the people of the Negro community of East Cleveland are prevented by the Constitution from trying to escape the racial stereotypes of the 'subculture' that his dissenting opinion describes" (Brennan Papers, file 453, Marshall Papers, file 194, Memo to the Conference, 2/16/77).

13. Petitioner brief, need cite. The ACLU only very briefly mentioned this right, pp. 15-6.

14. 431 U.S. 536.

15. Brennan Papers, file 453, Marshall Papers, file 194, Memo to the Conference from Chief Justice Burger, 11/22/76.

16. Brennan Papers, file 453, Marshall Papers, file 194, Letter to Chief Justice from Justice Marshall, 11/23/76.

17. Marshall Papers, file 194, Memo to the Conference from Justice Stevens, 4/11/77.

18. 431 U.S. 516-7, 519-20.

19. Marshall Papers, file 194, Memo to the Conference from Justice Stevens, 4/11/77.

20. Respondent brief, 18.

21. 431 U.S. 521.

22. See Brennan Papers, file 453, Marshall Papers, file 194: Letter from Justice Rehnquist to the Chief Justice, 11/23/76; Letter from Justice Stewart to the Chief Justice, 11/23/76; Letter from Justice Stevens to the Chief Justice, 11/23/76.

23. Petitioner reply brief, 1, 4; 431 U.S. 512.

24. The statute at issue, Section 16-6-2 of the Georgia Code Annotated, provided that "(a) A person commits the offense of sodomy when he performs or submits to any sexual act involving the sex organs of one person and the mouth or anus of another. . . . (b) A person convicted of the offense of sodomy shall be punished by imprisonment for not less than one nor more than 20 years." Despite the fact that this statute bars all such activity among both heterosexuals and homosexuals, the State of Georgia contended that it would not use the statute to bar heterosexual sex. Thus, this case became one that was used to determine

whether gays and lesbians had a right to privacy analogous with that of heterosexuals.

25. 478 U.S. 190-191.

26. Petitioner brief, 17.

27. Petitioner brief, 23.

28. In fact, this amicus contended that "[i]t would be most difficult to discern a connection between these traditionally cherished parental interests in rearing families and the privacy right of homosexual sodomy" (Catholic League, 7).

29. Rutherford Institute, 9, 10. This amicus claimed that same-sex relationships did not serve the same purpose as marriage and could be distinguished from marriage by its "fundamental features." According to amicus, "the fundamental feature of marriage is a bilateral dependency and fidelity," while a well-known feature of the "gay sub-culture" was extreme sexual promiscuity (Rutherford Institute, footnote 9, p. 16).

30. Petitioner reply brief, 7; Catholic League, 9.

31. Presbyterian Church, 6.

32. Respondent brief, 8-9, 11.

33. Bar Association of the City of New York, 4; National Gay Rights Advocates 7.

34. 478 U.S. 204. Hardwick did discuss privacy in the home at length (pp. 14-19), but Brennan and Blackmun's "2 prong" formulation bears a striking similarity to amici arguments.

35. Brennan Papers, file 714, Memorandum to the Conference from Justice Brennan.

36. 478 U.S. 206.

37. Brennan Papers, file 714, Memorandum to the Conference from Justice Brennan.

38. American Psychological Association, 8; National Organization for Women, 6-7.

39. Bar Association, 7.

40. Lambda Legal Defense Fund, 8; National Organization for Women, 7.

41. Lambda Legal Defense Fund, 11; Presbyterian Church, 6.

42. 478 U.S. 217.

43. 478 U.S. 205-206.

44. Bar Association, 12.

45. 478 U.S. 213-214.

46. Presbyterian Church, 9.

47. 478 U.S. 214.

48. *Palko v. Connecticut* 302 U.S. 319, 325 (1937).

49. 478 U.S. 192, 196.

50. 478 U.S. 194.

51. 478 U.S. 197.

52. In his Memorandum to the Conference, Justice Powell also accepted that homosexuality had been "recognized as deviate and not in the best interest of preserving humanity" for centuries. Marshall Papers, file 393, Brennan Papers, file 714, Memorandum to the Conference from Justice Powell.

53. Petitioner brief, 15-16.

54. Concerned Women, 8-16.

55. 478 U.S. 193-194.

56. Rutherford Institute, 12.

57. Rutherford Institute, 17. In fact, the Institute claims that departure from this historical basis will erode "the stability and identity of this society," because

it is "built upon a foundation inconsistent with the legalized practice of homo-sexuality" (Rutherford Institute, 16).

58. 478 U.S. 217.

59. 478 U.S. 211-212.

60. 478 U.S. 211-212.

61. Respondent brief, pp. 8-9 note 14, p. 13 note 23.

62. American Psychological Association, 13 note 27.

63. 478 U.S. 210.

64. 478 U.S. 211, note 5.

65. 478 U.S. 196.

66. 478 U.S. 209.

67. Respondent, 20. The respondent noted that there was "no moral consen-sus" about homosexual sodomy (p. 25), and that the statute had to serve some other goal than the "bald assertion of one possible moral view" (pp. 26-7).

68. 478 U.S. 209 note 3.

69. 478 U.S. 203 note 2. The APA had asserted that sodomy was both prevalent and harmless and reminded the Court that the vast majority of mental health professionals no longer view homosexuality to be a psychological disorder (APA brief, 10-12). The APA also contended that the statute restricted individuals' freedom to express intimacy and, in so doing, threatened their mental health. In addition, the APA discussed the amicus brief of David Robinson at length. It contended that Robinson's argument, which was that AIDS provides a rationale for state laws barring homosexual sodomy, is misguided and dangerous (APA, 20-22).

70. The Fund stated that "there is no such consensus that society views same-sex intimacy and oral/anal contact as wrong" (Lambda Legal Defense Fund, 12).

71. The Church stated that there is "no contemporary consensus about the objective morality of sexual orthodoxy" (Presbyterian Church, 7).

72. 478 U.S. 211.

73. American Psychological Association, 10-12, 20-22; Lesbian Rights Project, 22.

74. Respondent's brief, 8, 15. The respondent noted that this aspect of privacy was at play in *Griswold* as well as in other traditional search and seizure cases (pp. 17, 18).

75. According to Justice Blackmun, "the right of an individual to conduct intimate relationships in the privacy of his or her own home" was at "the heart of the Constitution's protection of privacy" (478 U.S. 208).

76. Respondent, 7. This view was seconded by New York State, which argued that the home was a "zone of prima facie autonomy" and that the presumption of privacy in the home was not easily overcome (NY, 9).

77. American Jewish Congress, 7.

78. NOW, 7.

79. Petitioner, 17-8; Catholic League, 10.

80. 478 U.S. 195-196.

81. 478 U.S. 196, footnote 8.

82. Marshall Papers, file 393, Brennan Papers, file 714, Memorandum to the Conference by Justice Powell, 4/8/86; 478 U.S. 197-198. The State of Georgia decided not to pursue its prosecution of Michael Hardwick; it was Hardwick who brought the action for declaratory judgment that sparked this litigation.

83. Lesbian Rights Project, 20; National Gay Rights Advocates 12-14.

84. 478 U.S. 203.

85. The state repeatedly argued that it would not punish hetereosexual sodomy, likely because it believed that such an application of this law would run afoul of both *Griswold v. Connecticut* and *Eisenstadt v. Baird*, which created a right of privacy for married and unmarried heterosexuals.

86. NOW, 8.

87. Rutherford Institute, 19.

88. 478 U.S. 203.

89. 478 U.S. 216-220.

90. Lesbian Rights Project, 16.

91. NOW, 7.

92. 478 U.S. 190.

93. 478 U.S. 194-5; 478 U.S. 197.

94. Catholic League, 11; Rutherford Institute, 16, 18.

95. 478 U.S. 199, 210.

96. Blackmun citing *Thornburgh v. American College of Obstetricians & Gynecologists* (1986), 478 U.S. 203.

97. 478 U.S. 211.

98. Lambda, 18; Lesbian Rights Project, 18-19.

6

Conclusions

The creation of a constitutional right to privacy has provided ample opportunities and a compelling need for amici curiae participation in a range of cases involving abortion, contraception, gay and lesbian rights, family relationships, and aid in dying heard by the Court over the last four decades. This book has highlighted the amici role in an attempt to understand the impact that these briefs have had on privacy doctrine. In examining amici influence in one doctrinal area across several decades, this book has aimed at filling a gap in the literature on judicial decision-making by providing a contextual analysis of interest group influence. This contextual approach has been urged by a number of scholars and reveals how the privacy right has changed over time, in large part because of the input of interested groups and individuals filing these briefs.[1]

By examining the Justices' personal papers and opinions in eleven cases, this book finds that amici have had a subtle but profound impact on the way the Court interprets the privacy right. The influence of amici arguments and data is manifest in at least two ways: first, this influence can be discerned in the Justices' *explicit* citation to these briefs; and second, and perhaps more important, this impact is revealed in the Justices' sometimes heavy reliance upon amici data and arguments without attribution. Patterns of amici influence on the decision-making process can be discerned over time, as can amici and party coordination and cooperation. This study strongly suggests that many of the same actors participated in these cases and that the Justices seem to have been "playing favorites" among the friends, that is, relying much more heavily on some than on others.

THE INFLUENCE OF AMICI ON
THE DECISION-MAKING PROCESS

The very construction of the privacy right in *Griswold*, which employed fundamental rights language and called upon the Justices to consider the history and traditions of our polity, coupled with the increasingly technical and scientific issues raised by these cases, probably ensured that amici who were able to provide much-needed information have a role to play. For this reason, it is perhaps not surprising that amici had a significant impact on the adjudication of these cases. To discern impact, this study has aimed at identifying those instances in which the Justices relied on some legal argument or extralegal concern that is presented either solely or principally in an amicus brief. The Justices rarely cited directly to an amicus brief: in *Poe v. Ullman*, *Griswold v. Connecticut*, *Harris v. McRae*, and *Moore v. City of East Cleveland*, there were no direct cites; in the other seven cases, there were thirty-five direct cites in total, and sixteen of these were in the *Quill* and *Glucksberg* cases. Most of the direct cites were to amici briefs that provided medical, scientific, historical, or sociological evidence that the Justices relied upon to bolster their position in the case. As Table 6.1 suggests, the Justices rarely cited an amicus brief as support for their position on a purely legal question. In the nine instances in which where a Justice directly cited an amicus for some legal position, only four of these were named amici, and three of these were to the brief of the United States. This finding suggests that Justices were very selective about which amicus they cited when discussing legal issues, but it belies the heavy *indirect* reliance on many other amici briefs that provided novel legal arguments or interpretations.

TABLE 6.1   Direct Cites to Legal Arguments Found in Amici Briefs

Case Name	Justice	Amicus Curiae	Argument that Justice Cited
Roe v. Wade	Blackmun (m)	"amici" (five cites, no named amici)	Some believe fetuses have constitutional rights; some believe abortion right should be absolute; discussion of state interests.
Akron v. Akron Reproductive Health Services	O'Connor (d)	United States	The abortion regulation must impose an undue burden before strict scrutiny should be employed.
Planned Parenthood of SE Pennsylvania v. Casey	Blackmun (c/d)	United States	The United States' reliance on the rational relation standard is wrong.
Vacco v. Quill and Washington v. Glucksberg	Rehnquist (m)	United States, Not Dead Yet	There is no principled basis for limiting this right.

Similarly, as in their direct cites to amici briefs for legal arguments, the Justices relied on only a handful of friends when citing to amici on extralegal questions. There were only slightly more direct cites to amici briefs for scientific, sociological, or medical information; but still, these cites were to very few friends, and most of the citations were in the *Cruzan, Vacco,* and *Glucksberg* cases. For example, in *Cruzan, Vacco,* and *Glucksberg,* nearly all of the cited briefs were filed by well-established medical and patient advocacy groups, like the American Medical Association, Concern in Dying, the Washington State Psychological Association, and the Coalition for Hospice Professionals, or by governmental entities, like the United States or state governments. Similarly, in *Casey* and *Bowers,* the Justices relied on the Solicitor General or the American Psychological Association and American Public Health Association. Only in *Roe* did Justice Blackmun cite to the briefs of groups that were neither medical nor governmental organizations. Here, the Justice juxtaposed the positions of the American Ethical Union and the National Right to Life Commission to point out that there is disagreement about when life begins. These direct cites, however, were anomalous, and in the cases that followed *Roe,* the Justices limited themselves to direct citation of only a few professional and governmental entities, even on extralegal issues.

While there are relatively few instances of direct citation to amici briefs, however, there are many instances of indirect reliance on these briefs. In other words, on many occasions the Justices relied on some legal argument or extralegal information provided either solely or principally in an amicus curiae brief, but did not attribute these arguments or data to the amicus. This is a much more subtle form of amici influence than is direct citation, but I argue that this approach makes sense in these cases, which involved some of the most contentious issues in American politics. In many instances, the Justices needed the information provided in these briefs because they lacked the technical or scientific background to fully understand the underlying issue in the litigation. In other cases, the Justices used the briefs to supplement the legal arguments offered by the formal parties. For example, in *Poe* and *Griswold,* the Justices' papers reveal that the Justices thought that the parties' briefs were poorly written and argued and were using the amici to supplement these briefs.

The significant extent to which the Justices relied upon these briefs is apparent in Tables 6.2, 6.3, and 6.4. These tables list all the instances in which the Justices relied upon some legal argument or extralegal data that was presented solely by an amicus. Table 6.3 reveals that the Justices were far less constrained in their *indirect* reliance on amici legal arguments than they were in their direct reliance upon these arguments. While nearly all of the direct cites were to the legal arguments presented

TABLE 6.2 Direct Cites to Extralegal Arguments Found in Amici Briefs

Case Name	Justice	Amicus Curiae	Argument that Justice Cited
Roe v. Wade	Blackmun (m)	American Ethical Union et al.	There is disagreement among religions about when life begins.
	Blackmun (m)	National Right to Life Comm., "amici"	Some believe life begins at conception.
Planned Parenthood of Southeastern Pennsylvania v. Casey (1992)	Plurality (O'Connor, Kennedy, and Souter)	United States	The United States has been urging us to overturn Roe in five cases heard over the last decade.
	Plurality	"amici"	Respondent and its amici would deny that women have come to rely on Roe.
Cruzan v. Director, Missouri Dept. of Health (1990)	Rehnquist (m)	American Medical Association (AMA)	Prognosis of those in a persistent vegetative state.
	Stevens (d)	AMA (two cites)	Incidence of death in hospitals and nursing homes; with advances in medical technology, this issue will continue to be important.
	Brennan (d)	AMA	Few individuals in a pvs will recover.
	Brennan (d)	American Academy of Neurology (AAN) (two cites)	AAN's position statement that views food and hydration as medical treatment; potential impact of this case on the decision about whether to begin life-support measures.
Vacco v. Quill and Washington v. Glucksberg (1997)	Rehnquist (m)	United States, State of California (two cites)	A variety of state interests were at issue in this litigation.
	O'Connor (c)	"parties and their amici" (amici not named)	Noted the position of parties and their amici about palliative medications that hasten death.
	Stevens (c)	Washington State Psychological Association	Mental health workers can make determinations about competency.
	Stevens (c)	Coalition of Hospice Professionals	Pain can't always be eliminated.
	Stevens (c)	AMA	The AMA endorses terminal sedation.
	Stevens (c)	Bioethicists for Respondents, Ronald Dworkin	Death should be in accord with one's life story.
	Breyer (c)	AMA, Concern for Dying (each amicus two times)	Palliative care is not always available.
	Souter (c)	Members	States don't punish suicide.
	Souter (c)	State Legislators	Court should allow states to experiment with legislation.
	Souter (c)	State Legislators	Regulatory proposals presented by [this] amicus look like what's in place in the Netherlands.
Bowers v. Hardwick (1986)	Blackmun (d)	Robinson, "respondent amici"	There is societal disagreement about whether the statute addressed some societal ill (noted the briefs of the State and of

TABLE 6.2   continued

			Robinson on the one side and the briefs of Hardwick and "respondent amici" on the other).
	Blackmun (d)	American Psychological Association, American Public Health Association	The ills that Georgia sought to avoid were specious since mental health professionals did not see homosexuality as a disease or disorder.

TABLE 6.3   Indirect Reliance on Novel Legal Arguments Found in Amici Briefs

Case Name	Justice	Amicus Curiae	Legal Argument Relied upon by Justice
Poe v. Ullman	Douglas (d), Harlan (d)	American Civil Liberties Union (ACLU)	State contraceptive bans violate the marital right to privacy.
	Douglas	ACLU	The right to privacy derives from the Fourth Amendment search and seizure provision and from the right to be let alone in one's home.
	Brennan (c), Harlan	Sixty-Six Physicians	The Justices reject the view that the law violates physicians' Fourteenth Amendment right to practice medicine.
Griswold v. Connecticut	Douglas (m), Goldberg (c), Harlan (c), White (c)	ACLU	Amicus reiterates Poe argument that state contraceptive ban intrudes on marital privacy (extensive elaboration of point briefly made by Griswold).
	Douglas	ACLU	Amicus reiterates Poe argument that ban implicates the search and seizure provision (complete overlap with Griswold brief).
Roe v. Wade [amici arguments seconding those made by parties—no novel amici arguments]			
Harris v. McRae [some seconding of party brief]	Marshall (d)	National Council of Churches	Amicus provides criteria for suspect classifications (cites footnote 4 of U.S. v. Carolene Products).
Akron v. Akron Reproductive Health [some seconding]	Powell (m)	Certain Law Professors	Under rational relation, virtually any abortion regulation can be upheld.
	O'Connor (d)	Certain Religious Organizations, Planned Parenthood (PP), American College of Obstetricians and Gynecologists (ACOG)	First Amendment rights of physicians are not raised in this litigation (extensive elaboration of point briefly made by City of Akron).
	Powell	College of American Pathologists	Disposal provision is unclear and implicates the due process clause.

197

TABLE 6.3 continued

Planned Parenthood of S.E. Pennsylvania v. Casey [extensive seconding of party briefs]	Stevens (c/d)	America21	The state's interest in fetal life must be subordinate to the rights conferred by the U.S. Constitution [uses the same immigration ex.].
Cruzan v. Director, Missouri Dept. of Health [some seconding of party briefs]	Rehnquist (m)	United States	The liberty clause is at issue in this case, not the right to privacy.
	Rehnquist	United States	A state may use a heightened evidentiary standard to safeguard against abuse.
	Rehnquist	United States, Association for Retarded Citizens (ARC)	The Court should reject the equal protection argument because there are differences in the decision-making abilities of incompetents.
	Brennan (d)	National Hospice Organization (NHO), American College of Physicians (ACP)	The right to be free from unwanted medical treatment can never be outweighed by state interests.
	Brennan	American Academy of Neurology (AAN)	The state has no unqualified interest in life—if it did, it would provide life insurance.
	Brennan	American Medical Association (AMA)	Informal statements can be used as evidence of intent.
	Brennan	AAN, AIDS Civil Rights Project	Choices about death are at the core of our liberty (and uses the same cases).
	Stevens (d)	Society for the Right to Die, Wisconsin Bioethicists	The state's interest was not in life, but in "biological persistence" (the same phrase used by amici).
	Stevens	ACP, AMA, ARC	The state should use the best interest test in treatment decisions for incompetents.
Vacco v. Quill, Washington v. Glucksberg [some seconding of party briefs]	Breyer (c)	ACLU, Gay Men's Health Crisis (GMHC)	The right is characterized as "death with dignity."
	O'Connor (c), Souter (c)	Bioethicists for Petitioners (B/P), Americans for Death with Dignity (ADD)	The right is characterized more narrowly than suicide or the right to die.
	Rehnquist (m)	American Hospital Association (AHA), American Center for Law and Justice (ACLJ), the State of California, Catholic Medical Association (CMA)	The Court should create no new substantive due process protections.
	O'Connor, Stevens (c), Breyer	U.S., Council for Secular Humanism (CSH), Center for Reproductive Law and Policy (CRLP), Surviving Family Members (SFM), J.Whitaker, M.D.	Pain and suffering are the linchpin for assessing whether due process liberty is implicated, and there is a strong due process interest in avoiding pain and suffering.

TABLE 6.3   continued

	Stevens	U.S., State Legislators (SL)	The patients here had a stronger liberty interest than did Cruzan because they were suffering pain.
	Souter	U.S., CRLP, AMA	There is a parallel between abortion law and assisted suicide.
	Rehnquist	American Geriatrics Society (AGS), American Suicide Foundation (ASF), B/P, U.S. Catholic Conference (USCC), ADD, U.S., Catholic Health Association (CHA), CMA, Members of the NY and WA State Legislatures (Members)	The equal protection clause is not implicated in these cases because there are real differences between those seeking to terminate life support and those seeking assistance in dying, particularly in their intent (extensive elaboration of point made briefly in states' briefs).
	Rehnquist	American Association of Homes and Services for the Aging, AGS, AHA, AMA, B/P, CA, Clarendon Foundation, CMA, Medical Society of NJ, U.S., USCC	Provides a catalogue of state court holdings distinguishing between cases involving the withholding or withdrawing of treatment and physician-assisted suicide.

Moore v. City of East Cleveland [extensive seconding of party briefs—no novel amici arguments]

Bowers v. Hardwick [some seconding of party briefs]	Blackmun (d)	Association of the Bar of the City of NY (Bar), National Gay Rights Advocates (NGRA)	There are two zones of privacy.
	Blackmun, Stevens (d)	Bar, American Psychological Association (APA), National Organization for Women (NOW), Lambda Legal Defense and Education Fund (Lambda)	The right to privacy encompasses the decision to engage in intimate relationships.
	Blackmun, Stevens	Lambda, Presbyterian Church (PC)	The right to privacy is based on the right of individuals to seek self-fulfillment.
	Blackmun	PC	Discusses *Loving v. Virginia* and the antimiscegenation statutes.
	White (m), Blackmun	American Jewish Congress, NOW, State of NY, PC	Application of the First Amendment freedom of expression and Fourth Amendment search and seizure provision (extensive elaboration of point made briefly in Hardwick's brief).

TABLE 6.3   continued

Blackmun	Lesbian Rights Project (LRP), NGRA	Application of the Eighth Amendment cruel and unusual punishment provision.
Blackmun, Stevens	Rutherford Institute, LRP, NOW	Application of the Fourteenth Amendment equal protection provision.

by the United States, the Justices indirectly relied upon novel argu-ments offered by a variety of friends, including not only governmental entities but also professional organizations, public interest groups, patient advocacy agencies, and religious organizations. These amici provided the court with legal arguments that were not present in the briefs of the formal parties but that appear to have been compelling for at least some Justices. In addition, in a number of cases, the amici seem to have played an important "seconding" function as well: even though their arguments were not novel, they may have helped to provide greater support and legitimacy for legal arguments provided in party briefs. This central finding, that the Justies embraced legal arguments presented solely by amici, is fascinating and runs counter to the princi-ple of justiciability, which strongly suggests that judges and justices should limit themselves to considering only those legal arguments presented by the formal parties.

The Justices' indirect reliance on the legal arguments presented in the amici briefs is striking, but it is their reliance on extralegal data that is the most profound. While the Justices directly cited to the briefs of only a few professional and governmental entities who provided this infor-mation, they relied extensively, albeit indirectly, on many other friends for scientific, medical, sociological, and historical data and insights. Table 6.4 suggests that the Justices relied heavily upon the information provided by a significant number of amici and that much of this infor-mation was central to their disposition of this case. It bears noting that, in some cases, the amici function was limited to elaborating upon or seconding points made by the formal parties. For example, in *Griswold* and *Casey*, there appears to have been extensive coordination of party and amici efforts: these briefs paralleled each other, often employing identical data. In other cases, perhaps most notably, the early abortion cases and the assisted dying cases, the Justices relied very heavily on the information presented by amici, often using data provided by a myriad of groups, including not only mainstream medical and legal organizations, but civil rights and women's rights groups, patient ad-vocacy groups, and religious groups. While the Justices relied solely on governmental entities or recognized experts in their direct citations to amici arguments or data, they appear to have read, and been influenced by, a much broader group of "friends."

Over time, the extralegal data found in the amici briefs appear to have become even more important to the Justices. In the early cases, most amici briefs were filed by public interest law firms or advocacy groups, and most of the party and amici briefs were concerned with legal or doctrinal issues. For example, in the 1960 case, *Poe v. Ullman*, the ACLU advanced the novel argument that the right to privacy had a constitutional basis and that state contraceptive bans ran afoul of marital privacy. This argument was incorporated into Griswold's party brief in *Griswold v. Connecticut*; in this 1965 case, the ACLU powerfully argued that these laws must be struck down because of their interference with the privacy right. Similarly, the adjudication of *Roe v. Wade* in 1973 focused on establishing a legal basis for the privacy right as it applied to abortion, and a number of patient advocacy groups filed in this case to argue in favor of this legal right. The amici continued to argue for, or against, the privacy right in all of the cases heard in the 1980s and 1990s; in fact, the amici probably played an important role in shaping the privacy right. By the 1980s, however, amici attention was increasingly devoted to providing the Justices with information about medicine, technology, sociological trends, and the historical record. Some of this focus on the extralegal record was an outgrowth of the legal standard itself: *Griswold* used fundamental rights language in establishing the right to privacy and, in so doing, called upon the Court to examine the "history and traditions" of the polity whenever the privacy right was employed. Some of the increased reliance on amici was also the result of the increasingly technical and scientific issues raised by abortion regulations like those promulgated in *Akron* and in *Casey* and in the aid in dying cases. In fact, the lion's share of the amici briefs filed in this study were in these five cases, and it appears that amici played an important role in providing the Court with information, particularly in the assisted dying cases.

Ironically, while the Justices probably had a greater need for this information in the 1980s and 1990s, the increasingly contentious atmosphere surrounding privacy cases may have made them less willing to explicitly cite to the briefs for the legal arguments and extralegal data they contained. This was probably most apparent in the wake of *Roe*, when the Justices found themselves at the vortex of an increasingly vicious debate about abortion. It is likely that after *Roe*, the Justices became increasingly wary about being perceived as open to interest-group lobbying on this issue, and one could reasonably expect that there would be less citation to briefs filed by interest groups in these cases. Clearly, this expectation is borne out in the abortion and gay and lesbian rights cases. These expectations are borne out in the abortion

TABLE 6.4 Indirect Reliance on Extralegal Data Found in Amici Briefs

Case	Justice	Amicus Curiae	Extralegal Data Found in Amicus Brief
Poe v. Ullman	Frankfurter (m), Warren (c), Brennan (m)	Planned Parenthood (PP)	The Justices rejected the amicus argument that state contraceptive bans have no basis in medicine, public morality, or religious belief, arguing that the Court didn't have enough information to make this assessment.
Griswold v. Connecticut [extensive seconding of information in party briefs]	Black (d)	Adams et al.	Reference to Gallup polls and to public opinion.
Roe v. Wade	Blackmun (m)	California Committee to Legalize Abortion (CCLA), National Legal Program on the Health Problems of the Poor (NLP), PP, ACOG	There is vigorous societal debate about abortion laws (discusses impact of these laws on population growth, racial equallity, and poverty).
	Blackmun	ACOG, Certain Physicians, Professors and Fellows of ACOG, NLP, National Right to Life Committee (NRLC), New Women Lawyers (NWL), CCLA, Texas Diocesan Attorneys (TDA)	At common law, there has always been a distinction between quick and unquick fetuses (Roe repeatedly uses the ACOG brief to discuss this distinction).
	Blackmun, Douglas (c)	ACOG, American Ethical Union, NWL, SCAA, American Association of University Women	Substantial burdens are imposed on all women by pregnancy.
	Blackmun, Douglas	ACOG, PP	Early abortion is safer than childbirth—calls into question the state's articulated interest in maternal health and life (Roe relied extensively on ACOG's and PP's analysis—on this point, the briefs are *identical*).
Harris v. McRae	Backmun (d), Brennan (d), Stevens (d)	NOW, NY	Abortion "choice" is illusory for poor women if they cannot afford to access abortion (extensive elaboration on point made briefly by McRae).
	Brennan, Marshall (d)	Association of Legal Aid Attorneys of the City of NY (Legal Aid), NOW	Indigent women are in a position of relative powerlessness.
	Brennan	National Council of Churches of Christ, Legal Aid, NY	The Hyde Amendment is an attempt to override *Roe*.

TABLE 6.4 continued

City of Akron v. Akron Reproductive Health	O'Connor (d)	U.S.	Federal courts should defer to state legislatures because legislatures have superior fact-finding abilities.
	Powell (m)	ACOG, American Public Health Association (APHA), Certain Law Professors (CLP)	Physician has a key role to play in effectuating the abortion right, and we must rely on standards of medical practice and on physician's judgment.
	Powell	APHA, Committee for Abortion Rights and Against Sterilization Abuse, National Abortion Federation (NAF), NOW	The ordinance imposes a heavy burden on women's access to abortion.
	O'Connor	ACOG	Medical advances make it possible that fetuses may be viable before the third trimester.
	Powell	ACOG, APHA	Abortions can be performed as safely in clinics as in hospitals.
	Powell	ACOG, APHA, California Women Lawyers (CWL), CLP, NAACP Legal Defense and Education Fund, NOW, PP	Regulations make abortions more costly and less accessible (extensive elaboration of point made briefly by clinic).
	O'Connor	ACOG	ACOG would sanction some mid-third trimester abortions and re-quire that they be performed in a hospital.
	Powell	ACOG, PP, NAF, Certain Religious Organizations	Informed consent provision does not present accurate information.
	Powell	ACOG, American Psychological Association, PP, NAF, CWL, NOW	Physician counseling and informed consent interfere with the physician-patient relationship and have negative effects—instead, we should use the ACOG/APHA/NAF counseling standards (extensive elaboration of point made briefly by clinic).
	Powell	ACOG	The waiting period is not neces-sarily in the patient's best interests.

Planned Parenthood of S.E. Pennsylvania v. Casey [extensive seconding of party data by amici suggests close party/amici cooperation—no novel amici arguments]

Cruzan v. Director, Missouri Depart-ment of Health	Rehnquist (m)	Free Speech Advo-cates, SSM Health Care System (SSM)	Use the standard that ensures that the individual's treatment decisions will be respected.
	Brennan (d)	American College of Physicians (ACP), AMA, American Hospital Association (AHA)	One's spiritual life informs his/her decision about how to die.

TABLE 6.4   continued

Brennan	AIDS Civil Rights Project (AIDS)	Statement about how death and dying should be defined with a lengthy quote about how medical technology has influenced the experience of death (quote without attribution).
Brennan	AMA	The state is using Cruzan as a symbol.
Brennan	Society for the Right to Die	Cruzan is living a degraded existence—(discusses statistics about the number of deaths in hospitals and nursing homes and the OTA quote about the timing of death).
Stevens (d)	United Methodist Church (UMC), ACP, Abrams et al., Burgoon	Life should be defined to encompass not only one's physiological condition, but the presence of one's spirit and one's activity matrix.
Stevens	UMC, SSM, NHO, Death is part of the cycle of life.	
Brennan	American Academy of Neurology (AAN), AMA	PVS patients are devoid of thought, emotion, and sensation.
Rehnquist	US, AMA	There is variation among states about how the decision to terminate treatment should be made for incompetents.
O'Connor (c), Scalia (c)	US, Association for Retarded Citizens, Focus on the Family, National Right to Life Committee	There is no consensus about whether courts should be involved in treatment decisions, and for this reason, states should be given a wide berth in crafting procedures.
Rehnquist	Milwaukee District Attorney's Office	Not all families are as loving as the Cruzans, so we must be careful of allowing families to make the decision to terminate treatment.
Brennan	AIDS	Lengthy quote (without attribution) about how the Missouri rule transforms human beings into "passive subjects of medical technology."
Brennan	Concern for Dying (CFD), Society of Critical Care Medicine (SCCM)	Concern about how medical technology is encroaching on individual rights.
Brennan	AIDS, AAN, AMA, Burgoon, CFD, SCCM	Concern about how this case will affect medical practice and undermine the willingness of physicians and families to begin treatment (may have used lengthy quote from *Olmstead* present in ACP's brief without attribution).

TABLE 6.4 continued

Vacco v. Quill and *Washington v. Glucksberg* [some seconding of party data]	Rehnquist (m)	Clarendon Foundation (CF), American Center for Law and Justice (ACLJ), American Association of Homes and Services for the Aging (AA), AMA, State of CA, Catholic Health Association (CHA), Catholic Medical Association (CMA), Institute for Public Affairs of the Union of Orthodox Jewish Congregations of America (IPA), Legal Center for Defense of Life (LC), National Legal Center for the Medically Dependent and Disabled (NLC), National Spinal Cord Injury Association (NSCI), Rutherford Institute (RI), U.S. Catholic Conference (USCC), Wayne County (WC)	Look to the history of our common law (thirteenth century forward) to determine whether assisted suicide bans are within our legal traditions, history, and practices.
	Stevens (c)	U.S., National Women's Health Network (NW), State Legislators (SL), Center for Reproductive Law and Policy (CRLP)	Look at history most broadly: there are no settled limits in fundamental rights jurisprudence, and rights are not frozen in their historical context.
	Souter (c)	NW, Sen. Hatch et al., 36 Religious Organizations (36), ACLU, WC	Look at *Poe v. Ullman* to assess due process right; look at eighteenth century forward.
	Breyer (c), Stevens	American Geriatrics Society (AGS), AMA, American Medical Student Association (AMSA), Coalition of Hospice Professionals (CHP), SL, Council for Secular Humanism (CSH), 36, Concern for Dying (CFD),	Discussion about whether palliative care is available and/or inadequate—note that all amici and Justices rely heavily on the New York State Task Force Report on Death and Dying.

TABLE 6.4 continued

	National Hospice Organization (NHO), LC, National Association of Pro-Life Nurses (NAPN), International Anti-Euthanasia Task Force (IAE), USCC	
Stevens	Bioethicists for the Respondents (B/R), CMA	The state's interest in life is not unqualified; for example, states employ capital punishment.
Rehnquist	AA, AGS, Agudath Israel (AI), CA, Evangelical Lutheran Church (ELC), Family Research Council (FRC), Members of the NY and WA State Legislatures (Members), Naional Catholic Office for Persons with Disabilities (NCOP), National Legal Center for the Medically Depen-dent and Disabled (NLC), NSCI, Not Dead Yet (NDY)	States can reject a "sliding scale" approach to rating the quality of life.
O'Connor, Souter	US, CA, NDY, CFD, CF, NCOP, Project on Death in America (PDA), USCC	States are justified in banning assistance in dying out of a fear of error about terminality, pain, and competency (petitioners cited the AGS and NHO) (extensive elaboration of a point made briefly by doctors and patients).
Rehnquist, O'Connor, Souter, Stevens	AA, CHA, ELC, Law Professors (LP), US	Physicians can subtly pressure their patients to choose death.
Rehnquist, O'Connor, Souter, Stevens	AMA, District Attorney of Milwaukee County (DA), NAPN, U.S.	Incidence of elder abuse.
Rehnquist, O'Connor, Souter, Stevens	American Life League (ALL), AGS, AMA, IAET, NAPN, NDY, PDA	Cost considerations may color decisions to hasten death.
Rehnquist	AMA, NAPN, AA, Christian Legal Society (CLS), CMA, ELC, FRC, LCDL, Medical Society of NJ (MSNJ), RI, US	Allowing physician-assisted suicide undermines the integrity of the medical profession.

TABLE 6.4   continued

	Stevens, Souter	ACLU, ADD, AMSA, B/R, CHP, SL	The physician may have an obligation to provide aid in dying.
	Souter	SL	The argument that medical ethics bars physicians from providing aid in dying has no greater purchase than in abortion debate.
	Rehnquist, Souter	SL, AGS, AMA, ASF, IAET, LCDL, NDY, NSCI, US, USCC	The Netherlands example highlights the problems of allowing assisted dying.
	Rehnquist, O'Connor	U.S.	We should rely on the democratic process to arrive at a solution.

Moore v. City of East Cleveland [extensive seconding of party data—no novel amici arguments]

Bowers v. Hardwick	Blackmun (d)	Association of the Bar of the City of New York (Bar)	Our commitment to pluralism bars statutes like this; employs the *Barnette* decision as evidence of this commitment.
	Blackmun	Presbyterian Church	We need to tolerate diversity.
	Blackmun	American Psychological Association (APA)	Over the last 2000 years, religious entities have barred homosexuality, but secular powers have not—this statute is an unconstitutional use of a state power to achieve a religious purpose.
	Blackmun	Bar, Presbyterian	History not sufficient to validate statute—and the "length of time" that such a statute is in existence, or the "passion of conviction" of the statute's supporters is not enough to validate it (Justice used identical words to those used in Bar's brief, without attribution).
	Blackmun	Bar, Lambda Legal Defense and Education Fund (Lambda), Presbyterian, American Jewish Congress (AJC)	This statute criminalizes activity that is widely seen as harmless, and there is no consensus that homosexuality is evil.
	White (m), Burger (c)	Catholic League for Religious and Civil Rights, Rutherford Institute	The Court should not interfere with legislative judgment.
	Blackmun	Lambda, Lesbian Rights Project	The Court must protect minority rights.

and gay and lesbian privacy cases, where the Justices relied heavily on information provided only in the amici briefs, and sometimes even "lifted" whole sections of these briefs, but did not provide any citation. Furthermore, the heavy direct reliance on amici briefs in the assisted dying cases was matched by extensive indirect reliance as well, with the Justices drawing heavily upon these briefs without citing to them.

In some cases, the Justices relied on only a few briefs. For example, in *Poe*, the ACLU had a prominent role, but the other amici made relatively insignificant contributions. The same can be said of *Harris*, where the Justices employed the briefs of the Association of Legal Aid Attorneys, the Council for Churches of Christ, NOW, and the State of New York, but disregarded the arguments presented by the other seven "friends." Similarly, in *Moore*, *Griswold*, and *Casey*, there was considerable overlap between the party and amici briefs, and so the Justices were not presented with novel amici arguments or data. In contrast, the Justices made use of all or nearly all of the briefs in *Bowers*, *Vacco* and *Washington* and in many of the briefs in *Roe*, *Akron*, and *Cruzan*.

Given the literature on judicial decision-making, we would have expected that the Solicitor General would have played an important role in these cases. The United States filed in four cases: *Akron*, *Casey*, and the aid in dying cases. Its influence in these cases, however, was variable. The Solicitor General's brief in *Akron* was perhaps its greatest success: it advocated the use of an undue burden standard for determining whether a regulation violated the right to abortion, and this standard was later adopted by a plurality of the Court in *Casey*. The brief of the United States was cited by Justice O'Connor favorably in her *Akron* dissent. By the time *Casey* reached the Court, however, Justice O'Connor and other members of the Court seem to have grown weary of the Solicitor General's lobbying effort and expressly rejected his office's repeated attempts to convince the Court to overturn *Roe*. The brief of the United States was also criticized by Justice Blackmun in this case, who argued that the Solicitor General's approach to determining fundamental rights and its reliance on the rational relation standard were wrong.

In the aid in dying cases, the Solicitor General's impact was also apparent. In *Cruzan*, Chief Justice Rehnquist relied on the legal arguments made by the United States with regard to the clear and convincing evidence standard. Similarly, both Justices O'Connor and Scalia echoed the United States' argument that courts should allow legislatures significant discretion in crafting procedures for making treatment decisions on behalf of incompetents. In contrast with the later abortion cases, however, the role of the Solicitor General in all of the assisted dying cases, and in particular in the 1997 cases, was quite prominent. Even though there were few direct cites to this brief in *Vacco* and *Washington*, the argument of the United States that one could have a liberty interest in avoiding severe pain and suffering was at the heart of the concurring decisions of Justices Stevens, O'Connor, and Breyer and may form the basis for a right to hasten one's death in the future. Similarly, the brief of the United States was relied on extensively by Justice Stevens, who argued that rights were not frozen in their historical context, and by Justice Souter, in his discussion of the parallels between abortion and aid in dying. In addition, the Chief Justice's discussion of the state interests at play in this litigation appears to have derived from the brief of the United States. Finally, the argument of the Chief Justice and Justice O'Connor that we should rely on the democratic process for resolution of this issue likely drew upon the Solicitor General's argument. Thus, the United States has played an important role in the abortion and assisted dying cases, although the Justices have not always accepted its arguments with absolute equanimity. Moreover, its influence appears to have been more long term in these cases: it planted the seed for the undue burden standard in *Akron*, which was later adopted in *Casey*, and it may have suggested an approach to future aid in dying cases that focuses on the degree of pain and suffering endured by individuals suffering from terminal illnesses.

For many of the same reasons that we would expect the Solicitor General to play a prominent role in these cases, we would expect that other governmental entities would occupy a central place. As some scholars have noted, amici briefs provide precise information to the Justices about the preferences of other actors, among these, Congress, the President, and state officeholders.[2] It bears noting that in some of these cases, members of Congress and the state legislatures played an important role, but participation in these cases was variable and so too was influence. For example, the role of state office holders was apparent in *Harris*, where New York State filed, and in *Casey*, where New York filed along with Representative Edwards et al. Similarly, in *Washington* and *Vacco*, California, State Legislators, Members of the New York and Washington Legislatures, and Orrin Hatch et al. all played an important role.[3]

In addition to the Solicitor General and other federal and state officeholders, we might have expected that organized interests would have a notable impact on the Court's decisions. While most scholars had assumed that the enhanced lobbying resources of these groups would carry over into the courts,[4] this is the first study that demonstrates the heightened influence of these groups. This study provides a foundation for these conclusions and suggests strongly that powerful, largely mainstream nongovernmental organizations tend to succeed in Supreme Court litigation. Certain groups were clearly more successful in these cases. For example, the ACLU, Planned Parenthood, the American

College of Obstetricians and Gynecologists, the AMA, the American
Public Health Association, and NOW figured prominently in these
cases and saw their arguments and data employed by the Justices.
Where other organizations offered arguments or information that conflicted with what was in the briefs of these amici, they were ignored.
For example, there was conflict among the amici in *Roe* about whether
early abortions were safer than childbirth, and the Justices accepted the
arguments of the American College of Obstetricians and Gynecologists
and Planned Parenthood that early term abortions were safer and
disregarded the arguments of Certain Physicians of American College
of Obstetricians and Gynecologists and Sassone, which contended that
abortion often resulted in serious medical complications for women.
Similarly, arguments by Certain Physicians about the "humanness" of
the fetus were rejected, and the arguments of the National Legal Program and Planned Parenthood, among others, that fetuses were not
entitled to legal protections were accepted by the Justices.

In *Cruzan*, the Justices took sides with the AAN and AMA against
Doctors for Life, the American Academy of Physicians and Surgeons,
the U.S. Catholic Conference, the Catholic Guild, the United States, and
the Milwaukee District Attorney and accepted that food and hydration
constituted medical treatment and not "ordinary care." In *Washington*
and *Vacco*, the Justices also resolved a number of conflicts by siding with
mainstream medical organizations against less mainstream medical
groups or nonmedical groups. For example, the Justices sided with the
American Geriatrics Society, American Suicide Foundation, and others
against Choice in Dying and Surviving Family Members in their disagreement about whether there are real differences in intent among
those who seek to withdraw life support and those who seek to hasten
their deaths by ingesting prescription medication. Moreover, the Court
accepted the views of a number of more mainstream organizations, like
the American Association of Homes and Services for the Aging, the
American Geriatrics Society, and the American Medical Association,
that states would not be able to limit a right to hasten one's death and
rejected the views of other groups, like the American Medical Student
Association, the Coalition of Hospice Professionals, and others, that
such a right could be contained.

Thus, it appears that when faced with disagreements over factual
issues, the Justices "played favorites" and accepted the views of larger,
more powerful friends, while ignoring conflicting data offered by their
opponents. For this reason, where an issue fell squarely within the
recognized expertise of an amicus, the Justices were much more likely
to use the expert amicus to resolve it than they were to rely on a less
well-known nemesis. This is an important finding, because it suggests
that the Justices will employ these amici as gatekeepers in areas where

there is disagreement or uncertainty over some factual issue. While there is pluralism on the Court, in that many groups have a chance of seeing their arguments or data show up in intra-Court discussions or in the Justices' opinions, the Justices tend to rely on mainstream organizations to resolve factual disagreements.[5] In addition, the Justices' heavy reliance on nonparticipant "amici," like the American Bar Association, whose Uniform Abortion Act appears to have provided the trimester approach adopted by Justice Blackmun in *Roe*, and the New York State Task Force *Report on Death and Dying*, which was cited repeatedly in *Washington* and *Glucksberg*, suggest the importance of input by expert groups.[6]

COOPERATION AND COORDINATION AMONG PARTIES AND AMICI

In addition to highlighting the significant impact that amici have had on the adjudication of privacy cases, this study brings into sharp focus the patterns of amici and party cooperation that have become apparent over the course of the last four decades. Many of the groups under examination here participated in a number of cases and, over time, likely developed an understanding of which arguments and which amici tended to be heard by the Justices. This pattern of cooperation is apparent as early as the *Griswold* case, in which the arguments of Griswold and her amici matched almost perfectly, and where each repeatedly cited and provided elaboration of each other's arguments. In *Roe*, there is even more compelling evidence of cooperation, as the amici provided extensive discussion of points only briefly mentioned by the petitioner. The *Roe* petitioners made extensive use of the briefs of the American College of Obstetricians and Gynecologists, Planned Parenthood, the American Bar Association, and New Women Lawyers and repeatedly cited to these sources. This elaboration function was apparent in amicus participation in *Akron* and *Casey* as well, and in these cases, as in *Roe*, the formal parties made use of standards or statements articulated by prominent amici like ACOG, the APHA, and the NAF. In *Cruzan*, the amici made many of their arguments independently of the parties, but in the 1997 physician-assisted suicide cases, there was a coalescing of amici and party arguments. The sole amicus participating in *Moore* simply seconded the party's argument and provided no novel arguments or data. But in *Bowers*, the amici took a much more independent role, and provided information and arguments distinct from those offered by the parties.

These cases suggest that amici and parties are less likely to cooperate in the cases that first bring a case to Court: for example, amici cooperation and coordination was noticeably absent in *Poe*, but apparent in *Griswold*, and there was much more coordination in *Akron* and *Casey* than there was in either *Roe* or *Harris*, which raised novel issues. Similarly, there was less coordination in the 1990 *Cruzan* case than there was in the 1997 *Washington* and *Vacco* cases. Finally, in *Bowers*, the first case to consider whether there was a privacy right to engage in sexual activities with a same-sex partner, there was relatively little cooperation.

Thus, where litigation is ongoing, as it was in the abortion debate, groups may learn to cooperate. In addition, this study suggests that in ongoing litigation, amici and parties learn which amici are likely to be heard by the Court. For example, by the time *Casey* was heard, participants in the abortion controversy were able to identify which amici might be most helpful or most damaging to their cause, and they expended significant energies trying either to shore up or to undermine these briefs. The same is true of *Washington* and *Vacco*; by 1997; the parties and amici concentrated on drawing the Justices' attention either toward or away from the briefs of amici who were perceived to be influential.

Moreover, the ability of parties and amici to coordinate their activities likely became more important between 1960 and 1997. First, the issues before the Court became increasingly complicated, and the amici and parties were called upon to present highly technical data. The *Poe* Justices were concerned primarily with a legal question: that is, was there a right to privacy that could be read as encompassing the procreative activities of married couples? By the time the Court heard the physician-assisted suicide cases in the 1997, the Justices had to consider a dizzying array of medical and scientific issues, most of which could not be "unbundled" from the privacy question.

Second, this heightened complexity corresponded with a change in the Supreme Court rules governing the filing of briefs. In 1984, the Court adopted a new rule that limited party briefs to fifty pages and amicus briefs to twenty-five pages. In the earlier cases, the parties and their amici had the opportunity to present every possible issue in their briefs, but after 1984, they were forced either to narrow their briefs or to parcel out issues to their "friends." This rule change intensified the need for cooperation and coordination and may have compelled the parties and their amici to work more closely together. This heightened coordination of party and amici briefs may have fundamentally altered the function of the amicus brief and placed the amici more squarely within the adversary model advocated by Felix Frankfurter in 1957.[7] While the briefs do provide information, consistent with Hugo Black's view of the amici function, they are less neutral now than they ever have been and are more likely to be friends of the parties than friends of the Court. Partisanship, not impartiality or neutrality, is now the most apparent characteristic of amici participation in Supreme Court litigation.

THE FUNCTION OF AMICI BRIEFS
IN PRIVACY CASES

A number of legal and extralegal factors have militated in favor of an expanded amici role in these cases. First, the nature of the privacy right, with its focus on fundamental rights, fairness, and justice, itself heightened the potential for amici influence. Second, the Court's willingness to focus on the underlying extralegal questions as a way of resolving the legal issue necessitated an informed and involved amicus "bar" in these cases. The law clearly mattered in these cases, but so too did medical technology, sociological trends, and our historical foundations.

The Continuing Importance of the Legal Model:
How the Right to Privacy Shaped Amici Participation
in These Cases

The right created by the *Griswold* Court was based upon natural law and notions of fairness that reached beyond the text of the Constitution. The penumbral approach adopted by Justice Douglas required that Justices think about the broader notions of justice and individual rights that were at the heart of the Bill of Rights. This approach invited the Justices to eschew the role of technician, mechanically applying the rules that had been arrived at before, in either the case law or the statutory law, and to see themselves as artisans, crafting decisions that were in keeping with the traditions and values that underlay the Constitution. Once they moved beyond the narrow legal questions at play in this case and the cases that followed, the Justices were faced with a tremendous challenge. They had to determine what was "fair" and "just" and in keeping with the American constitutional tradition.

In *Griswold*, a majority ruled that the right of married couples to use contraception was a fundamental right that emanated from the text of the Constitution even if it had not been articulated. In this case, the Justices assumed that our nation's history and traditions, and larger notions of liberty and justice could produce *only* this result. In the cases that followed *Griswold*, however, it began to become clear that varying conclusions could be drawn about what was "fair" and "just" under the Bill of Rights. Moreover, the question of examining our history and traditions became increasingly problematic as the justices were called upon to consider issues that were highly contentious in American society. While there may have been a social consensus about the right of married couples to use contraception, the abortion wars of the 1970s, 1980, and 1990s, intense lobbying efforts around "right to die" laws and laws that expand or restrict the rights of gays and lesbians and continuing debates about how families are to be structured strongly suggest that there is no broad consensus about these issues.

The right created in *Griswold* created a tremendous need for amici input. First, by signaling that they would not be bound by the text of the Constitution, the Justices created the opportunity for groups to step forward and to provide assistance in divining the broader meanings upon which the document was based. The fundamental rights test looked at whether an activity was deeply rooted in the nation's history and traditions or implicit in the concept of ordered liberty so that neither liberty nor justice could exist if it were sacrificed. By requiring that the nation's history and traditions be examined, the Court expanded the role of amici with expertise in the area of American history. Similarly, by requiring that the Court explore larger issues of liberty and justice, the Court created a role for social scientists, religious organizations, and advocacy groups to evaluate laws. This standard for identifying fundamental rights carried over not only to privacy cases, but to substantive due process, so when the Court began to move away from the right to privacy in the mid 1980s and back toward the due process clause, the expanded amici role was unaffected. Furthermore, we would expect amici influence to continue to be felt in cases involving the privacy right, especially since this right continues to have a firm foundation in cases involving residential privacy. The Court's unanimous decision in the 1999 case *Wilson v. Layne* suggests the continuing importance of this privacy right. In this case, the Justices found that by allowing journalists and photographers to accompany them on arrests and searches of people's homes, the police had violated the "right to residential privacy" at the core of the Fourth Amendment.[8] Similarly, the availability of RU-486 will likely reshape the abortion debate, by removing the act of "abortion" from clinics, hospitals, and doctor's offices to private homes.

Second, the right to privacy encouraged amici participation because in all of these cases, the Justices made it clear that they would not hesitate to evaluate the purposes for which laws regulating abortion, aid in dying, gay and lesbian relations, and family relationships had been adopted. To evaluate the state's purposes in adopting these laws, the Justices needed to rely upon outsiders, particularly those with expertise in the areas of medicine, science, and law. In *Roe*, Justice Blackmun explicitly recognized the role of science and medicine in the abortion debate and deliberately focused on what he called the "medi-

cal aspects of abortion and the medical-legal history of abortion statutes" as a way of steering clear of this larger societal debate.[9] In the
cases that followed, this data became increasingly important, as the
Justices were called upon to evaluate laws that involved increasingly
complex issues, like the withdrawal or withholding of life support, the
administration of lethal prescription drugs to hasten the death of a
terminally ill person suffering severe pain, and the rationale for antisodomy laws.

Over time, the Court's focus on historical, medical, and social scientific data has had two results. First, it has diverted the Justices' attention
away from developing more solid foundations for privacy jurisprudence. In fact, in the years since *Roe*, the Justices have steadily been
moving away from the right to privacy and signaling that they are
grounding rights in the due process liberty clause instead of the more
amorphous privacy right. Second, this emphasis on extralegal data has
enhanced the opportunities for interest-group influence in the Court's
decision-making process. In *Roe*, *Akron*, *Cruzan*, *Washington*, and *Vacco*,
where the Justices were focused on understanding medical procedures
or medical conditions, and in *Bowers*, where the Court was trying to
discern the historical foundations of antisodomy laws, the amici had a
prominent role to play. In *Poe*, *Griswold*, *Moore*, *Harris*, and *Casey*, which
involved more purely legal questions or the application of stare decisis,
the role of amici appear to have been less important, but even in these
cases, amici played an important role. For example, in *Poe*, amicus
ACLU was critically important: it for the first time offered a conception
of the right to privacy as emanating from the clauses of the Bill of Rights.
Similarly, in *Harris* and *Bowers*, the amici offered the dissenters alternative legal grounds upon which to base the privacy right. Thus, even
where legal questions were central to a case, the amici may have had an
influence by shaping these arguments.

The centrality of the amici in those cases that turned on extralegal
questions suggests that the framing of a case by the formal parties and
amici is critically important. Moreover, this project demonstrates that
the legal model continues to be indispensable to the study of judicial
decision-making, because legal arguments determine the focus of judicial inquiry. Moreover, precedent continued to be critically important
in these cases. Where the Justices were asked to consider the application
of case law in these cases, they were often willing to do so. As Epstein
and Knight wrote in their 1996 article, precedent affects not only the
decision reached in a case, but the decision-making process as well.[10]
From *Griswold* forward, the Justices indicated that they were willing to
rely on positions articulated in earlier cases to decide legal issues raised
in litigation. While some Justices did alter their positions in these
debates,[11] this study suggests that precedent plays an important role,

especially where cases were decided in a relatively short time span, as in the contraception, abortion, and aid in dying debates.

The Growing Significance of Extralegal Issues: the Friends as "Experts"

Since the Court considered *Muller v. Oregon* in 1908, it has indicated that it will consider both the legal arguments presented in the parties' briefs and extralegal information, as well. In this case, Oregon's attorney, Louis Brandeis, amassed a wealth of medical and social science data in support of the state law that limited the number of hours women would be permitted to work and opened the door for input by interested and expert outsiders. As was discussed in chapter 1, the prominence of experts' briefs began to become apparent in the 1954 *Brown v. Board of Education* case, when amici presented the Court with extensive data about the effects of segregation on schoolchildren.[12] In the years since *Brown* was decided, amici participation has become increasingly prevalent in litigation before the U.S. Supreme Court. The potential significance of amici participation in privacy cases was first apparent in the conference notes from *Poe*, where Justice Brennan decried the lack of information about whether contraception had a basis in medicine, public morality, or religious belief. These comments portended an important trend in how the Court would use expert information in future privacy cases.

All of the cases discussed in this book turned on questions that were outside the ken of the Justices and compelled the Court to consider the briefs submitted by the parties and their amici. In one case, *Moore v. City of East Cleveland*, the appellant itself acted as an expert and presented all of the social scientific data about the prevalence of extended families in the United States. In the other cases, however, information was either presented solely by the amici or by the amici in conjunction with the formal parties. As the cases became more complex and as the Court considered not only contraception but abortion, and not only the termination of life support but the provision of life-ending medications, the amici role became more important.

In all but a few of these cases, the Court was deluged with medical, scientific, and social scientific data intended to provide a more comprehensive view of the issue in question. In providing this information, the amici subtly shifted the way the Court functioned. Instead of having to rely only on the information provided by parties, the Justices were availed of additional information by the amici. By providing this information, the amici allowed the Justices to expand their understanding of the issues and to consider alternatives beyond what might have been offered by the parties alone. As a result, in these cases, the amici may have functioned to decrease the uncertainty attendant in the Court's decision-making process.[13] Furthermore, amici participation encouraged the Justices to consider the wider societal implications of their decisions, and this expanded policy space encouraged the Justices to move beyond the narrow constraints of the adversary system and to function more like legislators. In fact, in many of these cases, the decision-making process resembled that of a legislature: the Justices gathered the information provided enthusiastically by the amici and weighed and considered competing factual and legal bases. Some might argue that amici participation in these cases ensured that the Justices would be well-informed about the underlying issues at play and that this broader knowledge base would translate into a more compelling and viable decision.

In theory, this enhanced understanding of the underlying issues could have been provided by the parties, and in *Moore*, it was. It bears noting, however, that in all the other cases, the amici performed a critical information function, by presenting data on their own, by elaborating on statements made briefly by the parties, or by seconding points that had been discussed at length by the parties. Moreover, an amici was a well-respected and acknowledged expert in the field under investigation this information function was even more critical. Even where expert amici were merely seconding information presented in the party briefs, they were providing important cues to the Justices about how they should conceptualize the issue. In essence, where the expert amici were seconding information, they were validating it for the Justices and allowing them to accept it almost without question.

The role of amici in helping the Court to place a case in a wider context and to consider the policy implications of possible decisions was apparent from the beginning. Amici participating in the cases under review in this book devoted considerable energy to helping the Court to understand the impact of its decisions on the American people. The Court was clearly concerned about how its decisions would be received; and in nearly all of the cases, the Justices integrated this discussion into their decisions. The only case in which the policy implications were ignored by the amici was *Moore v. City of East Cleveland*, where the sole amicus, the ACLU, made a decision not to address these. This omission is glaring, especially when considered in light of other privacy cases, where the policy repercussions were central to the amici's discussions. In all of the other cases, the Justices were clearly receptive to arguments about the possible impact of their choices. In fact, in the four cases involving absolute bans on the activities in question, *Roe, Bowers, Washington,* and *Vacco,* the Justices were anxious to employ the amici briefs. In *Roe, Washington,* and *Vacco,* the Justices provided the greatest number of direct cites; in all four cases, the Court relied heavily on data drawn from amici briefs without attribution. Furthermore, in *Roe* and the aid in dying cases, the Court was engaged in a subtle balancing of state interests and individual rights. In these cases, the Court was most concerned about determining whether legislative choices were reasonable, not about whether they were constitutional. To engage in this balancing of state interests and individual rights, the Justices made use of much-needed data provided solely in the amici briefs.

While Epstein, Segal, and Johnson have argued that the Justices are policy seekers and not policy entrepreneurs and that the amici briefs are not the "source of important issues considered by the Court,"[14] this research suggests otherwise. In many of these cases, the amici served a number of critical functions. First, in cases like *Poe*, *Roe*, *Harris*, the aid in dying cases, and *Bowers*, the amici provided novel legal arguments. Despite the fact that the Justices are not supposed to consider issues not raised by the formal parties, in these cases some or most of the Justices did. Second, in all of the cases, the amici furnished the Justices with information: in some cases, they alone provided the information; in others, they elaborated upon or seconded the information provided by the formal parties.

THE ROLE OF AMICI IN THE FUTURE

This research strongly suggests that amici played an important role in litigation involving the right to privacy between 1960 and 1997. There have been anecdotal reports of amici influence, most recently, in the 1998 equal protection case, *Romer v. Evans*,[15] and the 1999 punitive damages case, *Kolstad v. American Dental Association*. In both of these cases, the Justices appear to have employed a legal argument provided only by an amicus. This is the first study, however, that employs a longitudinal approach to detect correspondence between the arguments and data employed by the Supreme Court Justices and those provided in the amici curiae briefs. This study demonstrates not only that amici participation is on the rise in Supreme Court litigation but that amici have played an important role in helping to mold privacy jurisprudence.

In this area of the law, amici have been instrumental in bringing about social change, as they have helped to shape the outcome of these cases and the process by which decisions have been reached. The amici, parties, and Justices have been engaged in a dance over the course of these nearly four decades, with all three groups working together to recognize the right to privacy and to interpret it in a range of situations. Moreover, the most influential amici have occupied a strange hinterland: they have become increasingly partisan, engaging in a pattern of cooperation and coordination with the formal parties, but have also become much relied upon "experts," whose briefs have likely been seen as providing much-needed, and neutral, data and arguments.

As some analysts have suggested, the Court is pluralistic, and groups with significant organizational resources have been quite successful in influencing the Justices. For example, the American College of Obstetricians and Gynecologists has had a strong influence on the Court's handling of abortion, but Certain Physicians for American College of Obstetricians and Gynecologists, a much smaller group with far fewer resources, has not. Similarly, in the assisted dying cases, groups like the American Medical Association and American Academy of Neurology, well-regarded groups with substantial resources, have seen their arguments and data accepted by the Justices, but smaller or less mainstream groups, like Doctors for Life, the American Academy of Physicians and Surgeons, the American College of Legal Medicine, and the American Medical Student Association, have been less influential.

Interest-group pluralism on the Court is apparent in these cases, as the Justices have chosen to adopt the arguments and data of groups with significant lobbying resources and have disregarded the often-conflicting information provided by groups with few organizational resources. Moreover, this tendency towards pluralism will likely become even more pronounced in the future, as the Court is increasingly called upon to consider cases that involve highly technical issues. For example, cases involving the new reproductive technologies, up until now heard only the lower federal and state courts, will likely reach the Court in the next few years. The most likely vehicle for considering these technologies will be a case involving the rights and ownership of embryos or preembryos created through a vast array of high-tech procedures and involving legal parents, gestational parents, and gamete donors.[16] It is highly likely that in seeking to understand these relationships, the Justices will rely on information provided by medical, scientific, and legal experts about the nature of these technologies and the role of social norms and traditions in determining parental status.

Moreover, in the future, amici influence will be even more apparent in cases decided in the lower courts. In the 1998–1999 Term, the U.S. Supreme Court wrote full opinions in only seventy-five cases, less than half the cases decided throughout the 1980s. The federal appeals courts and state courts of last resort are becoming the ultimate arbiters of the vast majority of cases heard in the American judicial system. Furthermore, the appellate courts are increasingly relying on the lower courts for their disposition of factual issues and instead are focusing all of their energies on the legal issues at play in the litigation. According to Simpson, amici are cited much more often in federal appeals courts and state courts, and we would expect that use of these briefs will intensify in the future.[17] Furthermore, researchers are turning their attention to the state courts, where interest-group litigation appears to be variable but widespread in some areas.[18]

Perhaps even more troubling, these lower federal courts are being called upon to evaluate evidence without the benefit of the Frye Rule, which required that all evidence admitted at trial had been published in a peer-reviewed journal. In the 1993 case, *Daubert v. Merrell Dow Pharmaceuticals*, the U.S. Supreme Court struck down this rule and determined that federal judges had the responsibility for determining whether the "underlying reasoning or methodology [of the evidence being offered] is scientifically valid" under the Federal Rules of Evidence.[19] While a number of groups urged the Court to retain the Frye Rule and argued that the publication requirement ensured that only valid scientific findings would come before the courts, the Supreme Court struck it down. After *Daubert*, lower federal judges have become the gatekeepers of most scientific evidence, even though these judges do not have the knowledge or expertise to evaluate this data.[20] A number of analysts have decried this development, arguing that it has allowed "junk science" to inundate federal and state courtrooms and that there is no quality control to allow the judges to differentiate between this pseudo-science and real science.[21] Some writers have proposed that the scientific community police itself, by subjecting amici curiae briefs to publication in relevant journals before they are submitted to courts.[22] Others have argued that amici should not advocate in favor of either side but simply provide information to the court.[23] Still other analysts have contended that the court should appoint experts who are not involved in the litigation or should use special masters, and still others argue in favor of governmental funding for independent research on contested issues.[24] None of these proposals has yet been adopted.

In the future, one would expect that organized interests will continue to have an impact on litigation in American courts. Furthermore, it appears that amici with significant organizational resources will have an even better chance of being heard, as Justices and judges try to sort out the increasing number of briefs being filed at all levels of the American judicial system. At the Supreme Court level, the rule adopted in 1997 that required that amici reveal the source of "substantial support" for the researching and writing of their briefs will likely mean that the Court will use the identity of amici as a sorting mechanism. Armed with this information, the Justices would ostensibly discount the briefs that were authored or sponsored by parties of amici seeking to evade the page limitations by filing multiple briefs.

This study of amici participation suggests strongly that interest groups will continue to play an important role in the future, as Justices and judges struggle to understand cases that present issues that exceed the expertise of lay men and women. Increasing technological complexity and the need for information will likely make the U.S. Supreme Court a more democratic place, but the democracy that will flourish in the marble palace will be pluralistic, and organized interests with significant lobbying strengths in the other branches will exercise considerably more influence than those less well endowed. Thus, lobbying the Court will continue to become more akin to lobbying the legislatures, and groups with fewer organizational resources will not likely overcome their political disadvantages by entering the judicial arena.

NOTES

1. See Lee Epstein, "Interest Group Litigation during the Rehnquist Era," 9 *Journal of Law and Politics* 694-5.

2. Epstein and Knight in Clayton and Gillman, 215, 222.

3. It bears noting that since the 1980s, state governments have made a concerted effort to improve the quality of their amicus briefs in hopes of increasing their chances of being heard in the United States. The National Association of Attorneys General and the State and Local Legal Center may be succeeding in their efforts. While New York and California have long been well regarded for the briefs that they file, other office holders appear to be filing briefs that are employed by the Justices as well.

4. Samuel Krislov was the first to argue that organized interests had advantages in lobbying the Court (see Krislov).

5. Kevin McGuire has written extensively about the role of repeat attorneys and has argued that these repeaters play an important gatekeeping function. Amici curiae briefs must be filed by lawyers who are members of the Supreme Court bar, and it may be that future research on the impact of amici curiae on Supreme Court decisions will highlight this role. (This project, however, did not provide evidence of improved success rates for attorneys who file in successive cases. There is some anecdotal evidence that the brief's author may boost its chances of being heard. For example, Graglia and others have argued that the high profile of Harvard Law professor Lawrence Tribe increased the chances that his brief would be heard in *Romer v. Evans* (Graglia, 427). Others have written about the impact of the Tribe brief on the Court's opinion in this equal protection case (see Janet E. Halley, "Romer v. Hardwick" 68 *University of Colorado Law Review* 429, 430).

6. See Acker for a discussion of how the Justices and brief writers tend to use government documents and reports rather than citing to undistilled periodicals and statistic reports (31).

7. Felix Frankfurter was concerned about how the filing of amici briefs by groups that used the Court "as a soap box or an advertising medium" might encourage the belief among the public that the Justices were open to outside pressures by groups with no real interest in the litigation. Thus, he argued that the Court had to "reconcile a liberality towards accepting amici curiae briefs with safeguards against their misuse." To this end, he argued that the parties should be prudent in considering whether to grant permission to amici who

wanted to file on their behalf, and that parties should inform the Court of the reasons that they had decided to withhold permission ("Memo and Copy of Proposal for Revision of Paragraph 9 of Rule 27 Relating to a Brief Filed on Behalf of an Amicus Curiae," Harlan Papers, file 481, 10/28/49.) Following the adoption of Rule 27, the Solicitor General began to automatically deny permission to file amici briefs in cases to which it was a party. This "untenable position" led Justices Harlan and Black to write a conference memo recommending that the process for amici filing be liberalized (Memo to the Conference, Harlan Papers, file 481, 10/15/57).

8. *Wilson v. Layne* (Docket No. 98-83).

9. 93 S.Ct. 709.

10. Epstein and Knight (1996).

11. For example, Justice White's position shifted between *Griswold* and *Harris*: he argued strongly in favor of the due process rights of married couples to access contraception in *Griswold*, and he argued that the Connecticut ban may have implicated the equal protection clause since it had a disparate impact on the poor, who had to rely on family planning clinics for access to contraception. In contrast, in *Harris*, Justice White emphatically rejected the argument that the Hyde Amendment violated the constitutional rights of poor women dependent on public funding for abortion services. In a longitudinal study of judicial decision-making, Epstein et al. recently concluded that Justices' positions are not necessarily static and may change over time (Lee Epstein et al., "Do Political Preferences Change? A Longitudinal Study of U.S. Supreme Court Justices," 60 (3) *Journal of Politics* 801-18 (1998)).

12. For further discussion of these briefs, see Simpson, 32.

13. This function was hinted at by Caldeira and Wright in their important study, "Amici Curiae before the Supreme Court: Who Participates, When, and How Much?" 52 (3) *Journal of Politics* 782-806, p. x (1990).

14. Lee Epstein, Jeffrey Segal and Timothy Johnson, "The Claim of Issue Creation on the U.S. Supreme Court," 90 (4) *American Political Science Review* 845-52 (1996).

15. Thomas Grey and others have argued that the Court employed the equal protection argument suggested in the amicus curiae brief authored by Harvard Law professor Lawrence Tribe and that the Court's emphasis on the purposes and effect of Colorado Amendment 2, which denied antidiscrimination protection to gays, lesbians, and bisexuals who had been discriminated against because of their sexual preferences, derived from this brief (Grey, 383). In addition, the decision that companies who are making good faith efforts to stop sexual harassment in their workplaces are not responsible for paying punitive damages was an argument encompassed only in the brief of amicus U.S. Chamber of Commerce ("Ruling Raises Hurdle in Bias-Award Cases," *New York Times* 6/23/99, A16).

16. For example, see Janet Dolgin, "An Emerging Consensus: Reproductive Technology and the Law," 23 *Vermont Law Review* 225 (1998); Judith D. Fischer, "Misappropriation of Human Eggs and Embryos and the Tort of Conversion," 32 *Loyola of Los Angeles Law Review* 381 (1999); Philip G. Peters, "Harming Future Persons: Obligations to the Children of Reproductive Technology," 8 *Southern California Interdisciplinary Law Journal* 375 (1999).

17. According to Simpson, between 1995 and 1998, 2539 appellate decisions referred to at least one amicus brief, and 428 opinions referenced an amicus brief three or more times. Of these, 237 opinions were in the federal appeals courts (Simpson, 8-10).

18. Lee Epstein, "Exploring the Participation of Organized Interest in State Court Litigation" 47 (2) *Political Research Quarterly* 335-51 (1994).

19. *Daubert v. Merrell Dow Pharmaceuticals* 509 U.S. 579 (1993). See also Freedman for further discussion.

20. Moreover, some analysts have argued that judges are at a serious disadvantage in performing this task, because science and law have much different standards for evaluating the truth. These writers point out that in most cases, judges and juries are instructed to accept an argument or data if there is 51 percent certainty that it is true, but in the scientific method, data is accepted only if there is a 95 percent or higher probability that it is accurate (see Nicholas Wade, "Method and Madness: Trials and Errors," *New York Times Magazine* 7/24/94, p. 10; William Glaberson, "The Courts vs. Scientific Certainty," *New York Times Week in Review* 6/27/99, sect. 7 pg. 5).

21. Michael Rustad and Thomas Koenig, "The Supreme Court and Junk Social Science: Selective Distortion in Amicus Briefs," 72 *North Carolina Law Review* 91, 113, 143-51 (1993); Foster, 1509, 1578-9.

22. Barrett, 211.

23. Rustad, 99.

24. Rustad, 152-3; Foster, 1614.

Sources

Poe et al. v. Ullman et al. (367 U.S. 502)

Brief of Petitioners, Poe et al. Filed in the Supreme Court of the United States, October Term, 1960, *Poe v. Ullman.*

Brief of Respondents, Ullman et al. Filed in the Supreme Court of the United States, October Term, 1960, *Poe v. Ullman.*

Amici in support of petitioners

American Civil Liberties Union

Planned Parenthood Federation of America, Inc.

Sixty-Six Physicians

Griswold v. Connecticut (381 U.S. 481)

Brief of Petitioners, Griswold et al. Filed in the Supreme Court of the United States, October Term 1964, *Griswold v. Connecticut.*

Brief of Respondent, State of Connecticut. Filed in the Supreme Court of the United States, October Term 1964, *Griswold v. Connecticut.*

Amici in support of petitioners

Adams et al.

American Civil Liberties Union

Catholic Council for Civil Liberties

Planned Parenthood Federation of America, Inc.

Roe et al. v. Wade et al. (410 U.S. 113)

Brief of the Petitioners. Filed in the Supreme Court of the United States, October Term, 1971, *Doe v. Bolton.*

Brief of the Petitioners. Filed in the Supreme Court of the United States, October Term, 1971, *Roe v. Wade.*

Brief of the Respondents. Filed in the Supreme Court of the United States, October Term, 1971, *Doe v. Bolton.*

Brief of the Respondents. Filed in the Supreme Court of the United States, October Term, 1971, *Roe v. Wade.*

Amici in support of petitioners

ACOG et al. in *Doe v. Bolton* and in *Roe v. Wade*

American Association of University Women et al. (Women's Organizations and Named Women)

American Ethical Union

California Committee to Legalize Abortion et al. (Organizations and Named Women)

National Legal Program on Health Problems of the Poor et al. in *Doe v. Bolton* and in *Roe v. Wade*

New Women Lawyers et al.

Planned Parenthood Federation of America, Inc. et al.

State Communities Aid Assn.

Amici in support of respondents

Americans United for Life

Attorney General of Arizona et al.

Certain Physicians, Professors and Fellows of the American College of Obstetrics and Gynecology

Ferdinand Buckley pro se

National Right to Life Committee

Robert L. Sassone in *Doe v. Bolton* and *Roe v. Wade*

Texas Diocesan Attorneys

Women for the Unborn et al.

Harris, Secretary of Health and Human Services v. McRae et al. (448 U.S. 297)

Brief of the Petitioner. Filed in the Supreme Court of the United States, October Term, 1979, *Harris v. McRae et al.*

Brief of the Respondents. Filed in the Supreme Court of the United States, October Term, 1979, *Harris v. McRae et al.*

Amici in support of neither side

Bergen-Passaic Health Systems Agency et al.

Coalition for Human Justice

National Council of Churches in Christ in the U.S.A.

United Presbyterian Church in the U.S.

Amici in support of petitioners

Representative Jim Wright et al.

United States Catholic Conference

Amici in support of respondents

American Ethical Union et al.

Association of Legal Aid Attorneys of the City of New York

National Organization for Women et al.

The State of New York et al.

City of Akron v. Akron Center for Reproductive Health, Inc., et al. (462 U.S. 416)

Brief of the Petitioners. Filed in the Supreme Court of the United States, October Term, 1982, *City of Akron v. Akron Center for Reproductive Health, Inc. et al.*

Brief of the Respondents. Filed in the Supreme Court of the United States, October Term, 1982, *City of Akron v. Akron Center for Reproductive Health, Inc., et al.*

Amici in support of neither side

American College of Obstetricians and Gynecologists

American Public Health Association

Americans United for Life

California Women Lawyers et al.

Certain Law Professors

Certain Religious Organizations

College of American Pathologists

Lawyers for Life

Legal Defense Fund for Unborn Children

National Abortion Federation

NAACP Legal Defense and Educational Fund, Inc.

National Organization for Women et al.

Planned Parenthood Federation of America, Inc., et al.

United States

Womankind, Inc.

Women Lawyers of Sacramento et al.

Amici in support of petitioners

American Psychological Association

Committee for Abortion Rights and Against Sterilization Abuse et al.

Amici in support of respondents

Feminists for Life

United Families Foundation et al.

Planned Parenthood of Southeastern Pennsylvania et al. v. Robert C. Casey (503 U.S. 957)

Brief of the Petitioner. Filed in the Supreme Court of the United States, October Term, 1991, *Planned Parenthood of Southeastern Pennsylvania et al. v. Robert P. Casey et al.*

Brief of the Respondents. Filed in the Supreme Court of the United States, October Term, 1991, *Planned Parenthood of Southeastern Pennsylvania et al. v. Robert P. Casey et al.*

Amici in support of petitioners

ACOG et al.

Alan Guttmacher Institute et al.

American Psychological Association

City of New York et al.

NAACP Legal Defense and Education Fund et al.

178 Organizations

Pennsylvania Coalition against Domestic Violence et al.

Representative Don Edwards et al.

State of New York et al.

250 Historians

Amici in support of respondents

Agudath Israel of America

America 21, Family Values for the Twenty-First Century

American Academy of Medical Ethics

American Association of Prolife Obstetricians and Gynecologists and the American Association of Prolife Pediatricians

Catholics United for Life et al.

Certain American State Legislators

Elliot Institute for Social Sciences Research

Feminists for Life of America et al.

Focus on the Family et al.

Hon. Henry J. Hyde et al.

James J. Crook

Knights of Columbus

Legal Defense for Unborn Children

Life Issues Institute

National Legal Foundation

National Right to Life Committee, Inc.

Nineteen Arizona Legislators

Rutherford Institute et al.

Southern Center for Law & Ethics

State of Utah

Texas Black Americans for Life

United States

United States Catholic Conference et al.

United States Justice Foundation

University Faculty for Life

Cruzan v. Director of Missouri Department of Health et al. (497 U.S. 261)

Brief of Petitioners, Nancy Beth Cruzan, by her parents and co-guardians, Lester L. and Joyce Cruzan, on Writ of Certiorari to the Missouri Supreme Court, filed in the Supreme Court of the United States, October Term 1989, *Cruzan v. Director of Missouri Department of Health, and Administrator of the Missouri Rehabilitation Center at Mt. Vernon.*

Brief of Petitioners, Nancy Beth Cruzan, by her parents and co-guardians, Lester L. and Joyce Cruzan, in Reply to Respondent's Brief on Writ of Certiorari to the Missouri Supreme Court, filed in the Supreme Court of the United States, October Term 1989, *Cruzan v. Director of Missouri Department of Health, and Administrator of the Missouri Rehabilitation Center at Mt. Vernon.*

Brief of Respondents, Director of Missouri Department of Health, and Administrator of the Missouri Rehabilitation Center at Mt. Vernon, on Writ of Certiorari to the Missouri Supreme Court, filed in the Supreme Court of the United States, October Term 1989, *Cruzan v. Director of Missouri Department of Health, and Administrator of the Missouri Rehabilitation Center at Mt. Vernon.*

Brief of Respondent, Thad C. McCanse, Guardian ad litem, on Writ of Certiorari to the Missouri Supreme Court, filed in the Supreme Court of the United States, October Term 1989, *Cruzan v. Director of*

Missouri Department of Health, and Administrator of the Missouri Rehabilitation Center at Mt. Vernon.

Amici in support of neither party

SSM Health Care System et al.

Amici in support of petitioners

AIDS Civil Rights Project

American Academy of Neurology

American College of Physicians

American Hospital Association

American Medical Association et al.

Barbara Burgoon and Ruth Fields

Concern for Dying

Frederick R. Abrams et al.

General Board of Church and Society of the United Methodist Church

John E. McConnell et al.

National Hospice Organization

Society of Critical Care Medicine et al.

Society for the Right to Die

Wisconsin Bioethicists and Other Health Professionals

Amici in support of respondents

Agudath Israel of America

American Academy of Medical Ethics

American Academy of Physicians and Surgeons, and C. Everett Koop, M.D. et al.

Association for Retarded Citizens of the United States, the Association for Persons with Severe Handicaps et al.

Catholic Lawyers Guild of the Archdiocese of Boston, Inc., et al.

Christian Action Council et al.

District Attorney of Milwaukee County, Wisconsin

Doctors for Life and Missouri Doctors for Life

Elizabeth Sadowski et al.

Families for Life et al.

Focus on the Family and Family Research Council

Frances Ambrose

Free Speech Advocates and Christian Advocates Serving Evangelism

Herbert Ratner, M.D.

International Anti-Euthanasia Task Force et al.

J.G. Morris

James Dunlap

Knights of Columbus

National Nurses for Life

National Right to Life Committee, Inc., et al.

New Jersey Right to Life Committee et al.

Paul Marx

Philip Dreisbach, M.D.

Right to Life League of Southern California, Inc.

Rutherford Institute et al.

United States

United States Catholic Conference

Value of Life Committee, Inc.

Vacco, Attorney General of New York v. Quill (521 U.S. 793) and *State of Washington v. Glucksberg* (521 U.S. 702)

Brief for the Petitioners. Filed in the Supreme Court of the United States, October Term, 1996, *Vacco et al. v. Quill et al.*

Brief for the Petitioners. Filed in the Supreme Court of the United States, October Term, 1996, *Washington v. Glucksberg et al.*

Brief for the Respondents. Filed in the Supreme Court of the United States, October Term, 1996, *Vacco et al. v. Quill et al.*

Brief for the Respondents. Filed in the Supreme Court of the United States, October Term, 1996, *Washington v. Glucksberg et al.*

Reply Brief for the Petitioners. Filed in the Supreme Court of the United States, October Term, 1996, *Vacco et al. v. Quill et al.*

Reply Brief for the Petitioners. Filed in the Supreme Court of the United States, October Term, 1996, *Washington v. Glucksberg et al.*

Amici in support of neither party

American College of Legal Medicine

American Geriatrics Society

Choice in Dying, Inc.

Amici in support of petitioners

Agudath Israel

American Association of Homes and Services for the Aging et al.

American Center for Law & Justice

American Hospital Association

American Life League

American Medical Association et al. in both *Vacco* and *Washington*

American Suicide Foundation

Bioethics Professors

Catholic Health Association of the United States

Catholic Medical Association

Christian Legal Society et al.

Clarendon Foundation

District Attorney of Milwaukee County, Wisconsin

Evangelical Lutheran Church in America

Family Research Council

Gary Lee, M.D. et al.

Institute for Public Affairs of the Union of Orthodox Jewish Congregations of America and the Rabbinical Council of America

International Anti-Euthanasia Task Force

Legal Center for Defense of Life, in both *Vacco* and *Washington*

Medical Society of New Jersey

Members of the New York and Washington State Legislatures

National Association of Prolife Nurses et al.

National Catholic Office for Persons with Disabilities and the Knights of Columbus

National Hospice Organization

National Legal Center for the Medically Dependent and Disabled, Inc.

National Right to Life Committee, Inc.

National Spinal Cord Injury Association

Not Dead Yet and Americans Disabled for Attendant Programs Today

Orrin Hatch et al.

Project on Death in America, Open Society Institute

Richard Thompson, Oakland County Prosecuting Attorney

Rutherford Institute

Schiller Institute

Southern Center for Law and Ethics

State of California et al., in both *Vacco* and *Washington*

United States, in both *Vacco* and *Washington*

United States Catholic Conference, in both *Vacco* and *Washington*

Wayne County, Michigan

Amici in support of respondent

American Civil Liberties Union

Americans for Death with Dignity and the Death with Dignity Education Center

American Medical Student Association

Bioethicists

Center for Reproductive Law and Policy

Coalition of Hospice Professionals

Council for Secular Humanism and the International Academy of Humanism

Gay Men's Health Crisis et al.

John Doe

Julian M. Whitaker, M.D.

Law Professors

National Women's Health Network and the Northwest Women's Law Center

Ronald Dworkin et al.

State Legislators

Surviving Family Members

36 Religious Organizations, Leaders and Scholars

Washington State Psychological Association et al.

Moore v. City of East Cleveland (431 U.S. 494)

Brief of the Petitioner, Inez Moore. Filed in the Supreme Court of the United States, October Term, 1976, *Moore v. City of East Cleveland*.

Brief of the Respondent, City of East Cleveland, Ohio. Filed in the Supreme Court of the United States, October Term, 1976, *Moore v. City of East Cleveland*.

Amicus in support of petitioner

American Civil Liberties Union.

Bowers v. Hardwick (478 U.S. 186)

Brief of the Petitioners. Filed in the Supreme Court of the United States, October Term, 1985, *Bowers v. Hardwick*.

Brief of the Respondents. Filed in the Supreme Court of the United States, October Term, 1985, *Bowers v. Hardwick.*

Amici in support of petitioners

Catholic League for Religious and Civil Rights

Concerned Women for American Education and Legal Defense Fund

David Robinson, Jr.

Rutherford Institute et al.

Amici in support of respondents

American Jewish Congress

American Psychological Association and the American Public Health Association

Association of the Bar of the City of New York

Attorney General of the State of New York

Lambda Legal Defense and Education Fund

Lesbian Rights Project et al.

National Gay Rights Advocates et al.

National Organization for Women

Presbyterian Church et al.

Selected Bibliography

Acker, JR. Mortal Friends and Enemies: Amici Curiae in Supreme Court Death Penalty Cases. *Criminal and Civil Confinement* (1993) 19:1–59.

Acker, JR. Social Science in Supreme Court Criminal Cases and Briefs: The Actual and Potential Contribution of Social Scientists as Amici Curiae. *Law and Human Behavior* (1990)14:25–42.

Alderman, E and C. Kennedy. *The Right to Privacy*. New York: Alfred A. Knopf, 1995.

Alexander, L. Sometimes Better Boring and Correct: *Romer v. Evans* as an Exercise of Ordinary Equal Protection Analysis. *University of Colorado Law Review* (1997) 68:335–47.

Allen, AL. Autonomy's Magic Wand: Abortion and Constitutional Interpretation. *Boston University Law Review* (1992) 72:683–98.

Arledge, PC and EV Heck. A Freshman Justice Confronts the Constitution: Justice O'Connor and the First Amendment. *Western Political Quarterly* (1992) 45:761–72.

Baker, LA. The Missing Pages of the Majority Opinion in *Romer v. Evans*. *University of Colorado Law Review* (1997) 68:387–408.

Barnum, DG. *The Supreme Court and American Democracy*. New York: St. Martin's Press, 1993.

Barnum, DG. The Supreme Court and Public Opinion: Judicial Decision Making in the Post–New Deal Period. *Journal of Politics* (1985) 47:652–65.

Barrett, GV and SB Morris. The American Psychological Association's Amicus Curiae Brief in *Price Waterhouse v. Hopkins*. *Law and Human Behavior* (1993)17:201–15.

Baum, L. *The Supreme Court* (6th ed.). Washington, D.C.: Congressional Quarterly Press, 1998.

Baum, L. What Motivates Supreme Court Justices? Assessing the Evidence on Justices' Goals. Presented at the 1995 Annual Meeting of the Midwest Political Science Association, Chicago.

Behuniak-Long S. Friendly Fire: Amici Curiae and *Webster v. Reproductive Health Services*. *Judicature* (1991)74:261–70.

Berry, JM. *Interest Group Society*. New York: Harper Collins Press, 1989.

Berry, MF. *Stability, Security and Continuity: Mr. Justice Burton and Decision-Making in the Supreme Court: 1945–1958*. Westport, CT: Greenwood Press, 1978.

Bickel, AM. *The Least Democratic Branch: The Supreme Court at the Bar of Politics*. New Haven: Yale University Press, 1962.

Blaesser, BW et al. Advocating Affordable Housing in New Hampshire: The Amicus Curiae Brief of the American Planning Association in *Wayne Britton v. Town of Chester*. *Journal of Urban and Contemporary Law* (1991) 40: 3–48.

Bloom, LH. Jr. The Legacy of *Griswold*. *Ohio Northern University Law Review* (1989)16:511–44.

Boucher, RL. Supreme Court Justices as Strategic Decision Makers: Aggressive Grants and Defensive Denials on the Vinson Court. *Journal of Politics* (1995) 57: 824–37.

Bowen, T. Consensual Norms and the Freshman Effect on the United States Supreme Court. *Social Science Quarterly* (1995)76(1):222–31.

Boyle, J. *Shamans, Software, and Spleens: Law and the Construction of the Information Society*. Cambridge: Harvard University Press, 1996.

Brace, PR and MG Hall . The Interplay of Preferences, Case Facts, Context, and Rules in the Politics of Judicial Choice. *Journal of Politics* (1997) 59:1206–1231.

Brace, PR and MG Hall. Judicial Choice and the Politics of Abortion: Institutions, Context and the Autonomy of Courts. Proceedings from the 1996 Annual Meeting of the American Political Science Association 1996.

Brace, PR and MG Hall. Neo-Institutionalism and Dissent in State Supreme Courts. *The Journal of Politics* (1990) 52:54–70.

Bradley, RC and P Gardner. Underdogs, Upperdogs and the Use of the Amicus Brief: Trends and Explanations. *Justice System Journal* (1985) 10.

Brenner, S and RH Dorff. The Attitudinal Model and Fluidity Voting on the United States Supreme Court. *Journal of Theoretical Politics* (1992) 4 (2):195–205.

Brenner, S and TM Hagle. Opinion Writing and Acclimation Effect. *Political Behavior* (1996) 18: 235–61.

Brenner, S and HJ Spaeth. *Stare Indecisis: The Alteration of Precedent on the Supreme Court: 1946–1992*. Cambridge: Cambridge University Press, 1995.

Brigham, J. Bodies of Law: The Supreme Court, the Justices, and Death. Proceedings from the 1996 Annual Meeting of the American Political Science Association, 1996.

Brisbin, RA. Antonin Scalia, Willian Brennan, and the Politics of Expression: A Study of Legal Violence and Repression. *American Political Science Review* (1993) 87:912–27.

Brisbin, RA. Justice Antonin Scalia, Constitutional Discourse, and the Legalistic State. *Western Political Quarterly* (1991) 44:1005–1038.

Buchanan, SG. The Right to Privacy: Past, Present and the Future. *Ohio Northern University Law Review* (1989)16:403–510.

Burger, WE. *It Is So Ordered: A Constitution Unfolds*. New York: William Morrow & Co., Inc., 1995.

Caldeira, GA and CE Smith. Campaigning for the Supreme Court: the Dynamics of Public Opinion on the Thomas Nomination. *Journal of Politics* (1996) 58: 655–681.

Caldeira, GA and JR Wright. Amici Curiae before the Supreme Court: Who Participates, When, and How Much? *Journal of Politics* (1990) 52:782–806.

Caldeira, GA and JR Wright. Lobbying for Justice: Organized Interests, Supreme Court Nominations, and the United States Senate. *American Journal of Political Science* (1998) 42:499–523.

Caldeira, GA and JR Wright. Organized Interests and Agenda Setting in the U.S. Supreme Court. *American Political Science Review* (1988) 82:1109–27.

Caldeira, GA and C Zorn. Of Time and Consensual Norms in the Supreme Court. *American Journal of Political Science* (1998) 42:874–902.

Calkins, S. Supreme Court Antitrust 1991-2: The Revenge of the Amici. *Antitrust L.J.*(1993) 61: 269–311.

Cameron, CM, JA Segal and DB Songer. Signals and Indices in the Supreme Court's Certiorari Decisions. Presented at the 1995 Annual Meeting of the Midwest Political Science Association, Chicago.

Caplan, L. *The Tenth Justice: The Solicitor General and the Rule of Law.* New York: Alfred A. Knopf, 1987.

Casper, JD. The Supreme Court and National Policy Making. *The American Political Science Review* (1976) 70:50–63.

Clapes, AL. Confessions of an Amicus Curiae: Technophobia, Law, and Creativity in the Digital Arts. *University of Dayton Law Review* (1994)19:903–74.

Colker, R. Feminist Litigation: An Oxymoron?—A Study of the Briefs Filed in *Webster v. Reproductive Health Services. Harvard Women's Law Journal* (1990) 13:137–88.

Cooper, PJ. *Battles on the Bench: Conflict inside the Supreme Court.* University of Kansas Press, 1995.

Cooper, PJ. The Solicitor General and the Evolution of Activism. *Indiana Law Journal* (1990) 65:675–96.

Costain, AM. *Inviting Women's Rebellion: A Political Process Interpretation of the Women's Movement.* Baltimore: Johns Hopkins University Press, 1992.

Cowan, R. Women's Rights through Litigation:An Examination of the ACLU's Women's Rights Project. *Columbia Human Rights Review* (1976) 9:373–412.

Dahl, R. *A Preface to Democracy.* Chicago: University of Chicago Press, 1956.

Davis, PC. *Neglected Stories: The Constitution and Family Values.* New York: Hill and Wang, 1997.

Davis, R. *Decisions and Images: The Supreme Court and the Press.* Englewood Cliffs, NJ: Prentice Hall, Inc., 1994.

Devins, N. *Shaping Constitutional Values: Elected Government, the Supreme Court, and the Abortion Debate.* Baltimore and London: Johns Hopkins Press, 1996.

Dolgin, JL. The Family in Transition: From *Griswold* to *Eisenstadt* and Beyond. *Georgetown Law Journal* (1992) 82:1519–71.

Dudziak, ML. Just Say No: Birth Control in the Connecticut Supreme Court Before *Griswold v. Connecticut. Iowa Law Review* (1990) 75:915–39.

Duncan, DW. A Little Tour in France: Surrogate Motherhood and Amici Curiae in the French Legal System. *Western State University Law Review* (1994) 21: 447–65.

Dupuis, M. Legal Mobilization Theory and the Impact of Law on the Gay and Lesbian Social Movement. Presented at the 1996 Annual Meeting of the American Political Science Association, San Francisco.

Eastland, T, ed. *Benchmarks: Great Constitutional Controversies in the Supreme Court*. Washington, D.C., Ethics and Public Policy Center, 1995.

Ennis, BJ. Effective Amicus Briefs. *Catholic University Law Review* (1984) 33:603–9.

Epstein, L. *Conservatives in Court*. Knoxville: University of Tennessee Press, 1985.

Epstein, L. *Contemplating Courts*. Washington, D.C.: Congressional Quarterly Press, 1995.

Epstein, L. Exploring the Participation of Organized Interests in State Court Litigation. *Political Research Quarterly* (1994) 47:335–351.

Epstein, L. Interest Group Litigation during the Rehnquist Era. *Journal of Law and Politics* (1993) 9:639–717.

Epstein, L et al. Do Sincere Preferences Change? A Longitudinal Study of United States Supreme Court Justices. Presented at the 1995 Annual Meeting of the Midwest Political Science Association, Chicago.

Epstein, L et al. Do Political Preferences Change? A Longitudinal Study of U.S. Supreme Court Justices. *Journal of Politics* (1998) 60:801–818.

Epstein, L et al. *Supreme Court Compendium*. Washington, DC: Congressional Quarterly Press, 1995.

Epstein, L and JF Kobylka. *The Supreme Court and Legal Change: Abortion and the Death Penalty*. Chapel Hill: University of North Carolina Press, 1992.

Epstein, L and J Knight. *The Choices Justices Make*. Washington, D.C.: Congressional Quarterly Press, 1998.

Epstein, L and J Knight. Mapping Out the Strategic Terrain: The Informational Role of Amici Curiae, in CW Cornell and H Gillman, *Supreme Court Decision-Making and New Institutionalist Approaches*. Chicago: University of Chicago Press, 1999.

Epstein, L and CK Rowland. Debunking the Claim of Interest Group Invincibility in the Courts. *American Political Science Review* (1991) 85:205–17.

Epstein, L, JA Segal and T Johnson. The Claim of Issue Creation on the U.S. Supreme Court. *American Political Science Review* (1996) 90:845–52.

Epstein, L, TG Walker and WJ Dixon. The Supreme Court and Criminal Justice Disputes: A Neo-institutional Perspective. *American Journal of Political Science* (1989) 33:825–41.

Erickson, RJ and RJ Simon. *The Use of Social Science Data in Supreme Court Decisions*. Urbana: University of Illinois Press, 1998.

Farole, DJ. *Interest Groups and Judicial Federalism: Organizational Litigation in State Judiciaries*. Westport, CT: Praeger, 1998.

Fein, B. *Griswold v. Connecticut*: Wayward Decision–Making in the Supreme Court. *Ohio Northern University Law Review* (1989); 16:551–60.

Fineman, MA. Intimacy outside of the Natural Family: The Limits of Privacy. *Connecticut Law Review* (1991) 23:955–72.

Fisher, L. Is the Solicitor General an Executive or a Judicial Agent? Caplan's Tenth Justice. *Law and Social Inquiry* (1990) 15:305–320.

Flemming, GN, DB Holian and SB Mezey. An Integrated Model of Privacy Decision Making in U.S. State Supreme Courts. *American Politics Quarterly* (1998) 26: 35–58.

Flemming, RB, J Bohte and BD Wood. One Voice among Many: The Supreme Court's Influence on Attentiveness to Issues in the United States, 1947–92. *American Journal of Political Science* (1997) 41:1224–1250.

Flemming, RB and BD Wood. The Public and the Supreme Court: Individual Justice Responsiveness to American Policy Moods. *American Journal of Political Science* (1997) 41: 468–98.

Formicola, JR. The Amicus Brief: A Judicial Tactic of the Catholic Bishops in the Abortion Battle. *Polity* (1995).

Funston, R. *A Vital National Seminar: The Supreme Court in American Political Life.* Palo Alto, CA: Mayfield Publishing Co., 1978.

Galanter, M. Why the Haves Come Out Ahead: Speculation on the Limits of Legal Change. *Law and Society Review* (1974) 9:95–160.

Galloway, R. *The Rich and Poor in Supreme Court History.* Greenbrae, CA: Paradigm Press, 1982.

Gangi, W. *Saving the Constitution from the Courts.* Norman and London: University of Oklahoma Press, 1995.

Garfield, H. Privacy, Abortion and Judicial Review: Haunted by the Ghost of *Lochner*. *Washington Law Review* (1986) 61:293–365.

George, TE and L Epstein. On the Nature of Supreme Court Decision Making. *American Political Science Review* (1992) 86:323–337.

Ginsburg, RB. Communicating and Commenting on the Court's Work. *Georgetown Law Journal* (1995) 83: 2119–2129.

Glaberson, W. The Courts vs. Scientific Certainty. *New York Times Week in Review* (6/27/99) 7:5.

Goldstein, LF. *By Consent of the Governed: Directions in Constitutional Theory*, in Epstein and Knight, *Contemplating Courts*, 275–95.

Graglia, LA. *Romer v. Evans*: The People Foiled Again by the Constitution. *University of Colorado Law Review* (1997) 68:409–29.

Grey, TC. *Bowers v. Hardwick* Diminished. *University of Colorado Law Review* (1997) 68:373–86.

Hagle, TM and HJ Spaeth. Voting Fluidity and the Attitudinal Model of Supreme Court Decision Making. *Western Political Quarterly* (1991) 434:119–28.

Hagle, TM and HJ Spaeth. Ideological Patterns in the Justices' Voting in the Burger Court's Business Cases. *Journal of Politics* (1993) 55: 492–505.

Halley, JE. *Romer v. Hardwick. University of Colorado Law Review* (1997) 68:429–52.

Harris, CA. Outing Privacy Litigation. *George Washington Law Review* (1997) 65: 248–273.

Haynie, SL. Leadership and Consensus on the U.S. Supreme Court. *Journal of Politics* (1992) 54:1158–1169.

Heck, EV. Justice Brennan and Coalition Building on a Changing Court: Freedom of Expression from Cohen to the Flag Burning Cases. Presented at the 1996 Annual Meeting of the American Political Science Association, San Francisco.

Hedman, S. Friends of the Earth and Friends of the Court: Assessing the Impact of Interest Group Amici Curiae in Environmental Cases Decided by the Supreme Court. *Virginia Environmental Law Journal* (1991) 10:187–212.

Henly, B. "Penumbra": The Roots of a Legal Metaphor. *Hastings Constitutional Law Quarterly* (1987) 15:81–100.

Hofrenning, DJB. *In Washington but Not of It: The Prophetic Politics of Religious Lobbyists*. Philadelphia: Temple University Press, 1995.

Howard, J. Retaliation, Reinstatement and Friends of the Court: Amicus Participation in *Brock v. Roadway Express*. *Howard Law Journal* (1996) 31:268–9.

Hrebenar, RJ and RK Scott. *Interest Group Politics in America*. Englewood Cliffs, NJ: Prentice Hall, 1990.

Irons, Peter. *Brennan vs. Rehnquist: The Battle for the Constitution*. New York: Alfred A. Knopf, 1994.

Ivers, G, and K O'Connor. Friends as Foes: The Amicus Curiae Participation and Effectiveness of the ACLU and the Americans for Effective Law Enforcement in Criminal Cases, 1969–1982. *Law and Policy* (1987) 9:161–78.

Jennings, G. The Amicus Curiae Brief in the State Courts 1950–1954: A Comparative Perspective. Presented at the 1993 Annual Meeting of the American Political Science Association.

Justice, WW. Recognizing the Ninth Amendment's Role in Constitutional Interpretation. *Texas Law Review* (1996) 74:1241–4.

Kairys, D., ed. *The Politics of Law: A Progressive Critique*. New York: Pantheon Books. 1997 (3rd ed.).

Kaye, JS. One Judge's View of "Friends of the Court". *New York State Bar Journal* (1989) 61:8–10+.

Knight, J and L Epstein. The Norm of Stare Decisis. *American Journal of Political Science* (1996) 40:1018–1035.

Kobylka, JF. A Court–Created Context for Group Litigation: Libertarian Groups and Obscenity. *Journal of Politics* (1987) 49:1061–78.

Kobylka, JF. The Mysterious Case of Establishment Clause Litigation: How Organized Litigants Foiled Legal Change, in Epstein and Knight, *Contemplating Courts*, 1995.

Kobylka, JF. *The Politics of Obscenity: Group Litigation in a Time of Legal Change*. Westport, CT: Greenwood Press, 1991.

Koshner, AJ. *Solving the Puzzle of Interest Group Litigation*. Westport, CT: Greenwood Press, 1998.

Krislov, S. The Amicus Curiae Brief: From Friendship to Advocacy. *Yale Law Journal* (1963) 72:694–721.

Lawrence, S. *The Poor in Court: The Legal Services Program and Supreme Court Decision Making*. Princeton, NJ: Princeton University Press, 1990.

Lazare, D. *The Frozen Republic: How the Constitution Is Paralyzing Democracy*. New York: Harcourt Brace & Co., 1996.

Lowman, M. The Litigating Amicus Curiae: When Does the Party Begin after the Friends Leave? *American University Law Review* (1992) 41:1243–99.

Maltzman, F and PJ Wahlbeck. Strategic Policy Considerations and Voting Fluidity on the Burger Court. *American Political Science Review* (1996) 90:581–92.

Maltzman, F and PJ Wahlbeck. May It Please the Chief? Opinion Assignments in the Rehnquist Court. *American Journal of Political Science* (1996) 40:421–43.

Maltzman, F and PJ Wahlbeck. Presented at the 1995 Annual Meeting of the American Political Science Association, Chicago.

Marshall, TR. Symbolic versus Policy Representation on the U.S. Supreme Court. *Journal of Politics* (1993) 55: 140–50.

Marshall, TR. *Public Opinion and the Supreme Court.* New York: Allen Unwin, 1991.

Marshall, TR and J Ignagni. Supreme Court and Public Support for Rights Claims. *Judicature* (1996) 78:146–51.

Mason, M. Trial and Error. *Health* (Jan/Feb 1994): 76–87.

McAffee, TB. A Critical Guide to the Ninth Amendment. *Temple Law Review* (1996) 69:61–94.

McCann, MW. *Rights at Work: Pay Equity Reform and the Politics of Legal Mobilization.* Chicago: University of Chicago Press, 1994.

McGuire, KT. Repeat Players in the Supreme Court: The Role of Experienced Lawyers in Litigation Success. *Journal of Politics* (1995) 57(1):187–96.

McGuire, KT. *The Supreme Court Bar: Legal Elites in the Washington Community.* Charlottesville: University of Virginia Press, 1993.

McGuire, KT and GA Caldeira. Lawyers, Organized Interests, and the Law of Obscenity: Agenda Setting in the Supreme Court. *American Political Science Review* (1993) 87:717–26.

McGuire, KT and B Palmer. Issue Fluidity on the U.S. Supreme Court. *American Political Science Review* (1996) 89(3):691–702.

McGurn, B. *America's Court: The Supreme Court and the People.* Golden, CO: Fulcrum Publishing, 1997.

McKeever, RJ. *Raw Juidicial Power? The Supreme Court and American Society.* Manchester, U.K.: Manchester University Press, 1993.

Mishler, W and R Sheehan. The Supreme Court as a Countermajoritarian Institution? *American Political Science Review* (1994) 88:87–101.

Mishler, W and R Sheehan. Public Opinion, the Attitudinal Model and Supreme Court Decision Making: A Micro Analytic Perspective. *Journal of Politics* (1996) 58:169–200.

Mohr, RD. Mr. Justice Douglas at Sodom: Gays and Privacy. *Columbia Human Rights Law Review* (1986)18:43–110.

Morris, TR. States before the U.S. Supreme Court: State Attorneys General as Amicus Curiae. *Judicature* (1987) 70:298–305.

Mulligan, ET. *Griswold* Revisited in Light of *Uplinger*: An Historical and Philosophical Exposition of Implied Autonomy Rights in the Constitution. *New York University Review of Law & Social Change* (1984) 13:51–82.

Murphy, WF. *Elements of Judicial Strategy.* Chicago: University of Chicago Press, 1964.

Nagel, RF. *Constitutional Cultures: The Mentality and Consequences of Judicial Review.* Berkeley: University of California Press, 1989.

Norpoth, H and JA Segal. Popular Influence on Supreme Court Decisions. *American Political Science Review* (1994) 88:711–24.

Note, Amici Curiae. *Harvard Law Review* (1921) 34: 773.

O'Connor, K. The Amicus Curiae Role of the United States Solicitor General in Supreme Court Litigation. *Judicature* (1983) 66: 256–64.

O'Connor, K. The Importance of Interest Group Involvement in Employment Discrimination Litigation. *Howard Law Journal* (1982) 25: 709–729.

O'Connor, K. *Women's Organizations' Use of the Courts*. Westport, CT: Greenwood Press, 1980.

O'Connor, K and L Epstein. Amicus Curiae Participation in U.S. Supreme Court Litigation: An Appraisal of Hakman's "Folklore." *Law and Society Review* (1981) 16:311–20.

O'Connor, K and L Epstein. Beyond Legislative Lobbying: Women's Rights Groups and the Supreme Court. *Judicature* (1983) 67: 134–43.

O'Connor, K and L Epstein. Court Rules and Workload: A Case Study of Rules Governing Amicus Curiae Participation. *Justice System Journal* (1983) 8:35–45.

O'Connor, K and L Epstein. The Rise of Conservative Interest Group Litigation. *Journal of Politics* (1983) 45:479–89.

Olson, M. *The Logic of Collective Action*. Cambridge, Mass: Harvard University Press, 1965.

Olson, SM. Interest Group Litigation in Federal District Court: Beyond the Political Disadvantage Theory. *Journal of Politics* (1990) 52:854–82.

Pacelle, RL.The Dynamics and Determinants of Agenda Change in the Rehnquist Court, in Epstein, *Contemplating Courts*, 251–74.

Pacelle, RL. Jr. *The Transformation of the Supreme Court's Agenda: From the New Deal to the Reagan Administration*. Boulder: Westview, 1991.

Pacelle, RL and BW Pyle. The Emergence and Evolution of Free Exercise Policy in the Supreme Court. Presented at the 1995 Annual Meeting of the American Political Science Association, Chicago.

Perry, BA. The Life and Death of the "Catholic Seat" on the United States Supreme Court. *Journal of Law and Politics* (1989) 6:55–92.

Perry, BA. *A "Representative" Supreme Court? The Impact of Race, Religion, and Gender on Appointments*. Westport, CT: Greenwood Press, 1991.

Perry, HW. *Deciding to Decide: Agenda Setting in the United States Supreme Court*. Cambridge: Harvard University Press, 1991.

Pfeffer, L. Amici in Church–State Litigation. *Law and Contemporary Problems* (1981) 44:83–110.

Plass, SA. The Foreign Amici Dilemma. *Brigham Young University Law Review* (1995) xx:1189–228.

Post, RC. *Constitutional Domains: Democracy, Community, Management*. Cambridge: Harvard University Press, 1995.

Provine, D. Case Selection in the United States Supreme Court. Chicago: University of Chicago Press, 1980.

Puro, S. and SS Ulmer, ed. *Courts, Law, and Judicial Process*. New York: Free Press, 1981.

Rains, RE. Fair-Weather Friend of the Court: On Writing an Amicus Brief. *Trial* (Aug 1990) 57–60.

Rakove, JN. *Original Meanings: Politics and Ideas in the Making of the Constitution*. New York: Alfred A. Knopf, 1996.

Rehnquist, WH. Remarks on the Process of Judging. *Washington and Lee Law Review* (1992) 49:263–70.

Rehnquist, WH. *The Supreme Court: How It Was, How It Is*. New York: Morrow, 1987.

Reynolds, GH. Sex, Lies and Jurisprudence: Robert Bork, *Griswold* and the Philosophy of Original Understanding. *Georgia Law Review* (1990) 24:1045–113.

Reynolds, GH. Penumbral Reasoning on the Right. *University of Pennsylvania Law Review* (1992)140:1333–48.

Roesch, R, SL Golding, VP Hans, and ND Repucci. Social Science and the Courts: The Role of Amicus Curiae Briefs. *Law and Human Behavior* (1991)15:1–11.

Roraback, CG. *Griswold v. Connecticut*: A Brief Case History. *Ohio Northern University Law Review* (1989) 16:395–402.

Rubin, ER. *The Abortion Controversy: A Documentary History*. Westport, CT: Greenwood Press, 1994.

Ruder, DS. The Development of Legal Doctrine through Amicus Participation: The SEC Experience. *Wisconsin Law Review* (1989) 1167:1167–91.

Rustad, M and T Koenig. The Supreme Court and Junk Social Science: Selective Distortion in Amicus Briefs. *North Carolina Law Review* (1993) 72:91–162.

Salisbury, RH. Interest Representation: The Dominance of Institutions. *American Political Science Review* (1984) 78: 64–76.

Salokar, RM. *The Solicitor General: The Politics of Law*. Philadelphia: Temple University Press, 1992.

Samar, VJ. *The Right to Privacy: Gays, Lesbians and the Constitution*. Philadelphia: Temple University Press, 1991.

Samuels, SU. Amici Curiae and the Supreme Court's Review of Fetal Protection Policies. *Judicature* (1995) 78: 236–241.

Scheingold, SA. *The Politics of Rights: Lawyers, Public Policy and Political Change*. New Haven, CT: Yale University Press, 1974.

Schlozman, KL and JT Tierney. *Organized Interests and American Democracy*. New York: Harper & Row, 1986.

Schmidt, CG. Where Privacy Fails: Equal Protection and the Abortion Rights of Minors. *New York University Law Review* (1993) 68:597–638.

Schnably, SJ. Beyond *Griswold*: Foucauldian and Republican Approaches to Privacy. *Connecticut Law Review* (1991) 23:861–954.

Schwartz, B. *The Unpublished Opinions of the Warren Court*. New York: Oxford University Press, 1985.

Segal, JA. Amicus Curiae Briefs by the Solicitor General during the Warren and Burger Courts. *Western Political Quarterly* (1988) 41:135–44.

Segal, JA et al. Ideological Values and the Votes of U.S. Supreme Court Justices. *American Political Science Review* (1989) 83:557–565.

Segal, JA and CD Reedy. The Supreme Court and Sex Discrimination: The Role of the Solicitor General. *Western Political Quarterly* (1988) 41:553–68.

Segal, JA and HJ Spaeth. The Influence of Stare Decisis on the Votes of United States Supreme Court Justices. *American Journal of Political Science* (1996) 40(4):971–1003.

Segal, JA and HJ Spaeth. *The Supreme Court and the Attitudinal Model*. Cambridge: Cambridge University Press, 1993.

Shapiro, SM. Amicus Briefs in the U.S. Supreme Court. *Litigation* (1984) 10:21.

Silverstein, M. *Judicious Choices: The New Politics of Supreme Court Confirmations*. New York: Norton, 1994.

Simpson, RW. *The Amicus Brief: How to Write It and Use It Effectively*. Chicago: ABA Publishing, 1998.

Skolnick, JH. Constitutional Privacy, Community, and the Individual: An Essay in Honor of Fowler J. Harper. *Northern Ohio University Law Review* (1989) 16:561–81.

Smith, GF and BE Terrell. The Amicus Curiae: A Powerful Friend for Poverty Law Advocates. *Clearinghouse Review* (1995) 29:772–792.

Smith, PM. The Sometimes Troubled Relationship between Courts and Their "Friends." *Litigation* (1998) 24:24–26.

Smith, RA. "Advocacy, Interpretation and Influence in the U.S. Congress" *American Political Science Review* (1984) 78:44–63.

Smith, RE. *Compilation of State and Federal Privacy Laws*. Providence, Rhode Island: *Privacy Journal: An Independent Monthly on Privacy in a Computer Age*, 1997.

Smolla, RA. *A Year in the Life of the Supreme Court*. Durham, NC: Duke University Press, 1995.

Smollin, DM. The Jurisprudence of Privacy in a Splintered Supreme Court. *Marquette Law Review* (1992) 75:975–1066.

The Solicitor General and the Evolution of Activism. *Indiana Law Journal* (1990) 65:675–96.

Songer, DR, CR Cameron and JA Segal. An Empirical Test of the Rational-Actor Theory of Litigation. *Journal of Politics* (1995) 57:1119–1129.

Songer, DR, S Davis and S Haire. A Reappraisal of Diversification in the Federal Courts: Gender Effects in the Courts of Appeals. *Journal of Politics* (1994) 56:425–439.

Songer, DR and A Kuersten. The Success of Amici in State Supreme Courts. *Political Research Quarterly* (1995) 48:31–42.

Songer, DR and RS Sheehan. Interest Group Success in the Courts: Amicus Participation in the Supreme Court. *Political Research Quarterly* (1993) 46: 339–354.

Spaeth, HJ. *Majority Rule of Minority Will: Adherence to Precedent on the U.S. Supreme Court*. Cambridge and New York: Cambridge University Press, 1999.

Stern, E et al. *Supreme Court Practice*. Washington, D.C.: Bureau of National Affairs, Inc.

Stewart, J and JF Sheffield. Does Interest Group Litigation Matter? The Case of Black Political Mobilization in Mississippi. *Journal of Politics* (1987) 49: 781.

Strossen, N. The Right to be Let Alone: Constitutional Privacy in *Griswold, Roe,* and *Bowers*. In T Eastland, ed. *Benchmarks: Great Constitutional Controversies in the Supreme Court*. Washington, D.C.: Ethics and Public Policy Center, 1995.

Substantive Due Process Comes Home to Roost: Fundamental Rights, *Griswold* to *Bowers*. *Women's Rights Law Reporter* (1988) 10:177–208.

Sunderland, LV. *Popular Government and the Supreme Court: Securing the Public Good and Private Rights*. Lawrence: University of Kansas Press, 1996.

Truman, D. *The Governmental Process: Political Interests and Public Opinion*. New York: Knopf, 1951.

Tushnet, M. *The NAACP's Legal Strategy against Segregated Education, 1925–1952*. Chapel Hill: University of North Carolina Press, 1987.

Tushnet, M. *Constitutional Issues: Abortion*. New York: Harold Steiner Books, 1996.

Ulmer, SS. Researching the Supreme Court in a Democratic Pluralist System: Some Thoughts on New Directions. *Law and Policy Quarterly* (1979): 153–80.

Ulmer, SS. Issue Fluidity in the U.S. Supreme Court: A Conceptual Analysis in SC Halpern and CM Lamb, eds. *Supreme Court Activism and Restraint*. Lexington, MA: Lexington Books, 1982.

Van Alstyne, W. Closing the Circle of Constitutional Review from *Griswold v. Connecticut* to *Roe v. Wade*: An Outline of a Decision Merely Overruling *Roe*. *Duke Law Journal* (1989) 1677–88.

Vose, C. *For Caucasians Only: The Supreme Court, the NAACP, and the Restrictive Covenant Cases*. Berkeley: University of California Press, 1959.

Wahlbeck, PJ, JF Spriggs and F Maltzman. Marshalling the Court: Bargaining and Accommodation on the U.S. Supreme Court. *American Journal of Political Science* (1998) 42:294–315.

Walker, JL. The Origins and Maintenance of Interest Groups in America. *American Political Science Review* (1983) 77:390–406.

Walker, JL. *Mobilizing Interest Groups in America*. Ann Arbor: University of Michigan Press, 1991.

Warren, S and L Brandeis. The Right to Privacy. *Harvard Law Review* (1890) 4:193–219.

Wedegar, KM. The Solicitor General and Administrative Due Process. *George Washington Law Review* (1967) 36:481–514.

Woliver, LR. Rhetoric and Symbols in the Pro-Life Amicus Briefs to the *Webster* Case. Presented at the 1992 Annual Meeting of the American Political Science Association, Washington, D.C.

Woodward, B and C Bernstein. *The Brethren: Inside the Supreme Court*. New York: Simon and Schuster, 1979.

Yeazell, SC. *From Medieval Group Litigation to the Modern Class Action*. New Haven, CT: Yale University Press, 1987.

Zemans, F. Legal Mobilization: The Neglected Role of Law in the Political System. *American Political Science Review* (1983) 77:690–703.

Index

Cruzan v. Director, Missouri Department of Health, 114–121, 198, 203–204

American Ethical Union (AEU)
Roe v. Wade, 55, 195, 196

American Geriatrics Society (AGS)
amicus influence, 151, 210
assistance in dying, 131, 134, 137, 141, 143, 145, 148–149, 199, 205–207, 210

American Hospital Association (AHA)
Cruzan v. Director, Missouri Department of Health, 115, 118, 121, 203
Vacco v. Quill, 134
Washington v. Glucksberg, 134

American Jewish Congress (AJC), 8
Bowers v. Hardwick, 178–179, 182–183, 199, 207
protected relationships, 178–179, 182–183, 199, 207

American Life League, assistance in dying, 206

American Medical Association (AMA)
abortion, 57, 62–63, 94, 195
assistance in dying, 112–122, 124–125, 128, 131, 134, 137, 143–144, 150, 196, 198–199, 203–207, 210, 219
Cruzan v. Director, Missouri Department of Health, 112–122, 150–151, 196, 198, 203–204, 210
influence on court, 122, 152, 195, 210
opinions of the Council on Ethical and Judicial Affairs, 140
Roe v. Wade, 57
Vacco v. Quill, 124–125, 128, 131, 134, 137–139, 143, 196, 199, 203–207

American Medical Student Association
assistance in dying, 131, 140, 145, 205, 207
influence of briefs, 219

American Psychological Association (APA)
abortion, 77–79, 88–89, 92–93

Bowers v. Hardwick, 173, 176, 178, 182–184, 187, 190n69, 197, 199, 207

City of Akron v. Akron Center for Reproductive Health, 77–79, 203
influence on Court, 195

Planned Parenthood of Southeastern Pennsylvania v. Casey, 88–89, 92–93
protected relationships, 173, 176, 178, 182–184, 187, 190n69, 197, 199, 207

American Public Health Association (APHA)
abortion, 71, 73–76, 78–80, 95, 203
amicus curiae briefs, 71, 73–76, 78–80
and medical practice, 73–76, 78–80
Bowers v. Hardwick, 172, 178, 187, 197
City of Akron v. Akron Center for Reproductive Health, 71, 73–76, 78, 79–80, 203
influence on Court, 195, 210–211
protected relationships, 178, 187, 197
Recommended Program Guide for Abortion Services, 76, 78–80, 203

Americans for Death and Dying (assistance in dying), 138

Americans for Death with Dignity, 126, 138, 140

American Suicide Foundation (ASF)
amicus influence, 210
Vacco v. Quill, 199, 207, 210
Washington v. Glucksberg, 199, 207, 210

American Suicide Foundation (assistance in dying), 138–139, 143

Americans United for Life, 79

Americans United for the Separation of Church and State, 8

Amicus curiae briefs, 2
Abrams, Frederick (amicus), 116, 122
abuse risk (assistance in dying), 138–139
Adams et al. (amici), privacy, 33–34, 37–41, 202

About the Author

SUZANNE U. SAMUELS is associate professor of political science at Seton Hall University. She has written widely in the area of law, politics, and society, and is keenly interested in the interplay of law and social and political institutions.